SCIENTISM

INTERNATIONAL LIBRARY OF PHILOSOPHY

Edited by: Ted Honderich

Grote Professor of the Philosophy of Mind and Logic
University College London

SCIENTISM

Philosophy and the infatuation with science

Tom Sorell

London and New York

First published 1991
by Routledge
11 New Fetter Lane, London EC4P 4EE
29 West 35th Street, New York, NY 10001

Paperback edition 1994

© 1991 Tom Sorell

Typeset in Bembo by
Florencetype Ltd.
Printed in Great Britain by
T J Press (Padstow) Ltd, Padstow, Cornwall

British Library Cataloguing in Publication Data
Sorell, Tom
Scientism.
1. Philosophy related to science.   2. Science realted to philosophy
I. Title
100

Library of Congress Cataloging in Publication Data
Sorell, Tom
Scientism/Tom Sorell.
p.   cm.
Includes bibliographical references and index.
1. Scientism. 2. Philosophy and science.   3. Scientism – History.
4. Philosophy and science – History.   I. Title.
B67.S69 1991
149–dc20   90–47550

ISBN 0–415–03399–3 (hbk)
ISBN 0–415–10771–7 (pbk)

NWST
1 AFJ6346

For Victor Sorell and Felix Wassermann

CONTENTS

CONTENTS

viii

CONTENTS

PREFACE

Scientism is a matter of putting too high a value on science in comparison with other branches of learning or culture. It is an occupational hazard in philosophy, for since the time of Descartes philosophers have not only been interested in the nature of science; they have often sided with science in its conflicts with religion, mysticism and even philosophy itself. In this book two forms of scientism in philosophy are criticized: one is relatively new and narrowly philosophical; the other is relatively old and much wider in scope. The new scientism is a reaction against those who write philosophy in ignorance of science, and who defer too much to prescientific intuition or common sense. It is also a reaction against the supposed metaphysical excesses of traditional philosophy, with its irreducible mental substances and events, its Platonic forms, and its transcendental egos. Philosophy in keeping with the new scientism only recognizes the existence of objects that science is already committed to, and it conveys a familiarity with the findings and habits of mind of practising physicists, biologists and psychologists. Sometimes it even reclassifies itself as a branch of science, as when epistemology is redefined as a chapter of psychology. I come to the new scientism at the end, in Chapters 6 and 7.

The rest of the book is devoted to the older scientism and the antidote to it. The older scientism insists on the need not only for philosophy, but for the whole of culture, to be led by science. This form of scientism has a history stretching back at least to the 1600s; in this century its spokesmen have included Carnap, Reichenbach, Neurath and other 'scientific empiricists'. The first chapter tries to give an impression of scientism by describing scientific empiricism, in particular its programme for co-ordinating the social sciences, humanities and fine arts with the natural sciences. The second chapter suggests how some of the excesses of this programme are anticipated in classifications of learning and science in writers as early as Bacon and Descartes, and in their valuations of reason relative to other human faculties. Long before the scientific empiricists, philosophers in the seventeenth century exaggerated the value of science in the scheme of learning, and the value of theoretical reason in the scheme of human capacities. Chapter 3 suggests that a much better balance is struck in Kant's philosophy, where a respect for science is not taken to the extreme of scientism, and where the limits of theoretical reason are as well advertised as its possibilities. Chapters 4 and 5 defend Kant's idea that the arts and sciences can each promote human improvement, and that they can do so harmoniously, rather than as competing sectors of the 'two cultures'.

The book concentrates on scientism in philosophy, but it does not deny that scientistic ways of thinking are to be found elsewhere, e.g. in business or politics or science itself, often in forms that have had a greater impact than any of the philosophical varieties. However, for reasons that I very briefly indicate in the first chapter, I am less keen to criticize these forms of scientism than the philosophical ones. It is possible that my emphasis will deter non-philosophers, but I hope not. I have tried to write for a wide audience. People who are new to philosophy should be able to cope with most of the book, and sections that contain technicalities – at the end of Chapter 6 and the beginning of Chapter 7 – are preceded and followed by more straightforward material.

A few friends read the book in draft and offered encouragement and advice: I should like to thank Stuart Brown, Nick Furbank and Vicent Raga. I was also helped by a seminar audience at the London School of Economics in October 1989 and by the opportunity to give two special lectures on scientism at University College, London in February 1990.

Material in the concluding section of Chapter 5 is drawn from 'The World from its Own Point of View', in A. Malachowski (ed.), *Reading Rorty* (Oxford: Blackwell, 1990). Almost half of Chapter 7 was previously published as 'Values and Secondary Qualities' in *Ratio* 27 (1985), 178–88.

1

SCIENTISM AND 'SCIENTIFIC EMPIRICISM'

WHAT IS SCIENTISM?

Scientism is the belief that science, especially natural science, is much the most valuable part of human learning – much the most valuable part because it is much the most authoritative, or serious, or beneficial. Other beliefs related to this one may also be regarded as scientistic, e.g. the belief that science is the *only* valuable part of human learning, or the view that it is always good for subjects that do not belong to science to be placed on a scientific footing. When, as has happened frequently since the seventeenth century, philosophers claim to have made morals, or history, or politics, or aesthetics, or the study of the human mind into a science, they take it for granted that for a subject to become a science is for it to go up in the world.[1] The idea that the acquisition of scientific status is always desirable seems to be mistaken: it exaggerates the value of science. But this and other scientistic ideas, I am going to argue, are not properly rebutted by attempts to denigrate science or to expose as empty its supposed pretensions. A framework is needed that enables one to recognize the considerable value of science alongside the considerable value of many other parts of learning. Fortunately, a framework of this kind exists, though not in an entirely satisfactory form. Kant has a theory about the arts, sciences and religion that implies that all are means of developing a moral culture. The theory sometimes looks scientistic itself, but I offer an interpretation that dispels this impression and then a defence of the general approach in the face of some influential theories opposed to it.

I will mainly be concerned with scientism in philosophy.[2] I do not consider at any length the enthusiasm for science among scientists, or among politicians or journalists or people in business,

1

though it can hardly be doubted that, until recently, scientistic beliefs have been strongly held in these circles and indeed throughout society, not only in the West but in the Soviet bloc, not only in the industrialized world but also in the developing countries. In the 1960s, for example, Jawaharlal Nehru, the first prime minister of independent India, wrote that

> It is science alone that can solve the problems of hunger and poverty, of insanitation and illiteracy, of superstition and deadening custom and tradition, of vast resources running to waste, of a rich country inhabited by starving people. . . . Who indeed could afford to ignore science today? At every turn we seek its aid. . . . The future belongs to science and to those who make friends with science.[3]

Views like Nehru's were once quite widely held, and, along with professions of faith in the 'scientific' political economy of Marx, they were perhaps typical of the scientism of politicians in the 1950s and 1960s. Other kinds of scientism were current at about the same time. In 1957 Anatole Rapaport suggested that on account of the values embodied in scientific practice – values such as tolerance, love of truth, co-operation and so on – scientific communities might be regarded as the prototype of moral communities.[4] Much more recently scientism seems to have left its mark even on ostensibly anti-scientific movements. Consider the rhetoric of those American fundamentalists who have demanded equal time for the biblical account of creation when school biology lessons describe evolution according to Darwin. It seems significant that what the creationists are asking to be taught alongside Darwinism is something called 'creation *science*'. The creationists agree with their opponents in using 'science' as an honorific term, and this is already scientistic or verging upon it. I am less keen to criticize scientism outside philosophy than scientism within philosophy, because it seems to me that outside philosophy scientism sometimes has the useful effect of bolstering up an appreciation of, and respect for, science in the face of anti-scientific and pseudo-scientific ideas. A scientistic Darwinian, for example, still overvalues science, but if he manages to show to people who are sceptical that Darwinism is scientifically superior to creation science,[5] he is more likely to convert the sceptical to an acceptance of a branch of genuine science than to win them over to scientism. In this way scientism outside philosophy can reduce the influence of anti-science or pseudoscience.

Within philosophy, on the other hand, at any rate as it is now practised in the English-speaking world, and as it has been practised for the most part in Europe since the seventeenth century, the anti-scientific attitude is that of a very small minority, and so the scientism that counteracts an anti-scientific attitude is out of its element. Hilary Putnam once said that all of the great philosophers who were interested in epistemology were philosophers of science in two senses of 'of'.[6] He meant that these philosophers were not only interested in the nature of science, but that they also set themselves up as spokesmen for science. The works that have come to be regarded as canonical in philosophy since Descartes are overwhelmingly the works of philosophers of science in the two senses of 'of'. In this strongly pro-scientific atmosphere scientism cannot be justified in the way it can sometimes be justified outside philosophy.

SCIENTISM IN TWENTIETH-CENTURY PHILOSOPHY

In this century scientism in philosophy has already had one high point, and it may be enjoying a resurgence. A programme for the unity of science, originally conceived in Vienna in the 1920s, was a vehicle for scientistic writing for the next thirty years. Much more recently a kind of scientism has become discernible in arguments for certain research programmes in the philosophy of mind and epistemology. For example, Patricia Churchland has written that 'there are remarkable new developments in cognitive neurobiology which encourage us to think that a new and encompassing paradigm [in epistemology] is emerging'.[7] Note the 'encompassing'. Churchland does not say, as members of the Vienna Circle did, that older forms of epistemology are suspect because they contain metaphysical statements that fail a test of verifiability. Her complaint is that the older forms of epistemology incorporate a worn-out paradigm. Thus, even if everything said by the traditional epistemologists makes sense, it is not any longer fruitful to carry on as they did. It is time for philosophical questions to catch up with the age of neuroscience and raise the questions that this age enables us to ask. Not 'How is it possible for us to represent reality?' or 'How is it that we can represent the external world of objects of space and time, of motion and colour?' but rather 'How does the brain work?'[8] Churchland seems to stand in a long line of philosophers who have urged the transformation of a branch of philosophy into a branch of natural science. And hers is not the only scientistic voice now audible. There are others who, for different reasons, have advocated a naturalization of ethics and a recognition of its basis in biology. As with earlier forms of scientism there is more to be said against the new versions than in their favour. Fruitfulness in philosophy is probably not the same as fruitfulness in other subjects, and redefinitions of questions that seem to produce it had better not discard live problems with dead ones. In particular, they had better not write off as dead questions those that are merely old. The questions that Churchland thinks have been superseded seem to me to be old and difficult rather than lifeless.

I shall return to the new scientism much later, preferring to begin with the form that was influential earlier in this century. This is the scientism whose spokesmen included Carnap, Reichenbach and Neurath, philosophers who believed that no field of enquiry was out of bounds to the positive sciences or unable to benefit from their methods. When I mention spokesmen of the earlier scientism I do not have in mind members of the Vienna Circle alone, or even adherents of logical positivism. Carnap has used the term 'scientific empiricism' for a wider movement of people[9] united in a sympathy for the empiricism of Hume and Mill, an admiration for the scientific method of nineteenth-century physics, and a willingness to apply, for the purposes of unifying both the laws and the language of different sciences, methods of logical analysis pioneered by Frege, Russell, Wittgenstein and others. Some of the views of the scientific empiricists make a good introduction to scientism in general. For one thing, they introduce a number of definite, mutually supporting, claims about science some of which are jointly sufficient for scientism.

Five theses of scientific empiricism

At least five claims about science seem to be characteristic of the scientific empiricists: (1) science is unified; (2) there are no limits to science; (3) science has been enormously successful at prediction, explanation and control; (4) the methods of science confer objectivity on scientific results; and (5) science has been beneficial for human beings.

The concept of science employed by these theses may be briefly indicated.[10] Science is a conjunction of well-confirmed scientific theories, and scientific theories, however disparate their subject matter, may be viewed as partially interpreted logical calculi. The calculi contain axioms and postulates from which observational truths are supposed to be derived. Taken together, the calculi of the different sciences add up to the body of truths of science ('a body of ordered knowledge' – Carnap). As for the means of reaching these truths, they vary. In the case of laws, including postulates, the truths can be abstracted from model experimental situations, while other truths are derived by pure deduction from the axioms and postulates. Turning to individual theories, each has two fundamentally different types of vocabulary – observational and theoretical – in addition to the strictly logical apparatus of the truth-functors, quantifiers, individual variables, individual constants and identity. The laws of a theory are assumed to be stable in theoretical and logical vocabulary alone. With the 'theoretical postulates' and 'correspondence rules' of the theory, as well as statements of initial conditions, the laws imply the truth of certain sentences in observational terms whose referents are specified either as physical objects or as sense-data. When some of the implied observation statements are discovered to be true, the theory is (partially) confirmed. 'Correspondence rules' either define or explicate theoretical vocabulary in terms of observational vocabulary, or indicate how theoretical statements of the theory can be applied to the phenomena in order to be experimentally tested. The 'theoretical postulates' typically serve to introduce whatever mathematical content is used by the theory proper to mathematize the data.

(1) Against the background of this view, which used to be called the 'Received View' of scientific theory,[11] the thesis that science is unified may be understood to be concerned with both the laws and the theoretical terms of different sciences. Among other things, the thesis holds that the laws of one theory can turn out to be logically derived from the laws of another, or that the theoretical terms of one theory can turn out to be definable in the terms of another. Examples of these derivations and definitional reductions are generally taken from physics, but the thesis we are considering is intended to apply outside the natural sciences as well, e.g. in anthropology and sociology. In the German-speaking world at the turn of the century there was a widespread acceptance of a categorical difference between the human sciences and the natural sciences. Scientific empiricism denied that there was any such

difference. There was supposed to be no ultimate dualism of natural and social science or of natural and human science.[12] According to Neurath there did not even have to be a dualism of the sciences and the humanities if a model of the unity of science was adopted such as that of the encyclopaedia.[13]

(2) There are no limits to science. Here Carnap's formulation in section 180 of the *Aufbau* may be used. Although the

> total range of life still has many other dimensions outside of science, . . . within its dimension, science meets no barrier. . . . When we say that scientific knowledge is unlimited, we mean: *there is no question whose answer is in principle unattainable by science.*[14]

A broadly similar account is given by von Mises: 'There is no field . . . into which scientific research can never carry any light; there are no "eternally unexplainable" areas.'[15] In Carnap's case at least, the claim about the limitlessness of scientific knowledge may be seen as a reflection of the meaning–empiricism of many in the unity of science movement. If intelligible questions are limited to those that some experience could provide an answer to, and if intelligible answers are drawn from the class of intelligible statements, in their turn identified with the class of scientific statements, in their turn identified with those that could be discovered by experience to be true or false, then by definition all intelligible answers to questions are scientific, since meaningful statements are scientific ones. (2) is sometimes also supported by a kind of induction: the previously intractable questions of the non–sciences have always given way to answers from the sciences; so perhaps the current and future questions will do so as well.

(3) Science has been enormously successful at prediction, explanation and control. Carnap's account[16] suggests that advances in physics from the mid-nineteenth century to the early years of the twentieth were given particular weight in scientific empiricism, but Hempel, in a later statement of this sort of thesis, mentions other sciences:

> Our age has often been called an age of science and scientific technology, and with good reason: the advances made during the past few centuries by the natural sciences, and more recently by the psychological and sociological disciplines,

have enormously broadened our knowledge and deepened our understanding of the world we live in and of our fellow men; and the practical application of scientific insights is giving us an ever increasing measure of control over the forces of nature and the minds of men.[17]

The idea of a successful forward march of science, led by the mature natural sciences and joined by psychology and sociology, runs through the writings of all of the scientific empiricists. Even philosophy is allowed a place. As Carnap has suggested in an autobiographical piece containing reminiscences of the Vienna Circle,[18] he and his colleagues believed that philosophy could aid scientific advance by improving scientific ways of thinking. Schlick's first book had suggested a role for philosophy in analysing or clarifying the foundations of science; and Wittgenstein's *Tractatus*, though not similarly motivated by a desire to contribute to scientific advance, had suggested that philosophy might have the task of clarifying propositions of natural science, a suggestion that might have been interpreted by Carnap and his friends as an echo of Schlick's idea.

(4) The methods of science confer objectivity on scientific results. This thesis is not often explicitly stated by scientific empiricists. At times it seems to be avoided; avoided either because the concept of objectivity is associated with a metaphysical concept of truth, such as truth as correspondence to fact, or because some methods – methods of discovery – were thought to belong to 'the context of discovery' which is the province of psychology, and not to the 'context of justification', which is the proper concern of the philosopher.[19] In any case, a connection between the method of finding inductive evidence and a weak form of objectivity for laws, namely the reasonableness of believing in them, is often assumed, or, where there is scepticism, as in Popper's writings, about whether inductive evidence confers objectivity, the objectivity of a law is taken to be borne out by the persistent failure of attempts to falsify it.

(5) Science has been beneficial for human beings. This thesis is crucial for the expression of scientism, since it is a natural explication of the claim that science is the most valuable part of human learning, which I am taking to define scientism. The scientific empiricists were neither the first nor the last of those to subscribe to (5), but unlike many of their predecessors, they were inclined to

insist that the scientific parts of culture or learning, such as religion or metaphysics, had no benefits, or benefits far outweighed by harms. Religion was viewed as 'primitive'[20] or as holding back progress by sustaining a belief in the supernatural.[21] Again, science was said to be beneficial because it enables people to get the better of undesirable effects and produce desirable ones. In a continuation of the passage quoted a moment ago, Hempel wrote that

> scientific knowledge and its applications [have] vastly reduced the threat of man's oldest and most formidable scourges, among them famine and pestilence; it has raised man's material level of living, and it has put within his reach . . . the active exploration of interplanetary space.[22]

Here the philosophical view of the benefits of science coincides with what was once a popular view. Another scientific empiricist, Carnap, mentions a less widely appreciated benefit: clearheadedness, and tells how it smoothed the proceedings of the Vienna Circle:

> The task of fruitful collaboration, often so difficult among philosophers, was facilitated in our Circle by the fact that all members had a first-hand acquaintance with science, either mathematics, physics or social science. This led to a higher standard of clarity and responsibility than is usually found in philosophical groups, especially in Germany.[23]

The five theses before us are up to a point mutually supporting. For example, thesis (4), which traces the objectivity of scientific results to method, may, if it is true, help to explain (3), which asserts the predictive and explanatory success of science. (3) in its turn is a possible explanation of (5). In other words, the fact that science has been successful at prediction, explanation and control, explains some benefits of science. (3) may be evidence for (2): the thesis that there are no questions out of bounds to science may be supported by the fact that science has dealt so successfully with questions it has addressed up to now. Finally, (3) may be partly explicated by (1), which takes the success of science partly to consist of a process whereby the laws of one theory are subsumed by those of another, the subsumption being what unifies at any rate some sciences.

The scientism in scientific empiricism

To see how scientific empiricism is scientistic, it is not always enough to consider theses (1) to (5) in the abstract. One has to consider how they are used. If some subject is claimed to lack scientific status and therefore to be of doubtful value because it is hard to see how it fits in with the body of established science, then, prima facie, that is a case of the scientistic use of thesis (1). Similarly, if the thesis that science has been beneficial is conjoined with claims about how much less beneficial some other non-scientific or anti-scientific subject has been, then, prima facie, that is a case of the scientistic use of thesis (5). But thesis (1) would not necessarily be used scientistically if it supported the conclusion that a subject did not belong to science and *nothing* was said about the value of non-scientific subjects. Similarly, if it is not accompanied by the claim that subjects outside science lack benefits, thesis (5) – the claim that science has been beneficial – is not scientistic either. What is crucial to scientism is not the identification of something as scientific or unscientific but the thought that the scientific is much more valuable than the non-scientific, or the thought that the non-scientific is of negligible value.

Against this background, where are we to find the key to the scientism in scientific empiricism? Carnap gives 'unity of science movement' as a synonym for 'scientific empiricism' and there is a clue to what we are looking for in the word 'movement', understood to mean a group of people formed to get something changed or reformed. Members of this movement held that by the turn of the present century the physical sciences enjoyed an implicit unity, which formalization would make explicit; outside physics, and especially in the social or human sciences, the unity had to be manufactured, by the introduction into previously unscientific subjects – ethics, for example, or history – of the concepts and methodology of established sciences. The thought behind the forging of this unity – that it is highly desirable for the concepts and methodology of established sciences to be spread, and unsatis-factory for, for example, ethics or history to be left in their prescientific state – captures the scientism in scientific empiricism. No one thesis from our list quite expresses this thought, though (1) and (5) together come close. As for theses (2) to (4), they fall into place as reasons why, in general, it is both desirable and possible for science to extend its territory.

The writings of a number of members of the unity of science movement proclaim the benefits of a scientific approach to psychology, history, the social sciences and philosophy. I come to these in a moment. There are also striking assertions of the capacity of science or unified science to improve everyday ways of thinking and speaking. In some remarkable passages from a monograph devoted to the question of how psychology could be put on a scientific footing, Neurath describes the difference it would make to children if unified science were to inform their way of understanding the world from the beginning.

> But how does the elimination of metaphysics proceed in practice? Men are induced to give up senseless sentences and freed from metaphysics. But must this always remain so? Must everyone in turn go through metaphysics as through a childhood disease – perhaps the earlier he gets it, the less dangerous it is – to be led back to unified science? No. *Every child can in principle learn to apply the language of physicalism correctly from the outset.*[24]

Neurath seems to have had in mind the teaching to children of a purified language.[25] The purified language would contain traditional words; but certain terms that resisted translation into the preferred formulations of physicalism would be eliminated – put on an index of prohibited words. Among the banned terms Neurath includes 'norm', 'transcendental', 'categorical imperative', 'intuition', 'immanent' and 'reality'.

Once children had been initiated into the language of physicalism, Neurath claimed, they would produce speech free of various kinds of senselessness. This would not be the only benefit: they would also become immune to the corruption of their language by philosophy. When they later

> become acquainted with academic philosophy, it will have become a foreign subject for them, to be studied only in an historical way, as theology was for many of their parents. . . .
> A new generation educated according to unified science will not understand the difference between the 'mental' and the 'physical' sciences, or between 'philosophy of nature' and 'culture'.[26]

Neurath was thinking of a new generation of German-speakers in particular. For he goes on immediately to say that 'in Western countries steeped in empiricism', such as the United States, there is no division of sciences into those concerned with nature and those concerned with *geist*, only an innocuous division of subjects into sciences on the one hand and non–sciences or arts on the other. Presumably English, or American English, already had affinities with the preferred physicalist language.

Neurath was not alone among the positivists in thinking that ordinary thought could be improved by being brought into line with science or the presuppositions of the unity of science movement. The creation of a cultural atmosphere favourable to science was thought by the whole of the Vienna Circle to be desirable.[27] In the wider scientific empiricist movement, too, especially the American branch of it, the desirability of extending the influence of science was strongly asserted. So much so that Charles Morris, one of the editors of the *Encyclopaedia of Unified Science*, argued that the Vienna Circle had not taken the advocacy of the scientific approach far enough:

> [B]y and large [Schlick's] group has looked at science from the point of view of the scientist, and not with the vision of one intent upon the bearing of the scientific attitude and results upon human culture.[28]

According to Morris, the American pragmatist philosopher Dewey had the appropriate vision. To Dewey,

> science is rich in potentialities for the control of human life, and for the enrichment and emancipation of the individual mind. He is impressed by the gap between the possibilities of 'this most potent social factor in the world' and the slowness of its extension into fields where value judgements hold sway. It is in these terms that he can write that 'the great scientific revolution is yet to come' and can conceive the task of philosophy today as the extension of the method of freed intelligence into ethical and social domains. And this extension is of course something advocated, and as advocate the philosopher has turned moralist.[29]

Morris advocates both the extension of scientific method into other fields and the adoption of Dewey's view of philosophy as advocacy. In outlining Dewey's approach Morris insists that it is a direct application of philosophy to life, rather than to esoteric specialisms dealing with morals and politics. It was a philosophy of life, but without the 'dogmatism and fugitive emotionalism' of the more usual philosophies of life.

Beyond the exact sciences

Turning from the supposed desirability of applying science to every-day life, let us consider how the scientific empiricists thought it would be beneficial to bring scientific method from its usual sphere, in the natural sciences, to the rest of learning. Eight monographs published under the series title 'Unified Science', and edited originally by Neurath, were largely devoted to this matter, as well as to detailed outlines of research programmes for a reformed economics, psychology and so on. The first of these monographs, written by Neurath himself and published in 1932, has already been quoted from. Entitled 'Unified Science and Psychology', it proclaimed the benefits to psychology of techniques for avoiding the senseless-ness sometimes encountered in psychology textbooks.[30] It then proposed a new discipline of 'behaviouristics' that would combine the lines of research of behaviourism and other branches of experi-mental psychology, with the approved vocabulary of physicalism.[31]

In another paper on psychology that appeared five years after Neurath's in the monograph series, Egon Brunswik argued for a view of the subject as 'an objective science of relations, namely the theory of the relations between happenings in and around a living being and the periodic constants of life, as well as other constants'.[32] The life constants of a living being might include its prey and enemy, offspring, tools and so on. Brunswik argued for a reorient-ation of theory away from events within an organism's body, to its relations with its environment, especially its 'successes' in its environment. Like Neurath, Brunswik thought that a reformed psychology would be particularly compatible with some forms of behaviourism.

Proposals for unifying psychology with other social sciences were also published in the 'Unified Science' series. A contribution by Clark Hull to the 1937 volume, which was intended to prepare the ground for an encyclopaedia of unified science, outlines a method of securing 'a genuine co-ordination of the scientific efforts of numerous workers of . . . diverse training and interests', namely, 'students of physiology, animal behaviour, psychology, sociology, cultural anthropology, psychopathology, juvenile delinquency, logic and mathematics'.[33] The method was a combination of empirical research and logic, with the logic unifying the results of the empirical research. First, experiments geared 'to the simplest possible situations and the simplest possible organisms' would be relied upon to suggest first-level postulates or approximations to laws of human behaviour in the form of equations; then the consequences of these postulates would be worked out by deductive methods for 'various possible dynamic situations and conditions', these consequences or 'theorems' in their turn being tested experimentally. Disagreements between experimental outcomes and theorems would then be taken as evidence of inadequacy in the formulation of the postulates, and of the need to set up new experimental situations to derive improved postulates.

According to Hull, the theorems yielded by these procedures, together with relevant postulates, would mark out the territory of an 'integrated empirical research programme'.[34] Such a research programme would be 'characteristically different from the scattered, opportunistic efforts usual in empirical investigations even in restricted fields'.[35] Hull went on to give a sampling of twenty out of, in all, sixty 'fertile points of attack' for such research programmes.[36] These ranged from the 'basic physiological principles of mammalian motivation' to the 'evolution of competition and aggression'.

Economics was another social science that attracted the interest of the unified science movement. In 1934 Neurath produced a monograph in the 'Unified Science' series devoted to the development of a scientific economic theory. The theory was to be concerned with the effect of economic systems on what, at a first approximation, could be called 'welfare'. Neurath's positive proposals for economics turned on the partially quantified concepts of 'life feeling' and 'life situations', which were used to produce measurements of economic value, and a survey of various models for predicting wage and profit levels.[37]

In the last volume of the 'Unified Science' series, Heinrich Gomperz attempted to extend methods of logical analysis to historical interpretation, his examples being drawn from the historical interpretation of philosophical and philological texts. Gomperz produced a highly systematic treatment of a branch of the humanities that has often been thought to be the most difficult to assimilate to the rest of science: hermeneutics. His monograph appeared in 1939.[38] It was not the last work to bring historical research within the scope of the unity of science. In 1942 Hempel published a paper in which he suggested that much of what could be said about general laws and explanation in the natural sciences applied to explanation in history.[39] After demonstrating the substantial parallels between historical explanation and explanation in the natural sciences, and the dependence of history on generalizations that were not themselves historical, Hempel concluded that

> it is . . . unwarranted and futile to attempt the demarcation of sharp boundary lines between the different fields of scientific research, and an autonomous development of each of the fields. The necessity, in historical inquiry, to make extensive use of universal hypotheses of which at least the overwhelming majority come from fields of research traditionally distinguished from history is just one of the aspects of what may be called the methodological unity of empirical science.[40]

Since Hempel seems to be pointing here to the *de facto* unity of history with the other empirical sciences rather than arguing for a scientific transformation of history that would result in its finding a place in the body of science, it is not entirely clear that this passage is quite in the spirit of the 'Unified Science' monographs. Elsewhere in the paper, however, where the would-be historical method of empathic understanding is unfavourably compared to that of trying to discover covering laws,[41] there are signs of the characteristic rejection of *geistwissenschaft*. Overall, Hempel's approach seems to be that of scientific empiricism.

There are affinities between the attitude of scientific empiricism to historical studies and the attitude of Marxists. Engels insisted that in Marx's writings history had already been raised to the level of science because it set out laws of historical development. The scientific empiricists did not agree, doubting the clarity and reliability of the dialectics that Marx adapted from Hegel. Nevertheless, at least the members of the Vienna Circle among the scientific empiricists tended to sympathize with Marxism and to assume the possibility of a convergence between Marxism and scientific empiricism. As Carnap recalled much later, 'All of us in the Circle were strongly interested in social and political progress. Most of us, myself included, were socialists.'[42] Again, replying to Robert Cohen in 1963, Carnap referred to the 'agreement on many points' between dialectical materialism and logical positivism, and tried to refute the charge that logical positivism was without a concept of reason that would permit realistic criticism of the world.

[S]ince Vienna, many of us, especially Neurath and I, have

criticized the existing order of society as unreasonable and have demanded that it should be reformed on the basis of scientific insights and careful planning in such a way that the needs and aspirations of all would be satisfied as far as possible.[43]

It was Neurath especially who called attention to political problems and who criticized any attempt to rise above political commitments in the 'technical' discussions of the Vienna Circle:

[W]e liked to keep our philosophical work separated from our political aims. In our view, logic, including applied logic, and the theory of knowledge, the analysis of language and the methodology of science, are, like science itself, neutral with respect to practical aims, whether they are . . . moral . . . or political. . . . Neurath criticized strongly this neutralist attitude, which in his opinion gave aid and comfort to the enemies of social progress. . . . Neurath's views about social problems were strongly influenced by Marx. But he was not a dogmatic Marxist. . . . He believed that our form of physicalism was an improved, non-metaphysical version [of materialism] which . . . should supersede both the mechanical and dialectical forms of nineteenth century materialism.[44]

In 1931 Neurath published *Empirical Sociology*.[45] This was meant to articulate the physicalist successor to dialectical materialism. Its approach was still being publicized by scientific empiricists twenty years after its appearance. Thus von Mises, writing in 1951 about the possibility of unifying the social and natural sciences, said that he could

agree with Neurath that sociology could be kept apart from history and that the Marx–Engels so-called materialistic conception of history represents a first long-range attempt to establish a relationship at large between the economic conditions of a class of people and other historical phenomena.[46]

In accepting Neurath's interpretation of Marxism, von Mises, as well as the members of the Vienna Circle, tended to follow Engels rather than Marx himself. Engels did not exactly play down the influence of Hegel on Marxist thought, but he seems to have liked the analogy between Marxism and Darwinism better. Marx's own understanding of the scientific claims of his theory have to be understood in quite a different, Hegelian, way.[47]

A place for the humanities?

Not only the social sciences but the humanities were incorporated into scientific empiricism. Neurath, in a paper on the form that he thought an encyclopaedia of unified science should take, stressed its inclusion of the humanities as an attraction.

> Many young people, to whom the sciences appear cold and distant in their isolation, will surely be attracted to unified science because of the possibility of connecting everything with everything else; and the desire to be many-sided, which is more frequent than is sometimes admitted, will be able to find a regular outlet in this field. The fact that this encyclopaedia deals with the history of art as well as crystallography, with education as well as technology, with jurisprudence as well as with mechanics, will, from the outset, counteract the view that logical empiricism is a matter for physicists and mathematicians. The basic idea that we have, finally, no firm basis, no system to fall back on, that we must always go on searching restlessly, and that we experience the most unexpected surprises if we want to test the fundamental assumptions which we have been using all along, this idea is characteristic of the attitude which we may call 'encyclopedism'.[48]

It was through the testing of ideas or fundamental assumptions that science, or at least scientific empiricism, could be spread to areas as far outside its sphere as the arts.

Neurath does not really go beyond naming some non-scientific subjects that an encyclopaedia could deal with. For an account that actually comments on a wide range of the arts and humanities from a scientific empiricist perspective, we can turn to von Mises. In Part Six of his *Positivism*, he considers the relations between science and other branches of learning and culture that on the surface are unscientific. These are metaphysics, poetry and the visual arts. His strategy in each case is to show that all have more in common with science than might be supposed, and that this being so, the scientific empiricist is not obliged to regard the arts as isolated productions without any use or value.

Though von Mises does not deny that there are differences between metaphysics and science (261–2), he thinks that their aims and problems are often the same or similar. Metaphysics lacks the clarity of science, and the scientific reluctance to recognize the reality of abstract entities corresponding to abstract expressions. In addition, it tends to assert a permanent independence of metaphysical from non-metaphysical fields, contrary to the belief of certain scientists and their philosophically minded supporters, that no field is necessarily out of the range of science. Nevertheless, metaphysics can share with science the same fundamental aim: 'to create a mental representation of the world, to describe reality, and to reveal interconnections that are suitable for guiding human actions' (264). Not only may metaphysics and science share the same aim, but the techniques used to realize this aim may start out by being metaphysical only to *become* scientific. Von Mises goes so far as to suggest that this is so as a rule, that metaphysics is not so much opposed to science and utterly divorced from science as a stage that thought passes through on the way to becoming scientific. Evidence from Hegel's writings of an attempt to reassimilate the results of natural science to metaphysics (266–7) are dismissed as aberrations or excesses that can be disregarded.[49] In general, 'metaphysics can be characterized as "science in its beginning". By asking questions that are still unconnectible one approaches problems whose clarification can be expected only by a further progress of science' (268). Von Mises goes on to associate metaphysical with religious systems, and calls both 'primitive' attempts at the solution of problems that are not yet treated by science (273).

The idea that metaphysics and science might not converge after all, because metaphysics has an unshakeable attachment to the a priori whereas science has no use for it, is met by a kind of psychological reduction of the a priori to feelings of certainty and to convictions of subjective evidence (277). These convictions and feelings may themselves be motivated, for example, by the desire for security and definitiveness. In any case, since the a priori is a psychological, rather than a logical, category, it has no tendency to show that metaphysics deals with a special sort of subject matter when it concerns itself with the a priori. A similar psychological story can be told to make intelligible the preference for holism in metaphysics. It is not that metaphysics treats of wholes and has a method of synthesis whereas science treats of parts and employs analytical techniques. For psychological reasons metaphysicians seek synoptic views, but this does not necessarily mean that metaphysics and science are concerned with different things (281–6).

Metaphysics is a kind of primitive science, according to von Mises, and poetry, in some of its forms, is a kind of metaphysics. It is metaphysics when it is mythological, and it has the relation to science that metaphysics has. As for other forms of poetry, these also have relations to science that can be clearly stated. Thus 'narrative poetry', including the novel, has a 'logical place' close to that of a thought-experiment in physics (291): assumptions are made that are not contradicted by experience, and a chain of events is constructed in thought that is also in accordance with experience, granted the assumptions. Though other forms of poetry differ in language and other conventions from 'narrative poetry', a creator of any kind of poetry invariably 'reports . . . experiences about vital interrelations between observable phenomena' (294). The subject matter of poetry, then, is not unconnected with that of science, though its use of language is very different. Even lyric poetry, at first sight completely cut off from science, communicates feelings that are based on knowledge and that originate in experience. No less an authority than Rilke is cited by von Mises in support of this claim (295).

When it comes to painting, an analogy with science is once again available, according to von Mises. A painter, he says, asserts something theoretical by means of his painting. In a landscape painting, for example, a use of colours can be tantamount to a theoretical identification in physics.

> This transition from green to brown *is* the river landscape, declares the landscapist Jacob van Ruisdael, and he accomplishes with this something similar to what the physicist does when he says that sounds are air vibrations. Every painting, every artistic creation is a *theory of a specific section of reality*. (303)

Von Mises intends this suggestion to contrast strongly with the traditional idea that art produces deception or illusion. He has other suggestions about the relation of science to painting. Not only is art supposed to be comparable to science in proposing theories of reality; it is itself supposed to be open to scientific study, as a branch of psychology and sociology (312).

Difficulties

Though he is much more definite than Neurath in his application of scientific empiricism to metaphysics, poetry and painting, von

Mises's account is much harder to accept. To begin with metaphysics, he simply does not show that its problems and solutions are primitive counterparts of scientific ones. It may be true that some scientific theories are answers to questions that were once addressed by metaphysical theories. It does not follow that all or even most metaphysical questions yield eventually to scientific answers. The idea that metaphysics prepares the ground for science at best fits parts of metaphysics. Not only is von Mises's account too general, it does not seem to account for the fact that certain metaphysical problems, such as the mind–body problem, keep up with scientific advance in reformulation after reformulation. The fact that certain metaphysical problems are perennial and adaptable does not seem to fit in with von Mises's idea of primitive questions withering away. The phenomenon of the perennial metaphysical question may also tell against von Mises's account of the aim of metaphysics. Perhaps metaphysics, especially after Kant, does not so much have the aim of producing a mental representation of the world or describing reality as the aim of exposing the limits of our understanding or of the significance of discourse. Finally, even if one accepts the idea that metaphysics can give way to science, and that metaphysics and science are both concerned with the description of reality, that way of putting it may be at too high a level of generality to show that science and metaphysics are continuous with one another. After all, to be concerned with what *must* be true of reality and what *is* true of reality are both ways of being concerned with reality, but they are not the same concern. For all von Mises establishes, this is how it is with metaphysics and physics: they do not necessarily have a common aim or common concern. So if science takes over from metaphysics, this may not be a case of science pursuing with more advanced, empirical techniques the sort of aims that metaphysics pursues primitively and speculatively. It may be a case instead of one aim being abandoned and a quite distinct one being taken up. Von Mises does not seem to allow for this sort of discontinuity in the process whereby metaphysics gives way to science. His account calls instead for the evolution of physics out of metaphysics; otherwise, there is no relating metaphysics to physics as primitive to advanced.

Turning now to von Mises's treatment of poetry, this too turns out to be unsatisfactory. Von Mises sometimes writes as if, in order to find a place for poetry in scientific empiricism, it is enough to show that poetry has something, not necessarily something important, in common with science or logic. For example, he says that 'every poem, except in rare extreme cases, contains judgements and implicit propositions and thus becomes subject to logical analysis' (289). This may be true, but it seems incidental to the status of something as a poem. Other of von Mises's attempts to minimize the differences between poetry and science focus on tenuous analogies. Thus, when von Mises tries to find the truth in the saying that poetry is without purpose, he confines himself to 'the fact that the artist does not always have in mind the concrete effect upon his listener or reader' (289). And he thinks this fact has a counterpart in science, in the case where research activity originally pursued with one aim goes off in an unexpected direction (289). Not only is this comparison tenuous – for one thing it likens the unexpected to the unintended – it badly explicates purposelessness in poetry. More central than the unintended or unexpected is the fact that there is no rigid determination of the content of a poem by its topic; another aspect of purposelessness is that the impulsion to write the poem is not completely recovered by specifying reasons. The operation of the unconscious in poetry may be significant. It is unclear that there would be analogous phenomena in science.

Two other weak points in von Mises's account of poetry may be mentioned. The first is concerned with 'connectibility'. Whereas different scientific theories are supposed to be in principle connectible, i.e. in principle locatable within a logically consistent system of sentences that regulate the use of a language (73), poems are not connectible, because the conventions followed in each

> admit of a usage in language in which many different meanings correspond to the same words and experiences and, above all, the same experiences can be expressed (approximately) in many different ways. If we call the single work of art a special theory of a section of reality . . . we must say that each of these separate 'theories' is written in a different language, so that they are not connectible, in principle, in the way that scientific theories are; connectibility is not even attempted in them. (293)

If correct, von Mises's claims about the conventions governing poetry only show that the conventions permit ambiguity. It is unclear, however, whether the possibility of ambiguity is sufficient for establishing different languages, or hence, whether it is sufficient for establishing the absence of connectibility. It is also unclear how, to recall another claim of his about poetry, a poem could be a theory of a section of reality and not be, even in principle, connectible. Of course, it is not very plausible that poems are always or typically theories of reality; so their being unconnectible may not matter. The point is, it is hard to see how von Mises can have it both ways, claiming that poetry is like science in being a vehicle for a theory of reality and unlike science in respect of being unconnectible.

Another weak point in von Mises's account of poetry is where he denies that feeling can be a source of lyric poetry. It is clear that unreduced poetic feeling is hard to accommodate in a scientific empiricist outlook, and so von Mises looks for a basis or source for poetic feeling that scientific empiricism *can* find room for. He claims that the feeling can have origins in knowledge and experience. But it does not follow from the fact that feelings can have origins in knowledge and experience that the knowledge and experience can by themselves be sufficient to inspire, and in that sense be the source of, lyric poetry. Nor does it mean, as von Mises claims (295), that the poems 'express' the knowledge and experience behind the feeling. The attempt to get feeling to cancel out in his account of poetry seems to fail.

Some of the defects of von Mises's account of poetry also affect his treatment of painting. Paintings, like poems, count for him as theories of reality, but the working out of the idea of painting as theory does not carry conviction. It is quite plausible that paintings are used by painters to, in von Mises's phrase, 'express themselves about an object exhibited' (303). But it is quite implausible to say that to express oneself about an object exhibited is the same thing as, or is naturally explicated as, giving a theory of an exhibited object or section of reality. This explication does not even fit all of von Mises's examples. He takes the case of Frans Hals's portrait of Descartes and says that it is used by Hals to assert: 'This is what Descartes looks like; these are the eyes of the sceptical thinker, who still keeps many things he knows to himself' (303). But how is this a theory? If the portrait reconstructed Descartes's appearance from scattered evidence that would be one thing; perhaps the portrait could even make a theoretical statement about Descartes's personality or character; it is hard to see how, if it is drawn from life, it can be a theory of Descartes's appearance. And if a portrait is inferentially constructed it looks like too unusual a specimen of painting to cite in favour of a theory of painting.

Von Mises has a second way of co-ordinating painting or art with science. He speaks of 'empirical esthetics' or 'empirical science of art':

> This field belongs to 'humanities', and we remember what has been said . . . about the relation of natural to humanistic science. There is no fundamental contrast in subject matter, in method, or even in the kind of understanding that comes to the fore here, but rather a change of emphasis with respect to the various elements that constitute a scientific exposition. . . . The description of the complex of phenomena to which the word 'art' points takes naturally at first the form of a historical, in certain cases a geographical–historical, study. . . . From historical descriptions, especially if one stresses the so-called humanistic point of view, there gradually develops, as one tries to perfect them, rudimentary 'theories' in the form of general statements about repeatable individual events. As a very far removed goal appears a closed deductive (axiomatic, tautological) system, which would display the relevant aspects of one or the other particular field. (310)

This is not exactly a proposal for bringing art within the sphere of science, but for bringing reactions to art within the sphere of science.[50] Von Mises leads up to his proposal with a criticism of philosophical theories of beauty, and he concludes his negative reactions about Kant's remarks on beauty with the claim that the words 'beautiful' and 'ugly' 'must not immediately appear in a theory that claims to be scientific. . . . The so-called search for absolute and objective beauty is inconsistent with the logic of the language' (306). Presumably, then, the empirical aesthetics that von Mises describes would make do without the concept of beauty in particular. But how, in these circumstances, one could be left with an aesthetic theory, as opposed to systematic art-history, is again quite unclear.

The criticisms of von Mises's claims about metaphysics, poetry and painting show, I think, that in order to represent these fields as continuous with science, he is forced to reinterpret them, sometimes in ways that are extremely implausible or one-sided. Von Mises's accounts of metaphysics, poetry and painting are not independently appealing, and their drawbacks may throw doubt on the possibility and desirability of unifying the humanities with the rest of learning and the exact sciences. The alternative to this sort of unification is not necessarily a picture of learning in which the humanities are cut off from the exact sciences; e.g. an historical account of the differentiation of the arts from the sciences would not leave out art in this way. Neither would the 'encyclopaedic' approach favoured by Neurath, so long as it was implemented in the spirit of his dictum that 'an encyclopaedia does not oblige collaborators to adopt a common programme, each reader must carry out the task of unifying and connecting for himself'.[51]

Doubts about the possibility of an ambitious form of unification arise as much for the social sciences as for the humanities, though in this case the proposed means of unification is admittedly clearer. As we saw, Clark Hull's description of the formulation and testing of postulates and laws suggests a methodological unification of some research programmes in the social sciences; Carnap's rather different idea of unification through the reduction of scientific language to phenomenalist language or to physicalist language, is another conception of the means of unifying science. The problem with these proposals is not that they are indefinite, but that they have proved virtually impossible to carry out.

2

THE ROOTS OF SCIENTISM?

Scientism in philosophy did not begin with scientific empiricism. Beliefs about the surpassing practical benefits, intellectual rigour and objectivity of science, beliefs about its central position in learning or culture, were widely shared by philosophers long before the twentieth century. Indeed, it is sometimes held that what I am calling scientism in philosophy is traceable to a number of related philosophical mistakes that were made by the early modern philosophers of science, figures such as Bacon, Descartes and Locke.[1] Tailoring their conception of the mind to what they believed suited the mind to science, these philosophers are supposed to have been attracted to foundationalism in epistemology, introspective theories of the mental in the philosophy of mind, and an exaggerated rationalism in the philosophy of science. Tailoring their conception of the mind to what science required, they put into circulation a deeply misleading metaphor for the mind, the metaphor of the mirror of nature. The mind was a medium for accurate representation of the world. In the scientific empiricists, a similar claim is made about language. It, too, is principally and essentially a medium for accurate description, as are some forms of pictorial representation, and the fact that the aim of accurate description can be found in painting as well as poetry, and in metaphysics as well as physics, shows that no sector of culture is entirely cut off from science. Von Mises, as we have seen, even reverts to unreconstructed talk of mental representation where he describes the common aim of metaphysics and science. In this way the excesses of scientism seem to be traceable to a seventeenth-century conception of the mind. In opposition to this account I shall suggest that as taken up by Descartes and Bacon the metaphor of the mirror of nature is largely harmless. I shall then suggest a different source in these philosophers for the scientism expressed in our century.

It will help to restate the five theses that were used in the last chapter to get at the scientism in scientific empiricism: (1) science is unified; (2) there are no limits to science; (3) science has been enormously successful at prediction, explanation and control; (4) the methods of science confer objectivity on scientific results; and (5) science has been beneficial for human beings. Of these theses it is the fourth which is hardest for philosophers to attack without seeming to abandon values that have been at the centre of the subject since Descartes. Even if one denies that there is a genuinely distinctive method or methods of science that account for its success, it is hard not to associate science with the achievement, perhaps by a number of different means, of an increasingly objective – an increasingly accurate – conception of the world. It is also hard to deny that this is something science does aim at and that is good for it to achieve. The fact that it is hard to rid science of these associations in philosophy, however, does not mean that one should not try, especially if incoherence or illusion is involved in bearing out the thought that part of the success of science is increasing objectivity. A number of philosophers have argued that incoherence or illusion *is* involved. Feyerabend is one;[2] Kuhn, on some interpretations, is another;[3] Rorty[4] is a third, and each of these writers claims many allies. I shall focus on Rorty, because he seems to see more clearly than the others how the values at stake in doubting the objectivity of science are crucial to the self-image of philosophy.

RORTY ON MIRRORING

'The picture which holds traditional philosophy captive', Rorty writes,

> is that of the mind as a great mirror, containing various representations – some accurate, some not – and capable of being studied by pure, nonempirical methods. Without the notion of the mind as mirror, the notion of knowledge as accuracy of representation would not have suggested itself. Without this latter notion, the strategy common to Descartes and Kant – getting more accurate representations by inspecting, repairing and polishing the mirror, so to speak – would not have made sense. Without this strategy in mind, recent

claims that philosophy could consist of 'conceptual analysis' or 'phenomenological analysis' or 'explication of meanings' or examination of the 'logic of our language' or of 'the structure of the constituting activity of consciousness' would not have made sense. (P&MN, 12)

Rorty tries to fight free of traditional philosophy and the captivation of its picture of the mind, following, as he thinks, in the footsteps of Dewey, Heidegger and Wittgenstein.

Starting with Descartes, philosophers are supposed to have looked for a class of ideas or representations which were certain, and which would serve as foundations of knowledge. From Descartes to Kant, Rorty suggests, philosophy as epistemology pretended to be somehow better than, because fundamental to, the rest of the sciences. It insinuated itself as the pre-eminent science, and was instrumental in making science seem the pre-eminent form of culture. The arrogance of epistemology-centred philosophy and its academic aridity are not the only defects Rorty uncovers. The subject is also full of confusion. Especially in the form in which it has come down to us from Locke and Kant, philosophy has confused the causes of knowledge with the justification of knowledge. And criticisms in our own century of the Myth of the Given and the analytic/synthetic distinction show that the confusion in post-Kantian epistemology is complicated and profound (P&MN, 209). The right response to this accumulation of criticisms, Rorty suggests, is to

> drop the notion of epistemology as the quest, initiated by Descartes, for those privileged items in the field of consciousness which are the touchstones of truth. . . . To understand the matters which Descartes wanted to understand – the superiority of the New Science to Aristotle, the relations between this science and mathematics, common sense, theology and morality – we need to turn outward rather than inward, toward the social context of justification rather than to the relations between inner representations. (P&MN, 210)

Descartes and ideas fit for science

Rorty overstresses the importance of the inner and of consciousness to Decartes's concerns. The mathematical content of the new science mattered at least as much to him as the impact of that content on consciousness, and there was much in consciousness that Descartes thought was of no use to science. Moreover, in the *Discourse and Essays*, which contained as much of a would-be demonstration of the superiority of the new science as the *Meditations*, the material on consciousness, on clarity and distinctness, and on doubt is passed over very quickly. Descartes deliberately kept the metaphysical content of the *Discourse* to a minimum, hoping that the fruitfulness of the specimens of the new science in the *Essays* would speak for itself. The full-scale metaphysical demonstration of the superiority of the new science was attempted only reluctantly, when troubles with the Jesuits and unexpected criticisms of the hypotheses in the *Essays* showed that he had to argue for the new science not by its results but from first principles. The point is that the metaphysical demonstration that he eventually produced in the *Meditations* was not the only demonstration of the viability of the new science that he thought could be given. In any case, the *Meditations* does not make quite the use of the veil of ideas and of inner and outer that Rorty's repudiation of Descartes requires.

In his first philosophy Descartes is trying simultaneously to explain why one body of learning with scientific pretensions – scholastic physics – should have proved bankrupt and why another body of thought – one largely outlined by Descartes himself – could live up to a billing as true science. Scholastic physics had proved bankrupt – it had thrown up anomaly after anomaly – because, as Descartes put it in the *Discourse on Method*, it drew its foundations from philosophy, in which nothing was certain, and because it relied on a purely qualitative, sense-based and fallible theory of natural substances and the causes of their observed effects. Scholastic physics was also embarrassed by its impious implications, as pyrrhonist critics in the early 1600s pointed out. For, on the one hand, in the spirit of Aristotle, it purported to deduce from necessary principles the necessity of observed effects. Yet, on the other hand, its principles were supposed to cohere with articles of faith, including the article of faith that God was a free and omnipotent agent who might have made natural effects different from what they are: scholastic physics could not both demonstrate the necessity of its effects and keep intact a thesis of voluntarism. Descartes wanted to side with critics of scholastic physics while also trying to demonstrate that a different, geometrical explanation of natural effects was freer of anomalies, independent of the sensory, and compatible with the idea of an omnipotent and benign

God. He needed a theory that would explain the shortcomings of the scholastic–Aristotelian theory of nature, and an alternative physics that would be free of these shortcomings. The theory had to explain why science had developed so little since Aristotle, but, being part of Descartes's propaganda for a new, largely untried approach to natural explanation, it could not feed pessimism about the further development of science. Thus it had to undercut the belief of some seventeenth-century Europeans that the human intellect was caught up in the decay of nature and was deteriorating in such a way that the achievements of the ancients would never be equalled after their time.[5] It had to suggest instead that the human intellect was capable of scientific progress once certain hindrances to it were removed. Descartes suggested that some of the hindrances were natural – contributed by the union of the intellect with a body during the natural life of a human being. Mind–body union accounted for the presence in the intellect of some ideas that, while useful for survival, gave no scientific insight, but were nevertheless improperly made into vehicles or sources of scientific theory.

The Cartesian theory of ideas had to contribute to explaining the backwardness of one sort of scientific theory without ruling out the possibility of a better one. 'Backward theory' meant one that was *ad hoc*, obscure in its explanatory terminology, that regularly misdescribed phenomena and proposed erroneous hypotheses. Now it is hard for a theory that explains error – false belief – not to commit itself to mental representations – representations by the mind of nature. So unless there is something suspect about the explanation of error, there should be nothing suspect about invoking mental representations of *some* kind or other. Yet surely if mental representations can be legitimately invoked by a philosophical theory of error, so can the metaphor of the distorting mirror. It may be true that some candidates for the role of mental represent-ation are bad candidates – Humean impressions, say, or, if the stock interpretation of Locke is right, Lockean ideas. It may be that some expressions of the metaphor are misleading. These, however, are not Rorty's complaints. Rorty thinks that the very idea of a mirror of nature, the very idea of accurate or inaccurate mental representation, is unnecessary and even harmful in philosophy. I claim, to the contrary, that, at least for the explanation of error, it may be necessary and helpful, and I claim that it is for this purpose that mental representations come into Descartes's philosophy.

It is not that Descartes mysteriously arrives at a 'veil of ideas' doctrine and then uses it to justify scepticism, as Rorty holds (P&MN, 94n); instead, scepticism is taken to be justified by errors, gaps and paradoxes in science (scholastic science) and then a certain theory of ideas is used to show within what limits these errors, gaps and paradoxes are avoidable. The theory of ideas that Descartes developed was a branch of what he called 'metaphysics': metaphysics in his sense dealt with principles about immaterial things that had to be known before a systematic natural science could be developed. Foremost among these immaterial things was the mind itself, which Descartes tried to clear of the pyrrhonist charge of being incapable of science. According to Descartes it really was within human powers to arrive at a systematic and true understanding of nature, for such an understanding was mathematical and its ingredients – ideas of simple natures – were present in the human mind. Being implanted by a non-deceiving God, the ideas could not be false. Nor was the possession of these ideas a contingent matter. To be able to think was to have these ideas, albeit latently. Sense-experience, far from drawing on these innate mathematical ideas, presented the sensible qualities of observed things, qualities that an undisciplined faculty of judgement could falsely ascribe to the natures of observed things. As if the natures of things could be gathered directly from natural phenomena. In fact, however, and as Descartes's optics indicated, all of sense-experience could be explained on the assumption that things acting upon the senses really were very different in nature from how the sensible qualities made them seem.

To explain the sensible qualities of observed things, it was unnecessary to suppose that corresponding real qualities actually inhered in the objects observed: the size, shape, position and speed of the parts of the observed things and their containing medium were by themselves sufficient to account for the quality of experience. This fact was a ground for doubting that the explanation of experience had to be qualitative at all. Thus, apples did not have to be supposed to possess a form of redness in order to seem red. The appearance of redness could be supposed to result from interactions of illuminated external bodies of such and such composition with human eyes and brains. And what went for redness went for all the other qualities, qualities that underpinned the division of nature into natural kinds by Aristotelian physics.

The lesson of the optics was reinforced by the metaphysics, which showed independently, in the form of the Dream Hypothesis, that qualitative conceptions of objects might have little or nothing in common with the objects themselves. Even the ideas of non-qualitative simple natures involved in the qualitative conceptions – even the ideas of extension and number involved in the idea of a single sweet, red apple – might have no basis in reality, for, as the Demon Hypothesis showed, it was conceivable that even one's ideas of simples were the products of a demon deceiver.

The Dream and the Demon Hypotheses are directed by Descartes against the pretensions of two types of sciences, on the one hand the sciences of 'complex things' (physics, medicine, astronomy, meteorology, etc.) and on the other sciences of simple things (geometry and arithmetic). The Dream Hypothesis showed that the sciences of complex things were conceivably very uncertain, because there might be very little correspondence between their understanding of the objects they studied and the natures of the objects. As for the sciences of the simple things (lines, numbers, proportions), though they were not discredited by the Dream Hypothesis, though they were more certain than the sciences of complex things, they were, for all that, not impervious to doubt, for they were conceivably the product of demonic manipulation, and so could not be relied upon to contain truths.

It is by way of the Dream and Demon Hypotheses that Descartes's metaphysics engages the traditional Aristotelian sciences and agrees with the pyrrhonists that they are thoroughly doubtful. It is by way of a theological proof of the objectivity of the simple natures that Descartes is able to give a pious vindication of the new mathematical sciences. The *Meditations* was not the first work to concede something to scepticism about the old science while sticking up for the new science. Mersenne, in the mid 1620s, had produced a monumental treatise along essentially these lines: *La Vérité des sciences*. But the *Meditations* was something different. It cunningly appropriated the form of a book of instruction for religious meditation. It introduced a very exacting and systematic type of methodological doubt to do duty for an informal pyrrhonist one, and it implemented a crypto-programme of laying down principles for an anti-Aristotelian physics in a text ostensibly answering a papal call to Christian philosophers to vindicate the belief in God and the immortality of the soul.

Ideas and veils of perception

I come now to the question of whether the ideas of simple natures or any other Cartesian ideas belong to a representative theory of perception or a veil of ideas doctrine. It seems doubtful that they do. Descartes's theory of ideas contributes to a theory of scientific error and scientific knowledge. As a contribution to the explanation of error it is concerned with establishing a discrepancy between hypotheses about the natures of objects that we might arrive at on the basis of sense-experience, and hypotheses that we might arrive at if matter were modelled on or even identified with geometrical space. Comparatively little of Descartes's text can be explained by reference to the point usually made by veil of perception theorists, namely that what we see when we look at an object is not the object itself but some appearance it presents, an appearance that changes as, for example, our vantage point does. None of Descartes's text indicates that he was interested in the usual sequel to the point about appearances, namely the task of phenomenalist reconstruction. Descartes does not try to construct the material world out of ideas or sense-data; on the contrary, he constructs the world out of the geometrical natures of length, depth, breadth and the laws of motion. Ideas come in only when one asks about the origin of the criterion of truth that he uses to justify his geometrical conception of the world. The criterion dawns on him at a stage in his metaphysical argument at which he is assuming that only he and his ideas are real, but it is only the criterion, not the solipsism, that survives to inform his physics. Nor, again, is much of his text illuminated by emphasizing his point that ideas and thoughts are one and all things of which the mind is conscious. He typically insists on this not when expounding his theory of ideas proper, but only when he is explaining how, in the context of the method of doubt, it has to be 'cogito, ergo sum' and not 'ambulo, ergo sum' or 'sto, ergo sum'.

The distinctive feature of ideas is not so much their accessibility to the conscious subject as what they are of or about. As Descartes says in the fifth paragraph of Meditation Three, to have an idea is above all else to think *of* a thing, to think of a man, a chimera, the sky, an angel or God. In other words, to speak of an idea is primarily to speak of a representation *of something*, and only secondarily a representation *to someone*. Without denying that Descartes writes at times as if there is an inner eye watching an inner arena, it seems possible to deny that these passages pick out what is central to Descartes's theory of ideas or to his theory of the mind.

Idols without veils of perception

Descartes, I am claiming, is committed at most to a harmless kind of non-pictorial mirroring in the form of thoughts of things. It is unlikely that he believes in veils of ideas or at least that veils matter much to his theory of ideas. Bacon's mirror metaphor is not enmeshed in a representative theory of perception either.

As in Descartes, Bacon's claims[6] about the distorting powers of the mind are part of an explanation of the backward state of science. He thinks that science has been held back by, among other things, the nature of the human mind, but the hindrance has not been a veil of ideas coming between the mind and reality. The senses put the mind directly in touch with the world, all right, but not with very much of it, according to Bacon, and not immediately with the part which matters to science. The senses take in what they do of nature by scraping the surface; what matter to science are the secret workings of objects below the surface – the 'working of the spirits in tangible bodies' and 'the subtle changes of form in the parts of coarser substances' (W IV, 58). The use of aids to the senses, such as the telescope or the microscope, enlarges the range of the senses, but these instruments are no real cure for the shortcomings of the senses: 'instances' and 'experiments' are what are needed (ibid.).

Bacon probably has as much or more to say about defects of mind apart from the shortcomings of the senses than about the senses themselves. He specifies some of these defects in *The Advancement of Learning* when he describes the branch of human philosophy that deals with the faculties of the soul. In the same general branch of the subject in which the will, appetites and affections are studied by moral philosophy, Bacon makes room for an account of the understanding and reason (W III, 382). These faculties are approached by way of four arts that bring them into play: an art of enquiry, an art of examining or judgement, an art of memory, and an art of elocution or 'tradition' (communication). An extended account of the defects of the mind, which anticipates the fuller theory given in Bacon's *Novum Organum*, is given in the course of a discussion of the art of judgement. Bacon follows tradition in saying that this art is concerned with valid proofs or demonstrations, as well as with *elenches* or the more common forms of departure from sound reasoning or judgement. Bacon's account of the *elenches* is unusual, however, for it 'hath a more ample latitude and extent than is perceived' (W III, 394). The doctrine takes in errors of reasoning caused by ambiguity, and distortions of judgement due to the overpowering effect of the imagination. But lastly, Bacon says, 'there is a much more important and profound kind of fallacies in the mind of men, which I find not observed or enquired at all' (ibid.), namely, those that he would later call the idols of the understanding.

He runs through these fallacies in a few pages (W III, 395–7). The mind of man, he says, is 'not a clear and equal glass' but 'an enchanted one', full of superstition. For example, by its nature, the mind is more inclined to believe in the reality of positive attributes than of privations. It can be overinfluenced by custom, and easily taken in by the false appearances created by words. In *The Advancement of Learning* Bacon suggests that the simple knowledge that we are subject to these false appearances helps to prevent our being taken in by them. But there is no escaping their influence entirely because 'they are inseparable from our nature and condition of life' (W III, 397). In *Novum Organum*, on the other hand, Bacon speaks as if people could rid themselves of the ill effects of some of these appearances by a kind of renunciation (First Book of Aphorisms, 68; W IV, 69), or at least by a method of refutation (W IV, 27). In general, Bacon advises 'every student of nature [to] take this as a rule, – that whatever his mind seizes and dwells upon with particular satisfaction is to be held in suspicion . . .' (W IV, 60). The rule resembles the first of the four given by Descartes in the *Discourse on Method*.

Novum Organum also suggests that there are innate and adventitious sources of misinformation and subjectivity in the human understanding. It is in this context that he compares the human understanding to 'a false mirror, which, receiving rays irregularly, distorts and discolours the nature of things by mingling its own nature with it' (W IV, 54). But when Bacon says that the human understanding is a false mirror he claims that not only the perceptions of the senses but also the perceptions of the mind 'are according to the measure of the individual' rather than the measure of the universe. He gives examples of tainted perceptions of the mind when he complains of the way pride in invention, investment of effort or simple familiarity can make some speculations and sciences seem superior to others (W IV, 59). Other doubtful perceptions of the mind flow from a mind's being specially sensitive to difference rather than similarity or are due to a mind's being prone to pay more attention to structure than to parts in isolation or vice versa (W IV, 60). The identification of these defects does not depend in any obvious way on a theory of the mind that emphasizes the inner/outer distinction, or on some intimate communion between the mind and its ideas. Yet Bacon's account of the defects does explicate the claim that the human understanding is a false mirror. The upshot is that the mirror metaphor can be detached from the objectionable Inner Eye/Inner Arena picture of the mind. If there is a ground in Rorty's writings for rejecting Bacon's scientism for its dependence on the mirror metaphor, then, we have yet to uncover it.

SEVENTEENTH-CENTURY PHILOSOPHY AND THE BENEFITS OF SCIENCE

We have been pursuing the idea that seventeenth-century philosophy of science is the source of some of what is wrong with the scientism of the scientific empiricists. In particular, we have been looking at the antecedents in seventeenth-century philosophy of thesis (4) of scientific empiricism, which is sometimes supposed to carry a distorted conception of scientific objectivity. Perhaps we do better to look at another scientific empiricist thesis for a stronger connection with seventeenth-century thought. Perhaps we do better to look at thesis (5), which advertises, and perhaps exaggerates, the benefits to humanity of applied science. This thesis is sometimes attributed to Bacon. For example, a reputable interpreter of Enlightenment thought, Maurice Cranston, has written,

> Bacon had died in 1626, but that did not mean that his message was out of date. On the contrary, it had a kind of actuality for eighteenth-century France which made him, to a greater extent even than Locke or Newton, a prophetic figure for the whole French Enlightenment. For Bacon was the first philosopher of science. It was not that Bacon made any scientific discoveries of his own; he simply proclaimed the doctrine that science could save us. . . . Once men knew how nature worked, they could exploit nature to their advantage, overcome scarcity by scientific innovations in agriculture,

overcome disease by scientific research in medicine, and generally improve the life of man by all sorts of developments in technology and industry.[7]

The power of science to improve human life was certainly insisted upon by the Encyclopaedists. Instruction in science was even seen as a source of moral improvement. In the *Encyclopaedia* article entitled 'Encyclopédie', Diderot wrote that the purpose of an encyclopaedia was to collect all available knowledge, reveal its overall structure to an audience of contemporaries, and preserve it for future generations, 'so that our children, becoming better instructed, may become at the same time more virtuous and happy' (*Oeuvres complètes*, vol. 7, p. 174). The association of science with virtue in the eighteenth century was also to be seen in Fontenelle's eulogies of deceased members of the Paris Academy of Sciences.[8] But the idea that science might save us – might be a panacea – is not easy to find in seventeenth-century writers, and it is not in Bacon. It is true that Hobbes claimed that through his own civil philosophy the arts and sciences would improve morals, just as, through natural philosophy, they had already improved agriculture, navigation and architecture.[9] But Hobbes would have denied that science by itself could save us.[10] As for Bacon, passages in the *Advancement of Learning* and *Great Instauration* do say that the arts and sciences can improve the human condition, but they also caution against expecting too much from the arts and sciences, and they indicate that confusion over the true purposes of the arts and sciences has harmed their reputation.

Scientism of a kind *is* to be found in Bacon, but it is much too muted to generate claims about the possibility of a scientific sort of salvation. If Bacon really had envisaged such a thing, he would have put it by saying that the arts and sciences were capable of undoing completely the Fallen condition of Man. And while he does relate the potential benefits of the arts and sciences to the Fall, he does not say that the arts and sciences are by themselves an antidote. He says that

> man by the fall fell at the same time from the state of innocency and from his dominion over creation. Both of these losses can in this life be in some part repaired; the first by religion and faith; the latter by the arts and sciences. (W III, 248)

Only one type of loss, that of dominion over creation, can be offset by the arts and sciences, and the arts and sciences cannot make up for it completely. It is possible that Bacon considers salvation to involve the recovery of this dominion; but it cannot consist of this alone. It must also involve a spiritual transformation brought about by religion, and religion, in Bacon's scheme, is neither an art nor a science. It follows that for Bacon out and out human salvation is not a possible by-product of the arts and sciences.

He did not even claim that the development of the arts and sciences could significantly increase people's earthly goods. Instead of providing a high standard of living, the arts and sciences were supposed to give relief from a very miserable one. In general, Bacon did not so much whip up optimism about the possibilities of science as try to counteract a debilitating pessimism about the powers of human beings. Unlike other writers who argued in the sixteenth and seventeenth centuries that the improvement of the human condition was possible, however, Bacon tended to play down the worth of inventions such as the compass and the printing press that were taken to show that the talents of the moderns could rival those of the ancients. Such innovations as had occurred haphazardly and without method, he tended to suggest, would be entirely overshadowed by the fruits of co-operative scientific work carried out according to approved canons of research. At the time of the *Great Instauration* almost everything remained to be accomplished: there was, according to Bacon, no real progress to take pride in. The benefits of science had yet to be enjoyed, but there was reason to think that, within modest limits, they one day could be.

A QUESTIONABLE PRE-EMINENCE FOR REASON AND SCIENCE

Reading what Bacon actually wrote about the benefits of the arts and sciences ought to encourage a doubt as to whether, laying so much weight on religion, and promising so little in the way of immediate benefits from the arts and sciences, he really anticipated the enthusiasm of the Enlightenment for science.

Nevertheless, another approach is possible, and this may reveal a genuine scientistic tendency, one that seventeenth-century philosophy shares with later intellectual movements like scientific empiricism. The more promising approach consists of locating the connection between scientism and seventeenth-century philosophy in thesis (1) of scientific empiricism ('science is unified') and asking whether figures like Bacon and perhaps Descartes overdo their enthusiasm for the new science, either by denigrating subjects which do not submit to its methods, or by pretending that there are no such subjects – that everything can be understood scientifically.

Bacon does not quite assimilate all of learning to science or philosophy, but he does subordinate non-scientific to scientific subjects, just as he subordinates the faculties which give rise to non-scientific subjects – memory and imagination – to reason. Descartes does not assimilate all of learning to science either, but he goes further in this direction than Bacon does, apparently absorbing both the doctrine of God's nature and morals almost completely into the body of science.

In Bacon's classification of the branches of human learning, the three main subjects of poesy, history and philosophy, correspond to three faculties of the understanding: imagination, memory and reason. Bacon's treatment of poesy is, by his standards, perfunctory, and it is also unflattering. Poetry is either of interest to the arts of eloquence only, or else it 'is nothing else but Feigned History' (W III, 343), that is, a type of narrative that removes the displeasing tedium, messiness and injustice of actual events and actions, and introduces a pattern more pleasing to the soul. Feigned histories contain 'a more ample greatness, a more exact goodness, and a more absolute variety, than can be found in the nature of things', or in a record of events involving these things. In its most familiar form, then, poesy is a kind of imitation of history, a wishful but uplifting narrative in words. Representative poesy is a parade of images of things as if they were present, rather than, as in a genuine history, as if they were past. Finally, allusive or parabolical poesy, as in the form of Aesop's fables, is history in which abstract ideas are made accessible in images that are vivid to the senses (W III, 344). Either that, or it is an adjunct to teaching or demonstration of a religious, philosophical or political kind (ibid.).

Bacon's taxonomy of narrative, representative and allegorical poesy does not seem to do justice to the variety of the writing he is trying to describe, and by making poesy a sort of failed history, he seems not to recognize the distinctive content and functions of the fine arts, or, to the extent that these functions might be thought to overlap with those of history and philosophy, the possibility that poesy or painting could be a way of representing the real. Partly as a consequence, Bacon seems unduly reluctant to concede that poesy could be beneficial. He concedes that it produces pleasure, but only the pleasure of feeding oneself uplifting illusions. He concedes no role to it in reconciling us to what is real, or consoling us about what is unpleasant in reality.

These problems with his account of poesy are foreshadowed in his account of the faculty that gives rise to poesy, namely the imagination. Unlike reason which 'doth buckle and bow the mind unto the nature of things' (W III, 344), the imagination bends the things it represents to the mind's standards. This is harmless in the sphere of poesy, but damaging in other branches of learning, for imagination is at the root of both credulity and the reporting of the fabulous (W III, 287–9). Imagination fits neatly on neither side of the divide between the Understanding and the Will (W III, 382). It acts as a kind of broker between the cognitive and the conative in man: it enables the practical decrees of reason to be acted upon by the will. And apparently it also transforms sensory information so that reason can make a judgement on the basis of it (ibid.). It mediates between Reason on the one hand and Sense and Will on the other, but in view of its responsibility for lending credibility to the imaginary, it is not to be trusted.

Memory is supposed to be more useful than the imagination, especially when it is methodically controlled, but it is a kind of servant to reason, as is history to philosophy. It is true that history, like philosophy, is a synoptic branch of learning, but it is inferior to philosophy in that it derives from philosophy the methods that make it effective. In particular, it owes the methods that make it effective to the rational part of human philosophy (W III, 383), the part that describes 'rational knowledges' and that teaches the Arts Intellectual of Invention, Judgement, Memory and Elocution:

> But to speak truly of things as they are in worth, Rational Knowledges are the keys of all other arts; for as Aristotle saith aptly and elegantly, That the hand is the Instrument of Instruments, and the mind is the Form of Forms: so these be truly said to be the Art of Arts; neither do they only direct, but likewise confirm and strengthen; even as the art of shooting doth not only enable to shoot a nearer shoot, but also to draw a stronger bow. (W III, 383)

In view of the possession by philosophy of the Art of Arts a kind of hierarchy emerges among the various branches of learning. Poesy is at the bottom, a sort of failed history, then history, and, at the top, philosophy or science.

Philosophy or science is the master branch of learning in more than the sense that it supplies methods for the other main branches of learning; it is the master science also in the sense that it treats of the sources of the other branches of learning. The faculties which give rise to the other branches are part of the subject matter of philosophy, as are, presumably, the branches of learning themselves and the causes of their relative state of development. Finally, philosophy or science is the master science in the sense that it is the one with the greatest benefits to mankind, the one uniquely able to transform things in nature for human benefit. The production of effects is, in Bacon's classification of learning, a pre-eminently philosophical or scientific function and not the office of history or poesy. In particular it is the function of natural philosophy, which is the pre-eminent branch of philosophy. Natural philosophy in Bacon's scheme overshadows natural theology (W III, 349) – the treatment of natural effects as evidence of God's power and understanding – and it contains human philosophy or morals and politics (W III, 366). It is in natural philosophy that at least three of the supreme Arts Intellectual, those of Invention, Judgement and Memory, have their main applications.

Bacon and practical reason

I have already complained that Bacon seems to overvalue philosophy in the scheme of learning, and it is plausible to hold that he overvalues reason in the scheme of the human faculties, where memory, and especially imagination, come off worse. A related problem is that Bacon inclines too readily toward an identification of reason with theoretical reason. It is true that practical reason of a kind is recognized, notably natural magic or the production of effects based on the knowledge of forms. But this is a species of practical reason that depends on theoretical reason. A different sort of practical reason, operating on knowledge of moral requirements, rather than forms in natural substances, might have been thought to operate in morals and politics. If Bacon recognizes such a faculty, however, it is hard to gather as much from *The Advancement of Learning*.

Bacon's failure to describe a practical reason fit for morals, his tendency to restrict practical knowledge to applied theoretical knowledge of nature, is evidence of his having associated philosophy or science too closely with natural philosophy or science. Bacon does not say that all of learning is science or that all science is natural science; he does not say in so many words that reason is better adapted to theoretical than to practical questions. But non-scientific branches of learning are sometimes denigrated, and the natural sciences are sometimes overprominent, in his scheme of learning. In the same vein, the uses of reason associated with natural science are too readily taken to be the central uses of reason. Scientism and naturalism combine to unbalance Bacon's account of learning.

Comparable difficulties affect other accounts of learning developed in the seventeenth century. In Descartes's reconstruction of knowledge on certain foundations at least one major subject from unreconstructed learning, namely theology, is entirely absent, while another – morals – is described, at first sight improbably, as an offshoot of physics. The distinction between certain and uncertain subjects, between scientific and unscientific branches of learning, inevitably devalues subjects like theology on the 'uncertain' and 'unscientific' sides of these divides, even though parts of learning without pretensions to conclusive truth can be valuable for being consoling, uplifting or simply absorbing or interesting.

We have come upon some genuine anticipations of twentieth-century scientism in seventeenth-century philosophy. The idea that science can be inclusive, the related idea that scientific reasoning is a master key to all sorts of intellectual and practical problems – these ideas are enduring elements of scientistic thinking. In the next chapter we see in outline the right sort of response to them.

3

REASON, SCIENCE AND
THE WIDER CULTURE

Art and religion, ethics, politics and history all stand in uneasy relations to science or philosophy in certain seventeenth-century classifications of learning. They are no better placed in the scheme of the sciences proposed by scientific empiricism. Either they are made to appear inferior to science for no compelling reason, or else they are questionably assimilated to science. Is there a way of overturning the low valuations of art and religion, and of asserting the autonomy of ethics and politics? Or are the classifications that we have been considering, though imperfect, along the right lines? Is science in fact the master branch of learning – in the sense that it is the most valuable branch of learning? Or must equal worth be accorded to some non-sciences? Is science in principle perfectly inclusive, or are certain branches of learning irremediably unscientific? Equally, must reason be regarded as the master faculty, superior to memory and imagination? Or is a different account possible?

The belief that a different account *is* possible is well represented in Western philosophy after the 1600s, and it is expressed in two conflicting sorts of theories. There are theories which, without dampening the seventeenth-century admiration for reason and science, revalue upwards other faculties and other branches of learning. This is the approach followed by Kant, who at the same time as he upgrades other faculties, introduces a concept of reason broader than Bacon's, one that embraces the theoretical and the practical without assimilating the practical to the theoretical, and without giving the theoretical the higher value. Kant is also responsible for a novel account of the relation between theoretical and practical sciences on the one hand, and the aesthetic on the other. He describes how each kind of science as well as the arts

41

contribute to human moral improvement. The arts are treated much more respectfully by Kant than poesy is treated by Bacon. History and religion are also accommodated, though perhaps not so satisfactorily.

A second way of bringing science and reason into harmony with other, relatively undervalued branches of learning, and with other, relatively undervalued faculties, is by revaluing science and reason downwards. Among the many different examples of this approach, some belong to the reaction against Kant in German philosophy, while others, better known in England and America in this century, are prompted by reflection on scientific theory proper and on the history of science and its 'success'. In this chapter the Kantian theory of the human faculties and the sciences will be considered;[1] toward the end of the next chapter something will be seen of the German reaction against Kant; and in Chapter 5 something will be seen of the deflationary philosophies of reason and science. Throughout I shall be arguing that the Kantian approach is to be preferred to the others.

FACULTIES OF THE MIND
AND FACULTIES OF KNOWLEDGE

Kant recognized at least three distinct faculties of the mind: knowledge, desire and pleasure (CJ, Intro.; Ak. 5, 177), and made the a priori principles of each the subject of the three great critiques. Knowledge is the faculty that corresponds most closely to what Bacon calls the understanding, but it is not given the pre-eminence in Kant's scheme that the understanding gets in Bacon's. It is not the source of all science, or even the science on which our flourishing most depends. Even its claim to be the source of the most certain science, mathematics, is counterbalanced by its giving rise to what traditionally is the most uncertain science: metaphysics. And while it is of great value in making us better able to satisfy desires, while it even enlarges human power, as Bacon recognized, the value it has in this respect is not to be compared with the value of a genuinely practical science – one that helps us to choose ends and not only means. Indeed, it is on practical science and the results of practical reason that genuine human flourishing most depends, according to Kant. Yet this science is associated not with the faculty of knowledge but with the faculty of desire. The closest Baconian counterparts of this faculty, namely will and appetite, play no such leading role in Bacon's scheme of learning.

The contrast between Kant and Descartes is equally striking. Not only is Descartes committed to the knowability of propositions (that God exists; that the soul is immortal) and to the reality of objects (the soul) that are beyond experience, and that therefore, according to Kant, are unknowable; Descartes actually makes the certainty of mathematics *depend* on knowledge of these unknowable things. As is clear from the preface to the French edition of *The Principles of Philosophy*, Descartes also makes knowledge of the precepts of a moral science depend on metaphysical knowledge, knowledge that, if Kant is right, is completely unavailable to us. As for desire, Descartes defines it as a perturbation of the soul caused by animal spirits (*Passions of the Soul* 86; CSM I 358; AT XI 393):[2] he is without resources to connect it in Kant's way with reason.

It is time to have some of the details of Kant's account of the faculties of desire and knowledge. Knowledge is a representation of an object either immediately or by means of concepts (CPR A320 = B377); desire is the faculty of causing the objects of representations by means of representations (MM, Gen. Intro.; Ak. 7, 211). There is more than one faculty of desire and more than one faculty of knowledge, and these sub-faculties, as we may call them, are distinguished as higher and lower. Thus, understanding is a higher faculty of knowledge than sense, and reason a higher sub-faculty of knowledge than understanding (CPR, A298–9 = B355). Similarly, there is a lower, empirically effective, faculty of desire, and a higher faculty of desire (CPrR; Ak. 5, 23, 24), the latter identified with reason (24). Reason in the role of the higher faculty of desire is practical reason or reason in its practical application. Reason in the role of the higher faculty of knowledge is theoretical reason. The practical and the theoretical are distinct applications of reason. Theoretical reason finds natural laws to explain experienced events and properties, and practical reason seeks a principled basis for entertained policies of action, a basis independent of what Kant calls inclination. Practical reason also generates policies of action from principles, just as, analogously, theoretical reason deduces consequences from laws and lower–order judgements.

Kant has a complicated and sometimes obscure account of the connections between theoretical and practical reason, but he also has something to say about the similarities and differences between the two, and some of the differences explain why he places a higher value on practical reason and reasoning than on theoretical. Theoretical reasoning turns out to have more limitations than practical, some of which it inherits from its dependence on the lower faculties of knowledge. It also turns out to promote far less well than practical reason the ultimate end or purpose of man, namely to become moral. Indeed, in its apparently valuable role of suggesting means to the satisfaction of lower desires, it enlarges the scope of *non*-moral motivation, according to Kant.

Reason and the lower faculties of knowledge

Reason is the highest of the three faculties of knowledge. Below it is the understanding, and below the understanding, sense. Understanding is the faculty by which the mind is able to turn what Kant calls 'appearances' into knowledge. An appearance is an 'undetermined object of empirical intuition' (CPR B34 = A20), that is, the bare registering of a thing through sensation. For appearance to become the stuff of knowledge it must become suitable subject matter for thought, and this is the effect of its being brought under a concept. An appearance is brought under a concept when it has applied to it a representation that could apply to other appearances. When an appearance is brought under a concept it makes an object thinkable, but for knowledge to be possible through a judgement about the object, a concept applied to the object must itself be thought of as subsumed by a concept applicable to other concepts. Kant gives the example of the judgement 'All bodies are divisible': in this judgement the concept of body conceptualizes one appearance among others that it could conceptualize, and the concept *divisible* is applied to the concept of body though it might have been applied to other concepts. The general application of the first-order concept *body* and the second-order concept *divisible* makes it possible for the mind to unite appearances, and unity of appearances, when it is objective, constitutes knowledge.

In the version of the Transcendental Deduction of the Categories given in the first edition of the *Critique of Pure Reason* Kant writes as if the purpose of the understanding is to find regularities or rules in appearances, ideally rules that are objective – what Kant calls 'laws'. Some of these laws, Kant holds, are synthetic and a posteriori – derived from the comparison of appearances (CPR A126) – but the most general of them

> issue a priori from the understanding itself. They are not
> borrowed from experience; on the contrary, they have to

confer on appearances their conformity to law, and so to make experience possible. Thus the understanding is something more than the power of formulating rules through comparison of appearances; it is itself the lawgiver of nature. (ibid.)

Kant is alluding to the categories – the pure concepts of the understanding – and the laws that they prescribe a priori to appearances, such as the law that 'in all change of appearances substance is permanent; its quantum in nature is neither increased nor diminished' (CPR B224 = A182) or the law that all substances interact (B252 = A211).

The understanding looks for rules, ideally laws, the most general of which it formulates a priori. In general, 'it secures the unity of appearances by means of rules' (B358 = A302). Reason, on the other hand, 'secures the unity of the rules of the understanding under principles'. How reason unifies rules is by inference from judgements to their grounds, and from their grounds to yet more basic judgements, until it hits upon the completely unconditioned (B364 = A307). Since the understanding relies on reason to find the unconditioned ground that unifies its judgements, reason is the superior faculty, but since reason relies on the understanding to supply it with judgements on which to base its inferences, reason seems to be limited by and dependent upon the understanding. Its pretensions to be a higher faculty than the understanding are suspect on another score, for while the laws implicit in the categories of the pure understanding make experience possible and therefore make available those appearances under which an independent reality is knowable for a mind, these pure concepts and principles do not similarly make empirical knowledge possible. At best they lend themselves to making miscellaneous items of empirical knowledge into a system. At worst, they are pressed by judgement into the role of concepts of the understanding and applied as if they were concepts of real things (B671 = A643), which they are not. According to Kant, this misuse of the concepts of pure reason, especially the concepts of God, the immortal soul and the free will, is, among other things, what made pre-critical metaphysics so uncertain and controversial.

Though reason cannot be the source of *empirical* knowledge, it can for all that be a source of knowledge, most notably in mathematics, through the construction of concepts in mathematics

(B741 = A713) and in philosophy (see B747 = A719). Even in relation to empirical knowledge reason is not useless, though it is not a source of such knowledge. It can provide concepts which inspire explanatory hypotheses or which suggest idealizations which enable explanatory hypotheses to be applied to appearances. Kant gives as examples of useful idealizations the concepts of pure earth, pure water and pure air, which enable the apparatus of mechanical explanation to be applied to chemical interactions (B673–4 = A645–6).

Nevertheless, what preoccupies Kant in his treatment of reason as a cognitive faculty is the possible misuse of reason and its relative fragility in the absence of knowledge of its own limits. Warnings of the futility of pursuing transcendental knowledge are sounded in the First Critique at virtually the same time as the concept of reason in general is introduced (B352 = A295), and, after being repeated often, the warning gives way (in the Transcendental Doctrine of Method) to practical precepts for keeping reason on the straight and narrow. Kant points out that there is an invitation to misuses of reason in its own principle of seeking the unconditioned as well as in the temptation to misappropriate mathematical method for philosophical purposes (B753 = A725ff), and in the attractions of scepticism about reason (B786 = A758ff).

PRACTICAL REASON

If reason is open to many kinds of misuse as a faculty of knowledge, if it takes a sophisticated critique and an elaborate discipline to ensure that it does not trespass on the territory of the understanding or attempt types of proof that are beyond it, then perhaps reason is not primarily cut out to be a faculty of knowledge. Perhaps its craving for a pure employment outside experience, while impossible to satisfy in the field of knowledge, can be met in some other area. This is the possibility explored by Kant close to the end of the First Critique (the Canon of Pure Reason) and taken up again at the beginning of the Second Critique.

In the opening section of the Canon of Pure Reason, entitled 'The ultimate end of the pure employment of reason', Kant considers the propositions which preoccupy reason in its transcendental employment, namely the propositions that we have free will, that the soul is immortal and that God exists. Kant asks whether insight into any of these could provide the material for any inference that reason would find useful in extending the field of knowledge based on experience. His conclusion is that 'these three cardinal propositions are not in any way necessary for knowledge', but that 'their importance, properly regarded, must concern only the practical' (CPR B827–8 = A799–800). Specifically, the propositions combine in the formulation of a very general problem, 'the problem *what we ought to do*, if the will is free, if there is a God and a future world' (B828–9 = A800–1). Kant thinks that this problem makes us deliberate in relation to the 'supreme end' or 'ultimate purpose', and that therefore nature has designed our reason to concern itself ultimately with moral interests.

Kant defines 'the practical' as 'everything that is possible through freedom' (B828 = A800), that is, through the free will, and he distinguishes between, on the one hand, exercises of free will dependent on empirical conditions, where reason has only a regulative function, choosing and co-ordinating a number of means so as to produce maximum satisfaction of empirical desires or happiness, and, on the other hand, exercises of the free will obedient to reason alone. In the former case, to the extent that reason can make the pursuit of happiness systematic at all, it can only prescribe 'pragmatic laws', that is, laws which relate courses of action to happiness, i.e. to the regular, prolonged and extensive gratification of sensuous desire (B834 = A806). In the latter case, not pragmatic but moral laws are prescribed. These tell us what we ought to do as rational beings and therefore apply and give us a reason to act no matter what our desires are. In co-ordinating our purely rational ends, moral laws promote the overriding aim of making us worthy to be happy (ibid.), just as pragmatic laws are supposed to contribute to making us happy simply.

According to the *Critique of Pure Reason*, happiness and worthiness to be happy are each a good, neither of which constitutes the complete good or the supreme good on its own. The complete and supreme good is happiness in exact proportion to worthiness to be happy (B842 = A814). There is a connection between thoughts about the production of the supreme good and moral conduct: in order for the conduct of life to be moral, reason must connect the moral law with something capable of arranging for the enjoyment of the supreme good in this or another world. Reason makes this connection by means of postulates about God and a hoped-for after-life (B841 = A813). Reason postulates the existence of God and the immortality of the soul in order to make morally desired conduct get what it deserves.

This, in outline, is Kant's way of transforming the speculatively useless ideas and propositions of pure reason in its transcendental employment into things that are useful to a morally legislating practical reason. Of course, the fact that certain ideas or concepts of pure reason have practical application does not by itself show that reason is primarily practical or that it is constituted to cater for a moral interest. Kant needs to base his argument for the practical utility of propositions of speculative reason on some claims about higher aims and higher interests (B825–6 = A797–8). These, however, are not the only considerations that Kant uses to connect the rational with the practical and the moral. In the section on ideas in general that opens the Transcendental Dialectic in the *Critique of Pure Reason*, Kant associates his use of the term 'idea' for concepts of pure reason, with ideas in Plato's sense. Plato, Kant says, was right to find instances of his ideas in the practical sphere. He was right, that is, to place the source of knowledge of morals and legislation beyond experience. But he was wrong to place the source of knowledge of *reality* there:

> For whereas, so far as nature is concerned, experience supplies the rules and is the source of truths, in respect of the moral laws it is, alas, the mother of illusion. Nothing is more reprehensible than to derive the laws prescribing what *ought to be done* from what *is done*, or to impose upon them the limits by which the latter is circumscribed. (B375 = A318–19)

The independence of 'ought' from 'is' in morality is supposed to be a ground for thinking that morality has a basis in reason rather than experience, rather than in some faculty for knowing nature. Another reason Kant has for connecting reason with morality is that the precepts of morality, unlike those for attaining happiness, form a system (B839 = A811). Finally, reason is the faculty for apprehending form, and the status of a practical precept as a moral precept is supposed to depend on its form (CPrR; Ak. 5, 28).

Practical reason in history

The idea that reason comes into its own only as a practical faculty, and that it is meant to serve the most elevated of practical interests, namely moral ones, is not expressed only in Kant's critical writings.

48

It emerges also, but in a different way, in his works of philosophical history, the writings in which Kant gives conditions for the development of freedom.[3] The 'Conjectural Beginning of Human History' is one such work. In it Kant attempts to fill out the account given in the biblical Book of Genesis with conjectures about the conditions that made it possible for human choice to enter natural history, for human beings subsequently to become conscious of being ends in themselves, and for them to develop after that a way of life in keeping with their recognition of this status. Reason turns out to be essential to each of these stages of development, but until the final stage, when the use of reason loses its merely pragmatic character in Kant's sense and becomes practical, its effects are not uniformly beneficial, and indeed are often harmful. Since pre-practical uses of reason for the choice of means to ends may be regarded as uses of theoretical reason (see CPrR; Ak. 5, 26n), Kant's conjectural history can be read as making once more the point about the superiority of practical to theoretical reason.

The conjectural history begins with a time when the first man, placed with a mate somewhere in a mild climate and with abundant nourishment, had developed his powers sufficiently not only to feed himself but also to think and speak. Under these conditions the first man's behaviour was still wholly instinctive. The first stirring of reason, however, made it possible for him to act contrary to instinct and experiment with food different from that recognized by instinct as nourishing (CB; Ak. 7, 111). This use of reason to depart from the patterns set by instinct was the first exercise of freedom, but since the order it permitted people to escape was the utterly benign order of God, freedom did no immediate good. On the contrary, the use of reason made possible the creation of desires that man previously did not feel impelled to satisfy. The tendency of reason to multiply desires was bad enough, but worse, aided by imagination, reason gave rise to perverted and unnatural desires. It now served not only to satisfy desire but to prolong it to the point where its satisfaction would produce most pleasure. Instincts for food and sex that began by being satisfied only on the occasion of felt hunger or felt sexual desire, were transformed into consciously cultivated and refined desires.

The ill effects of reason were partly counteracted by reason, for just as it was by reason that instinct gave way to the sensual, so it was by reason that sensual motivation started to prepare the ground for spiritual motivation (112–13). The fig leaf, Kant claimed, marked a first victory for reason over the sensual impulse, and in the transition from sensual to spiritual motivation there were also to be observed two further important developments: first, an evolution of a sense of what was agreeable into a taste for beauty, at first human beauty, but eventually natural beauty in general (113); and second, a proto-morality and a basis for sociability in the form of a sense of decency – 'an inclination to inspire others to respect by proper manners, i.e., by concealing all that might arouse low esteem'.

After the rational and impulsive stage, and the rational and spiritual stage, Kant discerns a third stage of human development due to reason, which we may as well call the stage of prudence: man began to be able to think ahead and act for the sake of his future welfare. As with earlier innovations by reason, the introduction of a capacity of foresight was a mixed blessing. The future that came into view when foresight was first developed was a future of troubles culminating in death (113). Apparently this stage of the use of reason was accompanied by a consciousness of reason – in the form of the confused thought that reason was somehow to blame for the troubles it caused people to foresee.

The fourth and final stage, in which the capacity for mere prudence gave way to the development in men of moral status, was also marked by a consciousness of reason, only this time a consciousness of reason as something that raises human beings as a species above other animals, and that makes individual human beings not only equal to one another, but even to higher beings (114–15). Reason in this form is what prevents the use of any human beings merely as a means, and because the dignifying power of reason suits men for a community of higher beings outside nature, it also brings about 'man's *release* from the womb of nature' (114). As it moves humanity toward a consciousness of moral status, then, reason alternately brings about an expulsion into nature and a welcome release from its demands.

Reason, culture and human nature

Where is human history headed under the influence of reason? Kant's answer is, toward a political life that allows the growth of culture, culture that in turn promotes the perfection of the species. In the 'Conjectural Beginning of Human History' Kant describes the steps that take man from the first inklings of his status as an end in himself, to out-and-out political life. Man first comes to the realization that he may make use of animals but not man for his own needs when he begins to keep herds. But the nomadic herdsman's existence eventually turns into an agricultural one, with a period of conflict between herdsman and farmer marking the transition (118–19). The intrusion of the herdsman's animals on the farmer's crops was probably the occasion of the first use of force to discourage encroachment. Farmers and herdsmen soon began to keep out of one another's way, however, and agriculture began to develop in earnest.

It was a small step from the setting in of agricultural life to the appearance of 'the first beginnings of culture'. Cultivation of the soil requires permanent housing on agricultural sites, and permanent housing requires an organization and division of labour on a much larger scale than that of the family. The formation of villages catered, through an elementary system of exchange, for the needs of agriculture and provided protection from the occasional raids of hunters and herdsmen. A byproduct of the system of mutual exchange was the possibility of 'art and entertainment' and the 'habit of industriousness'. Another byproduct – the most important of all – was the creation of a form of civil order and public administration of justice. At first this was concerned only to deal with violence by means more impersonal and moderate than revenge (119). Violent acts were punished by an authority which 'preserved the unity of the whole and was a kind of government' (ibid.).

All human skills owe their development to this early form of organization, and of all of these skills 'that of sociability and securing public safety is the most beneficial' (ibid.). Kant does not claim that the effects of early political life were wholly good. The primitive form of social order and public administration ushered in inequality, 'that rich source of so many evils, as well as of everything good' (ibid.). It also set the stage for the clash between the largely secular way of life of townspeople and farmers on the one hand, and that of nomadic herdsmen on the other. Though the two groups enjoyed liberty, war between them was an ever-present threat. The herdsmen were gradually drawn into the cities and, in a condition of subservience, were seduced by 'the incipient luxury' of urban life. The result was grim:

a despotism of powerful tyrants and – culture having barely begun – not only an abominable state of slavery, but along with it soulless self-indulgence mixed with all of the vices of an as yet uncivilized condition. A further result is also that the human species is irresistibly turned away from the task assigned to it by nature, the progressive cultivation of its disposition to goodness. (120)

Although Kant ends his conjectural history with a picture of this rather bleak state of affairs, he believed – as other writings of his show – that there could be an uplifting sequel, marked by the defeat of despotism within nations, and the ending of war between nations. What is important, given our concerns, is the way in which Kant concedes that the growth of culture, and with it the growth of the influence of reason in history, can have very bad effects in addition to good ones. When Kant enlarges on these bad effects, it turns out that it is not all kinds of reason that are unwholesome, but only applied theoretical reason, the kind that gives at most 'pragmatic' guidance to conduct. Pure practical reason does not turn out to have this bad side, and neither does the 'science' associated with it.

Kant considers the ill effects of culture in a digression of the conjectural history in which Rousseau's *Discourses* are mentioned favourably, and in which their line of thought is, to begin with, more or less endorsed. He starts the digression by comparing the human culture before and after the use of reason:

Before reason awoke, there was as yet neither commandment nor prohibition and hence also no violation of either. But when reason came to set about its business, it came, in all its pristine weakness, into conflict with animality, with all its power. Inevitably evils sprang up, and (which is worse) along with the cultivation of reason also vices, such as had been wholly alien to the state of ignorance and innocence. (115)

Though it sounds like Rousseau, the passage does not take Rousseau's line and blame vices on reason and the products of reason. Instead, it blames vices on a conflict between reason and animality, a conflict which reason loses, thereby entering the service of animality. Kant does not even follow Rousseau in saying that nature points us in one direction and reason in another; rather, it is nature itself that points us toward two different goals, and progress toward one interferes with progress toward the other (116–17). As Kant puts it, 'nature has given us two different dispositions for different purposes, the one for reason as an animal, the other for reason as a moral species' (116n). The growth of culture alters the conditions under which the aim of man's nature as an animal can be realized. The more people are altered by reason, the more difficult it becomes to satisfy the desires that are original to man. Eating only when one is hungry becomes difficult, because the desire for food is altered. Altered appetites in turn, especially those connected with luxury, slow the process by which man comes into his own as a moral being – a being whose policies of action have become as far as possible independent of his inclinations.

In the 'Conjectural Beginning', then, Kant seems to stop short of blaming reason and culture for the ills that attend human progress, and is inclined to blame the evils on the failure of nature and culture to develop in step with one another. A fuller and more systematic account of the same matters, but with a slightly different message, is to be found in the *Critique of Judgement*, written about four years after 'Conjectural Beginning'. In section 83 Kant tries to identify the ultimate end that nature has in store for mankind, and he proposes to himself the alternatives of happiness and culture. Happiness is a sort of end that is attainable if at all by human beings according to the provision of nature, Kant says. But neither external nature nor human nature is well adapted for securing human happiness. The human faculties are incapable of forming a stable conception of happiness, and whatever constitutes happiness at any one time cannot, even when achieved, please human beings, for they do not enjoy what they possess (Ak. 5, 430). Besides, external nature presents so many potential predators and other life-threatening dangers – famine, plague, flood and so on – that there is little hope of becoming happy. Even if external nature were more co-operative, 'the discord of inner tendencies betrays [man] into further misfortunes of his own invention' (ibid.).

Not happiness, then, but culture must be considered as the end of nature for man, and culture is 'the production in a rational being of an aptitude for any ends whatever of his own choosing, consequently of a being in his freedom' (431). Culture consists of the development of either skill or discipline. Human beings are skilled when they are able to take steps toward the fulfilment of ends of all kinds, that is, when they are good at implementing means to pre-selected ends. Skill, however, does not help one to choose ends, and yet this certainly falls within the scope of culture. Skill, therefore, does not make up all of culture. Discipline is able to supply what skill cannot. It promotes the choice of ends by preventing people from becoming slaves to impulse. It 'consists in the liberation of the will from the despotism of desires whereby, in our attachment to natural things, we are rendered incapable of exercising a choice of our own' (432). We have already encountered examples of desires, e.g. the desires for food and sex, that while not despotic in themselves can be altered by reason so as to be able to get the better of us.

The distinction between skill and culture enables Kant to be more precise than he is in 'Conjectural Beginning' about the ill effects of culture. It is culture in the form of enlarged skill that does the harm, not culture in the form of discipline, and yet even the harm of enlarged skill has its positive side, contributing, according to Kant, to a psychological transformation that aids moral improvement. The advance of the culture of skill – not of culture full stop – requires inequality among men, and indeed exaggerates it. The masses work hard to produce the necessities of life, themselves a contribution to culture-as-skill, and these necessities supply 'the ease and convenience of others who apply themselves to the less necessary branches of culture in science and art' (432). Eventually the fruits of this culture and science are enjoyed in some measure by the working majority, but inevitably the success of the culture of skill breeds a discontent among both upper and lower classes by making the previously superfluous come to appear necessary. If war is not to result, a civil community must be formed that reduces inequalities and allows the chances of developing natural tendencies to be more widely available.

Culture as skill does not necessarily bring about moral improvement, but it encourages moral improvement even when it seems to do the opposite. As Kant writes,

> The preponderance of evil which a taste refined to the extreme of idealization, and which even luxury in the sciences, considered as food for vanity, diffuses among us as the result of the crowd of insatiable inclinations which they beget, is indisputable. But, while that is so, we cannot fail to recognize the end of nature – ever more and more to prevail over the rudeness and violence of inclinations that belong more to the animal part of our nature. . . . Fine art and the sciences, if

they do not make man morally better, yet, by conveying a pleasure that admits of universal communication and by introducing polish and refinement into society, make him civilized. Thus they do much to overcome the tyrannical propensities of sense, and so prepare man for a sovereignty in which reason alone shall have sway. (433)

The reason that holds sway when man enjoys genuine sovereignty is practical reason. Theoretical reason is what is called upon when culture as skill develops, for it is theoretical reason that supplies the information about cause and effect which skill requires. Just as the *Critique of Judgement* enables Kant to be more precise about which side of culture is the bad side, so it enables one to assign different values to the different applications of reason.

OTHER FACULTIES

I have been trying to show that Kant's admiration for the faculty of theoretical reason is measured and that he reserves his real enthusiasm for practical reason. In the next section we shall consider whether Kant's sobriety about theoretical reason amounts to a sobriety about science that clears Kant of any charge of scientism, or whether, on the contrary, he does turn out to be scientistic, making inflated claims not for physics or mathematics but for a would-be science of practical reason. In this section, however, I shall be concerned with Kant's valuation of the non-cognitive faculties of the human mind other than practical reason, and with his valuation of non-scientific parts of culture. It will emerge that Kant is much better disposed to the non-cognitive faculties and the non-sciences than a scientistic philosopher could be expected to be.

The non-cognitive faculties, apart from practical reason itself, are the three that Kant defines either by reference to feeling, i.e. the general susceptibility to pleasure or pain, or by reference to feeling in relation to desire (practical pleasure). The instinctive or animal desires mentioned in 'Conjectural Beginning', such as the desires for nourishment and sex, are examples of feeling in relation to desire, and Kant thinks that these are perfectly wholesome and necessary to the species until reason redirects them to other than natural purposes. While Kant believes that there is a tension between feeling and reason, and while he places a higher value on the latter when the two are in competition, it is not clear that he thinks that there has to be a tension, or that reason must always be preferred to feeling when there is no tension. What he seems to think is that, once established, the tension will be difficult to eliminate.

'Inclination', or the ability to have desires partly determined by pleasure at what desire represents, is another non-cognitive capacity that Kant subordinates to practical reason, but this, too, has considerable value and Kant acknowledges as much even in writings in which he stresses the tension between moral activity and action from inclination. Thus, in Section One of the *Groundwork*, he says that the inclination to be kind or to honour are 'useful' and 'honourable', and 'deserve praise and encouragement' (Ak. 4, 398). I shall concentrate, however, on non-cognitive capacities in Kant's scheme other than inclination and appetite, namely capacities for contemplative pleasure that he thinks are activated in aesthetic experience.

Aesthetic feeling

'[T]he immediate pleasure in the beautiful in nature', Kant writes in the *Critique of Judgement*, 'presupposes and cultivates a certain "liberality" of thought, i.e., makes our delight independent of any mere enjoyment of sense . . .' (CJ; Ak. 5, 269). What is more, 'to take an immediate interest in the beauty of nature (not merely to have taste in estimating it), is always the mark of a good soul', and where this interest is habitual it is a sign of a 'mind favourable to moral feeling' (298). In the feeling for natural beauty our delight is independent of mere sensory enjoyment, because mere sensory enjoyment is private and unrepresentable, while the delight of the feeling of beauty derives from the fact that it can be shared and is much more than a purely personal and subjective response to an object. Feelings of beauty are a cut above pleasing sense responses because they have an apparent objectivity and tie people together through shared response or at least its possibility.

Feelings for natural beauty are also favourable to morality, because, like moral thought, they make available a certain kind of escape from the laws of nature. How they do this is by making us receptive to what the senses present by means other than the concepts that give appearances their necessary patterns or conformity to law. In aesthetic experience, according to Kant, we are receptive to objects by means of indeterminate concepts, ones that allow our attention to be engaged unthinkingly and in a way that does not promote cognition. Although the same faculties of understanding and imagination that make nature knowable are engaged when nature is found aesthetically pleasing, the relations between the faculties are different in cognition and aesthetic experience. In aesthetic experience the understanding and imagination do not synthesize or unify what is given in sense. Instead, receptiveness to an object, or to its form or purposiveness, sends the imagination and understanding into harmonious free play (see for example Ak. 5, 217), and the internal sense of this constitutes aesthetic pleasure.

A feeling for what Kant calls the 'sublime' in nature has the same 'liberalizing' effect on the mind as the feeling of beauty (269). A feeling for the sublime is the capacity for response to the formlessness as against the form of certain objects (193), to their being out of all proportion to our capacity to take them in, this last usually on account of very great power or magnitude. Mere terror or horror at what is much more powerful or much greater than oneself is not the feeling of the sublime. For one thing, the feeling of the sublime is in part a feeling of attraction, and for another its object is beyond nature. It is an attraction to what exceeds the possibilities of nature and of sensibility (CJ, S29; Ak. 5, 265). To be subject to the feeling of the sublime one has to have a faculty of cognition acquainted with ideas of reason – ideas that have no objects corresponding to them given in sense (ibid.). A feeling for the sublime enlarges the mind by making accessible the attraction of the transcendental, and, like the feeling for the beautiful, it constitutes a kind of escape from the tyranny of the laws of nature.

Aesthetic experience is valuable for Kant precisely because, in a number of ways, it creates conditions favourable for morality. It is an essentially public source of pleasure, and one that promotes sociability. To be open to aesthetic experience is to be willing to influence, and to be open to the influence of, the taste of others. Differently, aesthetic experience is an elevating source of pleasure, one that engages the higher faculties. It helps us to focus the attention, a requirement of the practice of virtue. Moreover, it is, in a deep and unusual sense, a way of taking pleasure in freedom from natural law, precisely the freedom one experiences in moral behaviour.

Genius

Aesthetic experience, though its value is considerable, does not begin to compare in worth with genuine aesthetic creativity, such as is capable of producing fine art. 'For estimating beautiful objects', Kant says '. . . what is required is taste; but for fine art, i.e., the production of some objects, one needs genius' (CJ, §48; Ak. 5, 311). In his theory of genius and of fine art, Kant's high valuation of the non-rational and the non-scientific is perhaps at its clearest. Genius makes certain demands on the cognitive faculties of imagination and understanding (S48; 316), but more on reason, either theoretical or practical. Its uses of the cognitive faculties, moreover, are quite different from any that produce knowledge. Imagination, which is called upon more than understanding in aesthetic creation, is set to work, not unifying representations suitable for conceptualization, but rather producing ideas to which no concept is adequate (§49; 314), and hence which afford no material for knowledge. The aesthetic ideas are the counterparts of the ideas of pure reason or intellectual ideas (ibid.), but they are not a subclass of these ideas. The use of these ideas in art is either to represent to sense things that are not found in experience, or to represent to sense an unexperienced character of things that *are* found in experience. Thus the artist has to convey a sense of the 'completeness' of things like love, or the vices that nature does not present complete.

In addition to presenting ideas independently of concepts, the imagination can sometimes present ideas that, as it were, invest concepts with a wider significance, or make links that express kinship between concepts (§49; 315). It is by this representation of forms that, for example, Jupiter's eagle, with lightning in its claws, can put us in mind of God. In this use the imagination produces specifically aesthetic ideas. Aesthetic ideas not only invest concepts with a wider significance not expressible in words, but produce a feeling which quickens the cognitive faculties. The essential features of genius are, first, a knack for producing aesthetic ideas, and, second, an ability to give them expression (§49; 317).

Genius, then, is an aptitude or talent that, despite its relation to ideas, is not a rational aptitude. It is nevertheless valuable, and not just because its product, fine art, has 'the effect of advancing the culture of the mental powers in the interest of social communication' (§44; 306). It is valuable because originality and exemplariness are valuable, and because the artist of genius produces original art that is at the same time exemplary (§46; 307–8). Originality is the primary property of genius: it consists of being able to produce something for which no definite rule of production could be given; something, therefore, which, on Kant's assumptions, is inimitable. Not that the works of a genius are produced according to no rules. Rather, the rules – whatever they are – are embodied in the individual's nature, specifically in the harmony of his faculties (§46; 307): they are not learned by the artist or able to be learned by would-be imitators (§47; 308).

In being beyond learning, genius in art contrasts with greatness in science, according to Kant. Newton was a great scientist, 'but all the steps that [he] had to take from the first elements of geometry to his greatest and most profound discoveries were such as he could make intuitively evident and plain to follow, not only for himself but for everyone else' (§47; 309). So however much talent it took to hit upon and arrange the steps, everyone can follow them. In general, then, the greatest inventor differs only in degree from the most laborious imitator, while the genius, according to Kant, is simply not in the same league as someone who paints by step-by-step instructions. I shall suggest later that Kant exaggerates the difference between great science and great art, and that he tends to overdraw the ineffability of genius. Indeed, Kant himself seems to sense this, for almost as soon as he has put genius out of bounds to imitation, he finds himself in difficulty saying how a work of genius can help a pupil of genius. He has already called the work of a genius exemplary, but in order to keep this from conflicting with his line on imitation, he says that it is one thing to imitate and another to follow a model (ibid.).

The fine arts and their value

Though all fine art is the product of genius, according to Kant, and valuable because genius is, not all fine art is equally valuable. All fine art has about it a certain artlessness or naturalness (CJ, §45; Ak. 5, 307), all is produced by makers of genius, all produces pleasure at representations considered as modes of cognition (§44; 305). But there are different fine arts, with different degrees of worth. Kant distinguishes between fine arts of speech, fine arts that are 'formative' and fine arts relating to the play of sensations (§51; 320). Rhetoric and poetry are the fine arts of speech; sculpture and architecture, painting and landscape gardening are the fine formative arts (§51; 322–3); and music and the art of colour make up the third type of fine art. A number of other fine arts are hybrids of the three main types: drama, for example, is rhetoric plus pictorial representation; song combines poetry and music, and so on (§52; 325–6). When assessed only in respect of agreeableness, Kant says, one of the most valuable arts is music (§53; 329). The same art, however, occupies lowest place in a scale of the fine arts according to their power of expanding the cognitive faculties. Indeed, music counts for far less from this point of view than any of the formative arts (ibid.), which stimulate the free play of the imagination while at the same time creating a 'product which serves the concepts of the understanding as a vehicle' (ibid.). As for the formative arts, they are inferior to what Kant considers to be the best art in aesthetic terms, namely poetry (see §53; 326). Poetry is both mind-expanding and invigorating. Its medium is aesthetic ideas – those imaginative representations calculated to produce the widest array of thought-provoking associations for a concept. It makes the mind feel a faculty which is able to throw nature into a light not afforded by experience. Finally, it 'plays with semblance', but not so as to deceive.

Poetry is one of two arts of speech. The other – rhetoric – seems to have little worth for Kant. It does not seem to compare in mind-improvingness to painting (§53; 330) or in agreeableness with the art of tone (§53; 328). Painting is the best of the formative arts, and, if I understand Kant, next only to poetry as a mind-improving fine art; it has this high status, because 'it can penetrate much further [than other formative arts] into the region of ideas and in conformity with them give greater extension to the field of imagination' (§53; 330). Only in the scale of agreeableness does another art come before poetry, namely the art of tone or play with sound.

The contrast between Kant's treatment of poetry and Bacon's treatment of poesy should already be clear. While Bacon identifies poetry with failed history, stressing the tension between it and true speech, Kant stresses the tension between what poetry captures and what is captured by concepts. He expressly denies that poetry is deceptive. Kant places a high value on poetry, and thinks its effects on the cognitive faculties are beneficial; Bacon seems to be ill-disposed to poesy and to think little of its effects. Another way of putting the difference between the two philosophers is by saying that for Kant there are wholesome non-cognitive uses of the imagination, while for Bacon there do not seem to be. It would be wrong to say, however, that in their views about poetry Kant and Bacon have nothing in common, for both think (perhaps accepting the association in Plato) that poetry and rhetoric are related arts, and both take what I believe to be an unduly dim view of rhetoric.

THE SCIENCES AND PRACTICAL SCIENCE

Kant's philosophy puts a high value on theoretical reason and natural science, but it puts a higher value on other faculties and other sciences. It makes practical, not theoretical, reason the pre-eminent faculty. It gives considerable worth to feeling and imagination. It holds that the arts as well as the sciences are important for the improvement and perfection of human beings, and it makes the pre-eminent science not a system that enables people to change external nature but a doctrine and a method that helps us to make our choices responsive to reason operating independently of nature. In Kant's philosophy the leading science is morals – not physics or mathematics. In view of the value he accords to the non-rational and to sciences other than theoretical ones, can Kant be considered to be scientistic at all? It would be easier to return a negative answer to this question if morals – the branch of learning that is crucial to our obtaining the highest good – had been reckoned an unscientific art instead of a science. But Kant seems to insist on a scientific status for morals. Perhaps this shows that Kant was in the grip of scientism after all, scientism in the form of the thesis that the most valuable or highest branch of learning, whatever it is, must be a science.

In this section I shall try to clear Kant of the suspicion of this mild scientism by arguing that, in his system, morals is in fact scientific in its doctrinal aspect but art in its method. For the most part Kant's philosophy turns out to be unscientistic. After indicating how this is so, I shall ask whether the avoidance of scientism depends on aspects of Kant's overall philosophy that are controversial, like the insistence on a strict divide between the phenomenal and the noumenal.

There are at least two places in Kant's writings where he seems clearly to claim that the guidance of pure practical reason amounts to a science, namely in the chapter on the Architectonic of Pure Reason in the First Critique, and in the Conclusion of the Second

Critique. In the First Critique he defines metaphysics as 'the system of pure reason, that is, the science which exhibits in systematic connection the whole body (true as well as illusory) of philosophical knowledge arising out of pure reason' (CPR B869 = A841). General metaphysics has two branches – the metaphysics of nature and the metaphysics of morals, and each contains 'all the principles which in an a priori fashion determine and make necessary *all our actions*' (ibid.). Is the metaphysics of morals a science? Kant says that the legislation consisting of the moral law forms, with the legislation of natural law, 'two distinct systems' (B868 = A840), and system is the mark of the scientific. As he puts it at the beginning of the chapter on the Architectonic, 'systematic unity is what first raises knowledge to the rank of science, that is, makes a system out of a mere aggregate of knowledge' (B860 = A832; see *Metaphysical Foundations of Nature*, preface, Ak. 4, 468). Or, in other words, if the metaphysics of morals is organized by an idea that gives it unity, it is a science. It *is* so organized – by the idea of freedom.

The idea of a scientific metaphysics of morals is anticipated in some of Kant's pre-critical writings, notably a prize essay of 1763 for the Berlin Academy in answer to the question whether the first principles of metaphysics – specifically those of natural theology and morals – could be proved with as much certainty as the truths of geometry.[4] A letter of 1772 which seems to outline the approach of the later critical works also gives a place in a general theory of the theoretical and practical for 'basic principles of morality'.[5] In the Second Critique, the belief in a scientific metaphysics of morals or a science of morals is reaffirmed:

The fall of a stone and the motion of a sling, resolved into their elements and the forces manifested in them treated mathematically, finally brought that clear and unchangeable insight into the structure of the world which, as observations continue, we may hope to broaden but need not fear having to retract.

This example recommends to us the same path in treating of the moral capacities of our nature and gives hope of a similarly good issue. We have at hand examples of the morally judging reason. We may analyse them into their elementary concepts, adopting, in default of mathematics, a process similar to that of chemistry, i.e. we may, in repeated experiments on common sense, separate the empirical from the rational, exhibit each of them in a pure state, and show what each by itself can accomplish. Thus we shall avoid the error of crude and unpractised judgement and (which is far more important) the extravagances of genius. . . . In a word, science (critically sought and methodically directed) is the narrow gate that leads to the doctrine of wisdom. (CPrR; Ak. 5, 163)

The analogy between natural and moral science is not elaborated at much length, but it is sufficiently worked out to suggest that it is more than an afterthought. Finally, and in the same vein, there is the opening of Part Two of the *Critique of Practical Reason*, which insists that practical reason has a methodology, as a science has, not merely a manner, as in the case of common knowledge (151). Though its methodology is not the same as that appropriate to theoretical reason – its job is to give pure reason in practice and not organize knowledge into a system – it is nevertheless still a methodology, and therefore something that raises the doctrine of practical reason to the level of a science.

If presenting morality as a set of principles unified by the concept of freedom is what is involved in making a science out of it, then the idea of a science of practical reason seems modest enough, so long as the principles are not over-assimilated to those of a natural science. Kant consistently emphasizes the differences between practical and theoretical principles, and the ways in which the philosophical categories of 'architectonic', 'methodology' and even 'metaphysics' have to be reinterpreted when transferred from theoretical to practical science. Kant does not, for example, try to derive the precepts of morality from the biological purposes of a human being or from the quasi-naturalistic idea of human happiness. Most of the possible bases for a link between practical science and theoretical science are excluded as alien to what he means by a science of practical reason. So are the usual problems with denying the distinctness of its subject matter by modelling it on a theoretical science, or of making it a byproduct of biology or psychology, avoided. Another kind of difficulty, however, may attend his claim that there is a methodology of pure practical reason. For if he means by 'methodology' a definite technique for acquiring morality or for becoming wise, it seems implausible to say that practical reason has a methodology.

It may seem, however, that Kant cannot avoid this implausibility, since, when he contrasts art in general and fine art in particular with science, he divorces art from definite rules or techniques or mechanical learnability, and yet associates science with those things (see CJ, §43; Ak. 5, 303–4; §47; 308–9). These are unwanted associations if the methodology of morals is supposed to make people wise: the idea of a definite technique for becoming wise verges on incoherence. Either Kant must drop the claim that wisdom can be acquired by science, or drop the claim that science is mechanically learnable. What he does in fact is to keep the terminology of 'science' and 'methodology' but to outline a technique that keeps morality from becoming merely mechanically learnable.

In the part of the Second Critique called the Methodology of Practical Reason, Kant points out that, without any particular training, human beings are good at arguing from assumptions about the motives behind actions to conclusions about whether actions are morally good or not. Not only are they able to argue competently about these things: people enter into debates about them with pleasure. Kant's methodology taps this ability. He proposes that 'after laying the foundation in a purely moral catechism', moral teachers should make use of

> biographies of ancient and modern times with the purpose of having examples at hand of duties they lay down, so that, by comparing similar actions in different circumstances, they could begin to exercise the moral judgement of their pupils in marking the greater or less moral significance of their actions. (CPrR; Ak. 5, 155)

This would implant a good foundation for righteousness and an admiration for virtue in others. An additional method, however, is required to cultivate virtue oneself – to act not out of any gratification at the merit of what we do, but just because it is our duty (159). The method consists, first, of getting used to judging actions on the basis of moral laws, and, second, of making sure that whatever the moral law prescribes in a given case is done just out of the recognition of one's duty. In this latter connection one is helped by examples which show what it is to act out of the recognition of duty alone (160–1). These examples help to focus attention on what it is to act out of freedom, and help to give an agent a sense of what is inferior about acts not done freely or independently of inclination. Consciousness of this inferiority creates conditions for loss of self-respect if one does not oneself act with purity of moral disposition, and the fear of loss of self-respect keeps the agent on the straight and narrow, i.e. sustains the morally upright agent in trying to do his duty for its own sake.

Kant thinks morality can be learned by the method that he outlines, but it is clear that the method is not a recipe or algorithm, or even in its initial stages simple conditioning to virtue by precept, reward and punishment. As the *Metaphysics of Morals* makes clear, the moral catechism which starts off moral education is the delivery of the doctrine of duty to learners by means of mutual questioning (Ak. 6, 477). The teacher's questions present the learner with certain concepts, while the learner's questions show how far the pattern of the teacher's questioning is taking effect or suggests how the pattern should be altered to achieve its purpose. Presumably there is no one pattern suitable for the moral instruction of everyone, and therefore, within the loose framework provided by the steps that Kant described, there is scope for learning to become moral in a variety of ways. For example, Kant does not prescribe a canonical set of instructive biographies or actions for discussion. And there is presumably more than one way of getting used to judging one's policies of action by reference to the moral law.

What goes for the method of applying practical reason and cultivating virtue in general, goes for cultivating the particular virtues. Here again, there is no question of settling in advance how to be, for example, charitable or respectful in absolutely every situation. On the contrary, it is of the essence of what Kant calls 'duties of wide obligation' that the conditions of their fulfilment can only be indicated in broad terms. For example, the duty to develop one's natural powers as far as possible is

> merely ethical or of wide obligation. No principle of reason prescribes in a determinate way *how far* one should go in cultivating one's powers. . . . Then, too, the different situations in which men find themselves make a man's choice of the sort of occupation for which he should cultivate his talents quite arbitrary. With regard to natural perfection, accordingly, reason gives no law for actions. (Ak. 6, 392)

A similar indeterminateness is inevitable in the rule that one sacrifice oneself for others, and similar duties.

It is emerging, then, that while morality or the doctrine of pure practical reason lends itself to being applied methodically, the method is not strict or fully determinate. Perhaps in the case of morality, or at least in the observance of its duties of wide obligation, method gives way to manner and science gives way to art. Adapting the distinction that Kant makes in the case of aesthetics (CJ, §49; Ak. 5, 318), we may say that the difference between a method and a manner of practical reason is that the steps one follows are unified by feeling in the latter case and by reason in the former case. An action that is not specifically called for by a duty of wide obligation but that seems to conform with it, may be done because on the occasion it produces a feeling of appropriateness. As for the more general suggestion that it may be thanks to art, rather than science, that we are able to become wise or moral, this seems to be in line with what Kant himself says in 'Conjectural Beginning', where he comments on the characteristic conflict between culture and impulse. 'Natural impulse', he says, 'interferes with culture until such time as finally art will be strong and perfect enough to become a second nature. This indeed is the ultimate moral end of the human species' (Ak. 7, 118; see CPR B776 = A748). Surely art becomes strong and perfect enough when moral education has reached its final stage and one accustoms oneself to art just in the way that duty directs one to act.

DIFFICULTIES

In the last section I tried to dispel the scientistic air surrounding Kant's claim that pure practical reasoning has a scientific methodology. If I have succeeded, then Kant's philosophy should appear to the reader, as it does to me, to be at once admiring of science and unscientistic, at once admiring of reason and yet not infatuated with it. How, finally, does it compare with seventeenth-century accounts of learning? Does it correct all of their excesses, or are some of those reproduced? Does it manage to strike a balance between arts and sciences, and between reason and instinct, only thanks to an unacceptable theory of the mind, or thanks to an unacceptable distinction between a practical reason with access to a reality beyond experience and theoretical reason with no such access?

The Kantian apparatus

To take the last suggestion first, it does not seem to me that Kant's method of balancing the values of the arts and sciences depends particularly on a theory of the mind as consisting of faculties, let alone on a theory that distinguishes as sharply as Kant's does between faculties of sense, judgement and reason. It is true that he relates the aesthetic to the capacity of objects to send the cognitive faculties into a felt free play and harmonization, or to provoke certain sorts of thought, but there may be ways of recovering these ideas or similar ones without Kant's classification of faculties or even reference to faculties. One of Kant's ideas is that aesthetic experience is pleasure at features of objects that relate to their design, but not to a would-be purpose that the design serves. It does not require a theory of mental faculties to make strict sense of this thought, only a theory of subpropositional or prepropositional content and some such concept as that of registration: aesthetic pleasure would be pleasure at a certain registration of pattern (say of colour or sound) rather than pleasure at thought of something by way of its sort or type. As for the thought-provokingness of aesthetic experience and the sense of free play in response to something considered beautiful, this might be captured not by a theory of psychological mechanics, but of the appropriate content for the expression of aesthetic appreciation or criticism. In the case where the reaction was beyond concepts, the devices used in some new criticism of stretching beyond the limit the signifying relations of vocabulary, by puns, neologisms and so on would help to bring out what was involved.

Again, reasons and reasoning, rather than a faculty of reason, are important to Kant's account of the theoretical and practical sciences. It is important that there can be inference from observation to law and back again, and from policy of action or appraisal of action to moral principle and back again; it is not crucial that the inference be the work of a distinguishable faculty of the mind. Even if one dispenses with a faculty of reason one is still able to make out a type of operation – inference – that is at work in both thought and action. A theory of practical and theoretical reason is not Kantian, however, unless the three following conditions are fulfilled: (1) it denies that conditions for being real are independent of conditions for being humanly experienced or thought; (2) it has apparatus for distinguishing between what is thinkable and what is not, or between what is able to be experienced and what is not; and (3) it makes the main task of practical reason the articulation and application of a moral code binding on everyone to whom it is addressed. These conditions can be satisfied without using Kant's own apparatus.

Conditions (1) and (2), for example, can be satisfied by a theory that equates what can be experienced and thought with what can be meaningfully expressed by sentences in a natural language, anti-realistically interpreted. And condition (3) can be satisfied by a number of theories of reasons for action, such as that given by Nagel in *The Possibility of Altruism*.[6]

Two distinctive elements of Kant's philosophy not obviously captured by conditions (1) to (3) are its association of theoretical reason with a certain predisposition for illusion, and its claim that human reason is better adapted to practice than to theory. Can these features be accommodated by a post-Kantian theory without the use of suspect Kantian machinery? The craving for generality, the tendency to over-objectify and over-reify are at least counter-parts of the ills that Kant thought human reason was subject to, and there is no incompatibility between recognizing these ills and holding a theory that meets conditions (1) to (3) above.

As for Kant's association of reason with practice, this seems to be a case of something distinctively Kantian that, even in Kant himself, is not always expressed with the aid of Kant's theoretical apparatus. For as we saw in connection with the methodology of pure practical reason, Kant thinks that there is a more or less *native* talent and taste for arguing

> about the moral worth of this or that action, from which the character of some person is made out. Those who otherwise find everything which is subtle and minute in theoretical questions dry and vexing soon take part when it is a question of the import of a good or bad act that is recounted; and they are exacting, meticulous and subtle in excogitating everything which lessens or even casts suspicion on the purity of purpose and thus on the degree of virtue to an extent that we do not expect of them on any other subject of speculation. (CPrR; Ak. 5, 153)

An explanation of this flair for analysis that is so conspicuously lacking in theoretical questions is that human reason is more easily applied to these than to other matters.

Enough should by now be before us to show that what is antique or controversial in Kant's way of according value to arts and sciences, and in making out the superiority of practical to theoretical reasoning, may not be essential to a Kantian theory. It may be possible to recover many of Kant's ideas within a theory of the mind and of reasoning and content that is not Kant's but that is Kantian in spirit. So objections against Kant's approach to scientism based on objections to his apparatus of mental faculties and the like need not be regarded as decisive. Three other areas of difficulty in Kant's philosophy, however, remain to be considered. The first concerns Kant's valuation of the change from the use of instinct to the use of reason. Does he overestimate the moral benefits of civilization afforded by the use of reason and underestimate the costs of the loss of the instinctive life? The question can only be raised in this chapter. Second, does Kant's philosophy recognize a wide enough array of distinct non-scientific subjects with something to contribute to learning and culture? Granted that fine art and the arts generally are given their due, are some other subjects under-valued? If so, then Kant's scheme of learning, while it may be superior to, say, Bacon's, may not be good enough. Finally, how satisfactory after all *is* Kant's treatment of the arts? Does he assign enough value to arts other than the fine arts, and does he assign the right sort of value to the fine arts? Are the fine arts valuable mainly because they promote moral perfection, or should they be regarded, contrary to Kant, as having an entirely independent kind of value? The latter question, which can only be broached in this chapter, will be pursued in some depth in Chapter 5. I begin, however, with the suggestion that in Kant's science of learning both history and religion, which are prominent in Bacon's scheme, are almost wholly eclipsed by science.

The status of history and religion

History and religion appear on the surface to be unsatisfactorily positioned in Kant's scheme. 'Historical' is associated in the *Critique of Pure Reason* (B864 = A836) with knowledge that is merely 'learned', hence that is inferior to philosophical knowledge, while religion seems to be, if not assimilated outright to morals, then at least not given much of an autonomous existence, being defined in terms of one of the central concepts of morals as the recognition of all duties as divine commands (CPrR; Ak. 5, 129. CJ; Ak. 5, 481. Rel.; Ak. 6, 154. MM; Ak. 7, 487). History is merely the systematic presentation of knowledge of facts; the value of its contribution to knowledge and culture is not clearly indicated by Kant, and the interdependence of natural history and natural science is not repeatedly insisted upon, as in Bacon. In short, though history is one of the two main branches of knowledge, its contribution to knowledge is underspecified, with the result that it seems to be an area of negligible interest. Religion, on the other hand, has a clear enough role in culture, but not, apparently, one that is independent enough of morality.

Can Kant be defended against the charge that he is too indifferent to history and too insensitive to the factors – social and emotional – that help to give religion a life of its own? If one distinguishes between philosophical history and empirical history,[7] then it is false to say that Kant was indifferent to history. For he took an interest in the philosophical history of human beings, and also in philosophical history in the form of cosmology. We have already seen how important one of his works of philosophical history – the 'Conjectural Beginning' – seems to be to understanding the relation between the practical and theoretical as well as between the arts and sciences. Other essays of his in philosophical history, in particular 'Idea of a Universal History from a Cosmopolitan Point of View', were apparently intended to influence the writing of empirical history: Kant could hardly be expected to write proposals of frameworks for empirical history if the subject had no importance for him. So at least in the light of this last essay evidence of his interest in history is evidence of his interest in history at large. That he did not undertake the project in empirical history that he outlined does not mean that he thought it was of small importance.

There is further evidence of a respect for empirical history in Kant's 'methodology of pure practical reason' as well as his 'methodology of taste'. Presumably biography is an example of empirical history, and, as we have seen, that is claimed by Kant to be an invaluable aid to moral training. It makes available examples of people and actions on which learners can sharpen their moral judgement. In the case of taste models are no less necessary, only this time they are apparently made available by 'histories of nations'. In section 60 of the *Critique of Judgement* Kant writes of the exemplary nations of old that first managed to strike a balance between the cultured sections of the community and the simple and original but less cultured sections of the community. From these cultures there is something to be learned not only by their immediate successors but by their successors, and their successors' successors:

> Hardly will a later age dispense with those models. For nature
> will ever recede farther into the background, so that eventually,

with no permanent example retained from the past, a future age would scarce be in a position to form a concept of the happy union, in one and the same people, of the law-directed constraint belonging to the highest culture, with the force and truth of a free nature sensible of its proper worth. (Ak. 5, 356)

If the concept *is* formed, it is presumably thanks to a written history that is at least partly empirical. Turning now from history to religion, we can once again distinguish between 'empirical' or historical religion, with a strong institutional presence developed over a long time, and philosophical religion – a rationally communicable core of belief and practice. Historical religion embraces the variety of beliefs outside Christianity and includes their historically transmitted traditions and sacred texts, their historically developed hierarchies of religious leaders, codes of law and so on. Philosophical religion or religion within the bounds of reason alone is a different matter. It is a pattern of faith and practice that is required by the moral perfection indicated by Kant's philosophical history: it is not a pattern drawn from the actual evolution of individual religious practices or religious practice in general.[8]

One destination of the human species in history guided by reason is life within society; and following Rousseau, Kant thinks that society both benefits human beings and puts them in jeopardy. They benefit by being able more efficiently to provide for and protect themselves; but they start to become overconcerned with their image in other people's eyes, and so become subject to 'lust for power, greed and the malignant inclinations bound up with these' (Rel., Bk III, E 85). In this situation people are constantly exposed to evil. The only response to this situation compatible with the ultimate end of the species – namely happiness commensurate with worthiness to be happy – is for people to set up an ethical society (86). Now an ethical society is one in which moral behaviour is not externally coerced, but produced by the will to do the right thing. But this inner will cannot be required by merely human legislation; people cannot see into the hearts of one another and tell whether no external incentives are prompting them to do right. Only God can have the necessary insight and therefore occupy the role of legislator (Ak. 6, 99).

This is how it becomes necessary to see moral requirements as God's commands, how it becomes necessary to find a place for

71

religion in the pursuit of the highest good. To form themselves into a genuinely moral community, people must regard themselves as a people of God, collectively a church under God's decrees (ibid.). The empirical institution of religions involving different sections of humanity can be seen as approximating to the ideal of a non-empirical and pure religion involving all of humanity. And there can be progress from the unsatisfactory situation where people form themselves into different empirical churches to the point where they belong to a pure religion, to the one great church, by a process of enlightenment. The process has the effect of making people regard their own religions as failed attempts to be the pure one (Ak. 6, 121).

Nothing in this account obliges Kant to deny that there is something beyond reason in the pattern of faith and practice of any empirical religion. Nothing obliges him to deny, in particular, that revelation cannot function independently of religion as an introduction to religion.[9] Nothing in his account, either, obliges Kant to deny that the only function of empirical religion is that of providing (confusedly) for the possibility of a genuinely moral community.

The arts and the purposes of the arts

I come now to a third sort of problem in Kant's philosophy, a problem with his treatment of the arts. Might not this treatment turn out to be unsatisfactory because arts other than the fine arts are not accorded any or enough value? And, more generally, might there not be something wrong with supposing that the value of even the most valuable arts is derived from their moralizing or civilizing function? Might not art even have a higher value than morality? The larger of these questions cannot be considered now: I shall take them up in the next chapter. Something *can* be said, however, about arts other than the fine arts.

In the *Critique of Judgement* Kant divides the arts in general into mechanical and aesthetical ones (CJ, §44; Ak. 5, 305). The mechanical arts – really crafts and applied sciences – had been rather exalted by Diderot in the *Encyclopaedia* article on 'art', but in Kant they are firmly subordinated to the aesthetical ones, on the ground that they are disagreeable in themselves and draw what positive value they have from their results (304). But whether it is derivative or not, the value of the mechanical arts is certainly acknowledged. The same is true of the aesthetical arts other than the fine arts, the so-called 'agreeable arts' of knowing how to keep a conversation going over dinner, choosing music for an occasion, and, in general, play of every kind that does no more than make the time pass unnoticed. Because of the connection there is between these arts and an inclination to inspire others to respect by proper manners, which, in 'Conjectural Beginning', is called 'the real basis of all true sociability', the value of these arts for Kant cannot be negligible. Yet it is true that he subordinates the agreeable arts to the fine arts. He does so by making them out to be the source of a lower sort of pleasure – pleasure consisting only in sensations as distinct from pleasure consisting in modes of cognition (305). Probably it is controversial to divide the fine arts from others in the way that Kant does, for there is no necessity to suppose that every example of fine art can provide intellectual rather than sensory pleasure. Indeed, the fact that one of the kinds of fine art is the 'art of the play of sensations' (§51; Ak. 5, 321) indicates a vagueness of boundary. What is at issue, however, is whether Kant is without resources to give considerable value to arts other than the fine arts, and there is no evidence that he *is* without these resources. There is a corollary. Because there is scope in Kant's theory for giving value to arts that are agreeable without being intellectual, and because the distinction between agreeable and fine arts seems to be as exhaustive as the distinction between low and popular culture without quite coinciding with it, Kant seems to be safe from accusations that he cannot concede any value to popular culture.

Large questions nevertheless remain concerning the source of value of the fine arts in Kant. It is not quite right to say that the fine arts are valuable *only* because they contribute to the process of perfecting human beings. It is clear that they are valuable also in respect of the sort of intellectual pleasure they produce, and in respect of the value of genius. Both of these sources of value, however, are inferior in Kant's scheme to the value of producing the maximum purity of heart and will and perhaps *this* valuation is controversial. Perhaps genius is incomparably valuable. And, to revive a theme that was prominent earlier, perhaps fine art does not make a contribution to culture comparable to that of science, as Kant says; perhaps it makes a bigger and more significant contribution. These are ideas to be considered in the next chapters.

4

MORAL CRITICISMS OF THE ARTS AND SCIENCES

The account given by Kant implies that science and the arts alike are valuable, and that both contribute to a morally improving culture. Theoretical science contributes to a culture of skill, making the satisfaction of human desires more efficient, and therefore helping us to become happy. Practical science – the system of morality – contributes to a culture of discipline. It tells us what ends we ought to pursue and also which of our policies of action are consistent with those ends. Trying to live by this science is what makes us worthy to be happy. As for the arts, they increase our pleasure, and the best of them do so by exercising faculties that we need for fulfilling the requirements of morality.

Kant's account is coherent, but perhaps it exaggerates the moral benefits of the arts and sciences. Kant himself concedes that in view of the social inequalities they depend upon for their development and the appetite for luxury they encourage, the arts and sciences are a mixed blessing. But perhaps this is to underestimate the drawbacks of developed arts and sciences. Perhaps the arts and sciences only get their point from morally bad motives and practices; perhaps the evil they enable people to do overwhelmingly outweighs the good they make possible. There is a wide range of possible moral objections to the arts and sciences. In this chapter I begin by trying to answer those that are sometimes encountered in the philosophical literature.

Afterwards I defend Kant's procedure of determining the worth of different parts of learning or culture by reference to moral value. I defend it in particular against Nietzsche's rival conception. Nietzsche held that things were valuable to the extent that they were, in a special sense, life-enhancing. He thought that morality, or at any rate conventional morality, only made sense against the background of beliefs that were both false and debilitating to the best human beings. I shall argue that while this view is extremely arresting it is accompanied by an unconvincing argument against conventional morality.

FIVE OBJECTIONS TO SCIENCE

Science and pride

The view that science is harmful is often supported by a line of thought connecting science or, more generally, the drive to acquire knowledge, to the sin of pride. There are many versions of this line of thought. According to one version there are some kinds of knowledge that it is bad for us to acquire, though pride makes us think otherwise. This version is discernible in the biblical story of the Fall. The tree whose fruit gave knowledge of good and evil was present in the garden of Eden, but Adam and Eve were forbidden by God to eat from the tree, for the knowledge was considered to belong to God alone. When Adam and Eve disobeyed God's command, they tried to acquire knowledge meant only for God and so proudly tried to become gods themselves. Not only was their act gratuitous – everything they could reasonably desire had already been given to them in Eden – but it brought about the loss of all of the goods that they already enjoyed in Paradise.

A pride related to Adam's and Eve's has sometimes been thought to motivate science. Once again it is a type of pride that makes people try to find out things that they are not naturally equipped to find out, and that they do not need to know. It is the pride people take in their powers of discovery. In the *Discourse on the Sciences and Arts*,[1] one of the best-known philosophical tracts against science, Rousseau claims that pride is necessarily associated with science because science is conducted in the belief that human intellectual powers are equal to uncovering the causes of things. The fact that it is difficult for human beings to discover causes, and that they often fail to discover them, ought to strike people as a sign that causes are not meant to be found out (DSA 13; OC III 15). Instead of taking the hint, however, human beings proudly persevere and suffer 'ills caused by . . . vain curiosity [which] are as old as the world' (DSA 7; OC III 9) – as old, that is, as Eden and the Fall.

Rousseau followed in the tradition of earlier writers influenced by pyrrhonism. In 1526 Henricus Cornelius Agrippa von Nettelsheim wrote a treatise, 'On the Vanity of the Arts and Sciences', in which virtually every branch of learning was claimed to be either of no help to mankind or positively harmful. The sciences were harmful, according to Agrippa, when they fed intellectual pride and created contempt for the simplicity of scripture. Faith and not science, Agrippa said, was the way to truth. Montaigne, who read Agrippa but was especially influenced by Greek pyrrhonist arguments, developed related ideas in his *In Defence of Raymond Sebond*. Chapter 3 of the work, entitled 'The Futility of Learning', says that the 'effort to increase in wisdom and knowledge was the original cause of the downfall of the human race',[2] and recommends the practice of suspending judgement instead. Science is criticized as an impious attempt to make divine activity intelligible to an inadequate human understanding.

The pride that Montaigne and Agrippa complained of is the pride of persevering in a task to which one is discoverably unequal. Science – the systematic discovery of causes or principles – seemed to many people in the sixteenth and early seventeenth centuries to be beyond them; the widespread belief that the best discoveries had already been made by the ancients, and that the passage of time would only produce an intellectual winding down, made the line of thought seem natural. Not that everyone accepted it. Descartes claimed that if approached with the right method, practically any scientific problem would be tractable. Before him a number of other writers had proclaimed the powers of special arts of discovery. But the fact remains that pessimism about science was also and perhaps more generally felt. The pessimism lost its force with the increasing success of scientific explanation and prediction from the mid seventeenth century on. This success, however, created the conditions for a new kind of pride. Some people began to think that perhaps human science was equal to the solution of *any* theoretical problem.

The new kind of pride seems to have had its most forceful expression in the nineteenth century. In 1889 a German zoologist called Ernst Haeckel wrote a reply to a widely discussed lecture that identified seven riddles or problems supposedly incapable of scientific answers. The problems were to do with the nature of matter and force, the source of motion, the origin of consciousness, the possibility of free will, and some other questions in biology. Haeckel claimed that six of these problems were not only soluble, but virtually solved already, while the seventh – the one concerning free will – was a pseudoproblem not calling for solution. In general, according to Haeckel, 'the number of world riddles has been continually diminishing in the course of the nineteenth century through the . . . progress of a true knowledge of nature'.[3] The clear implication was that soon there would be no big problems left for science to solve.

Haeckel's pride is more extreme than that of the scientific empiricists. They did not believe that big scientific problems were running out, only that any that cropped up were in principle soluble by science. Even this milder confidence in science, however, is not a necessary accompaniment to, or a sustaining cause of, successful science. It is perfectly possible to hold that science has been successful in explanation and prediction, that it will go on being successful, and also that it can only ever be successful within limits, because some problems, whether soluble or not, fall outside science, and because others, though they fall within science, may defeat all of those who happen to investigate them.[4] This does not amount to humility about science, but neither does it amount to unreasonable pride. More humble positions – to the effect that there are many problems that not only can but must defeat the human intelligence – are nevertheless defensible.[5]

Science and evil ends

Science enables things to be produced or policies to be pursued that serve evil ends or that make possible mass destruction: does this show that science is bad or that it is bad on balance? It may show that *some* science is bad, e.g. the sort that is conducted expressly to enable mass destruction to be carried out. But it is implausible to say that all science is conducted with such an intention, or even that very much of it is. What about science that, while not morally bad in its purpose, creates a significant and foreseeable risk of mass destruction? Even if the answer here, too, is that it is morally impermissible to develop such science, it is not clear that the same can be said in the intermediate cases. Suppose a significant risk has been created for the sake of a significant benefit, as when, for the sake of reducing energy costs to manufacturers, designs for experimental nuclear power stations emerge from a scientific research programme. Even if the power stations pose a risk of environmental pollution, the case for saying that there is something morally wrong with the research programme is not so clear cut, even if the risk of something going wrong with the power stations is more than negligible.

The intermediate cases aside, doesn't it often turn out, even where the harm that science makes possible is actually felt, that science is not harmful in itself, but that it is appropriated for bad ends by those in control of it? Might it not be arguable that science has no ill effects (and perhaps no benefits) to call its own? Though it is tempting to draw this conclusion, the facts do not always agree with it. As at least one case study seems to show, the conduct of science, the beliefs and interests of influential people in the scientific community, and morally abhorrent but politically popular ideas can coalesce in such a way that it is false to say that science is taken over and made to serve bad ends by non-scientists. Science, scientists and evil politics can sometimes display an unforced harmony.

In a book entitled *Murderous Science*,[6] Benno Müller-Hill documents the willing involvement of German geneticists, psychiatrists and medical anthropologists in the selection of mental patients, Jews, gypsies and sick children for extermination and life-threatening experiments during the Hitler era. His account begins in 1900, more than thirty years before Hitler became Chancellor of the Reich. For it was at the turn of the century that the work of Mendel was rediscovered, and deployed in new ways by people in and out of the scientific community who believed that European culture was in danger of dying out. Their idea was that human intellectual capacities were a matter of genetic inheritance and that the genetic characteristics that had contributed to the growth of European culture could only be preserved by selective procreation. The genetically superior members of the superior races would be the preferred breeders of the new Europeans.

Academic journals and societies promoting the elaboration and application of this way of thinking began to be founded in Germany in the early years of the century, and as early as 1908 ideas about the necessity of racial hygiene were reflected in legislation: existing mixed-race marriages in German Southwest Africa were annulled, and all future such marriages were forbidden. One of the medical scientists who was later to become prominent in the application of theories of racial superiority in Germany itself, Eugen Fischer, seems to have conducted his first significant investigations into mixed-race marriages in 1908 in Southwest Africa. In a book that brought together his findings in 1913, Fischer recommended that people of mixed blood be given the minimum protection which was due to them as an inferior race, and that, when they were no longer useful to Germany, 'free competition should prevail, and lead to their decline and destruction'.[7]

In 1920 the writings of racial theorists like Fischer began to converge with those of psychiatrists and lawyers who argued that genetically inferior individuals, including the incurably mentally ill, could legitimately be subjected to euthanasia. Textbooks on genetics began to put forward principles of racial hygiene. The second (1923) edition of the textbook by Fischer, E. Bauer and F. Lenz, came into Hitler's possession while he was imprisoned in Landsberg, and influenced the opinions about race in *Mein Kampf*. In 1929 Fischer became head of a new Kaiser-Wilhelm Institute of Anthropology, Human Heredity and Eugenics at Berlin-Dahlem.

In the 1920s, then, ideas about race that were congenial to the Nazis gained currency in the scientific community, but apparently not as a direct result of the improvement in the political fortunes of the Nazis themselves. Indeed, Nazi ideas about race were up to a point rejected by Fischer and the co-authors of his genetics textbook. In the third edition, published in 1931, one of the co-authors, Fritz Lenz, wrote that 'we must of course deplore the one-sided "anti-Semitism" of National Socialism. Unfortunately, it seems that the masses need such "anti" feelings . . . we cannot doubt that National Socialism is honestly striving for a healthier race'.[8] Two years later, in a lecture given to 'the elite of Berlin', as Müller-Hill puts it, Fischer also pointed out disagreements with the race theories of the Nazis. He denied that people of mixed race are always intellectually inferior, and he denied that all Jews were necessarily inferior. The most assimilated of the German Jews, he claimed, were 'different', not inferior.[9] Other race-hygienists recoiled from these views and showed their displeasure by removing Fischer from the presidency of the German Eugenics Society. When the press attacks on Fischer as a friend of the Jews mounted, and he was denounced to the Ministry of the Interior, he wrote a memorandum saying that while he had always been anti-Semitic by inclination, he was a scientist and had to stand by views that were arrived at scientifically.

In later years, however, Fischer's differences with the Nazis seem to have evaporated. On 28 March 1943, he wrote in the *Deutsche Allgemeine Zeitung* that 'it is a rare and special good fortune for a theoretical science to flourish at a time when the prevailing ideology welcomes it, and its findings can immediately serve the policy of the state'.[10] Again, replying to an invitation from the Reichminister for the Occupied Eastern Territories to act as a chairman of a session at an international 'Anti-Jewish Conference' in Cracow in 1944, Fischer congratulated him on the idea of creating 'a scientific front line for the defence of European culture against the influence of Jewry'.[11] The admiration that Fischer came to have for the Nazis was reciprocated, despite the doubts that had arisen about his 'scientific' approach to the racial inferiority of the Jews. Himmler wrote this tribute to Fischer and Lenz in a letter to Hitler's staff in 1938:

> I am convinced that through their scientific work, they have both made a considerable contribution, in the last few years, to the theoretical basis and scientific recognition of the racial components of National Socialist ideology. . . . I am convinced that Fischer and Lenz can be allowed to join the Party. In fact I believe that their enrolment is a matter of political necessity, since we can hardly use the talents of these two men to provide scientific support for our ideology while rejecting them as members of the Party.[12]

Fischer and Lenz were medical anthropologists. But representatives of other medical specialities also had ideas that were attractive to the Nazis, or took advantage of Nazi extermination to pursue their research. There were psychiatrists who called for the sterilization of psychopaths[13] or who practised euthanasia by starvation on the mentally ill.[14] A law proclaimed in July 1933 allowed for compulsory sterilization in cases of 'congenital mental defects, schizophrenia, manic–depressive psychosis, hereditary epilepsy . . . and severe alcoholism'.[15] In 1935, F. Kallman, a Berlin psychiatrist, claimed at an international conference on population problems that

> it is desirable to extend prevention of reproduction to relatives of schizophrenics who stand out because of minor anomalies, and, above all, to define each of them as being undesirable from the eugenic point of view at the beginning of their reproductive years.[16]

In 1939, at least nine professors of psychiatry and thirty-nine medical doctors, acting as 'experts', participated in a systematic survey of mental patients for euthanasia. Some 75,000 are known to have been selected.[17]

Though a few psychiatrists wanted their profession to have

nothing to do with the euthanasia programme, they were a minority and seem to have had little success in persuading their colleagues not to collaborate with the government. In the summer of 1940 the heads of departments of psychiatry in German universities were urged by a Dr Jaspersen from the Bethel mental hospital to protest collectively against euthanasia.[18] They did nothing. Between January 1940 and September 1941, more than 70,000 mental patients were killed by carbon monoxide gas in six extermination centres.[19] The techniques for mass-killing pioneered in this euthanasia programme were later used in concentration camps like Auschwitz.

What was to be done with the remains of the mass-killings ordered by the Nazis? A department head at the Karl-Wilhelm Institute for Brain Research had some ideas. In the transcript of an interview with American officers after his arrest, Professor J. Hallervorden describes how he took the initiative:

> I went up to them: 'Look here now, boys, if you are going to kill all these people at least take the brains out, so that the material could be utilized.' They asked me, 'How many can you examine?' And so I told them an unlimited number – 'the more the better'. I gave them fixatives, jars and boxes, and instructions for removing and fixing the brains and they came bringing them like the delivery van from the furniture company. . . . There was wonderful material among those brains, beautiful mental defectives, malformations and early infantile diseases.[20]

Hallervorden was not alone in making use of the research opportunities afforded in the 1940s. The infamous Dr Mengele had certain gypsy inmates of Auschwitz killed for their eyes: the eyes exhibited hereditary discolourations of the iris that Mengele was interested in. The organs of dwarves were sent off to the Anthropological Institute at Berlin-Dahlem, where Mengele's former teacher, Otmar von Verschuer, had succeeded Eugen Fischer as Director. And so the cases go on.[21]

It seems that the scientists whose activities Müller-Hill documents did not have to be coerced or enticed into working with the Nazis. Many benefited from laws that resulted in the removal of Jewish academics from institutes and universities. They willingly placed themselves at the disposal of the authorities and were active in helping to formulate and implement legislation concerning sterilization, euthanasia and mixed marriage. Müller-Hill's interviews with those involved revealed that because there were always scientists willing to fill posts that fell vacant, it was easy for those who were asked to participate in the euthanasia programme to request other work instead. Those who participated, then, apparently did so freely. To what extent, if any, was the willing collaboration due to a frame of mind associated with science, and to what extent was it traceable to the special circumstances of Germany and the German scientific community before the Second World War?

Müller-Hill, himself a professor of genetics, is inclined to place a considerable part of the blame on the scientific frame of mind:

> Scientists espouse objectivity and spurn value judgements. But pure objectivity leads to regarding everything as being feasible. The killing of mental patients? If it is objectively necessary on economic grounds, and if it can be objectively organized, why not? The use of mental patients, the Jews, and the Gypsies as experimental animals before or after their necessary deaths? If the authorities allow it, why not?[22]

Though one can see what he means, Müller-Hill's suggestion is not very convincing when applied to the anthropologists, psychiatrists and others whom he discusses. For one thing, it is very far-fetched to say that all or many displayed pure objectivity even in their purely theoretical work. The basis for deciding that certain 'external appearances' were definitive 'Jewish traits', for example, seems to have been non-existent, and 'expert' opinions about racial ancestry were rendered on the basis of blurred photographs of people's grandparents. The confidence that quarter-Jews could be identified by 'race-biological assessment' went against elementary facts about the variety and distribution of human genes and chromosomes.[23] The objectivity of the 'expert' judgement that the Ukraine and Crimea had a climate unsuitable for people of Nordic stock, and would have to be forested if Germans were to resettle there, is equally open to doubt. Then there was the disagreement over the inferiority of Jews between Fischer on the one hand and other race-hygienists with similar scientific training on the other. Not only is it doubtful that the collaborating scientists were in the grip of an objective frame of mind: it is unclear that objectivity could have made a case for extermination seem strong, when it was based on economic considerations alone. A judgement is objective when it gives appropriate weight to all relevant considerations. The money-cost of maintaining mental patients is one consideration relevant to a judgement about the treatment they should receive. But it is not the only relevant consideration. That is why it cannot be objectively necessary on economic grounds alone to do one thing rather than another with mental patients. Perhaps Müller-Hill confuses objective judgement with judgement based on precisely quantifiable factors, such as the money-cost of treating mental patients. Finally, what has objectivity got to do with believing that, just because the authorities allow it, a certain course of action is permissible? Surely this is not objectivity but deference to those in authority, who *may* have the facts on their side, but who then again may not.

The habit of problem-solving or of being arrested by the task of thinking out how a thing could be done if one wanted to do it is a more plausible source in science for some of what went on in Germany under the Nazis. It was in this spirit, perhaps, that the design of gas-chambers effective for mass-executions was conceived. It was in this spirit, perhaps, that apparatus was thought up for the covert sterilization of quarter-Jews by X-ray. A letter of 1941 to Himmler showed with what ingenuity the scientists had applied themselves to this problem:

> One way of carrying out the sterilization would be, for example, to have the person concerned step up to a counter where questions have to be answered or forms filled in; this would keep the person occupied for two or three minutes. The official, who would be sitting behind the counter, could use the apparatus during this time by turning on a switch which would activate both tubes simultaneously, since irradiation from both sides is necessary.[24]

Though the technical problem of sterilization may have had a fascination for those who liked solving technical problems, and though a fascination for solving technical problems may be part of what one gets from learning and practising science, it is hard to see how even this keeps one from asking why sterilization should be contemplated, and whether it should be carried out. The idea of sterilization has to be part of the scientific orthodoxy if means of carrying it out are not to raise eyebrows, and it became part of that orthodoxy in certain quarters in Germany not solely because of what science is like, but also because of the state of Germany and German science at the time.

Müller-Hill himself gives considerable weight to these environmental factors.[25] To explain how scientists could have been active in implementing the plans of a Fascist government in Germany but not in countries like Spain or Italy, he speaks of the humiliation felt in Germany after its defeat in the First World War, and the consequent decline of German science and industry, which had previously been pre-eminent. According to Müller-Hill, the workings of the Weimar Republic caused resentment among German professors and their assistants, who were inclined to blame both the military defeat and the growth of capitalist democracy on Jews and Communists. In this way, according to Müller-Hill, the German scientific community, especially those with theories of race-superiority and eugenics, was predisposed to welcome National Socialism. The importance of these factors seems to me to undercut the claim that the scientific frame of mind played a very significant role in its own right in the collaboration of scientists with the Nazis.

I shall return to the question of whether aspects of scientific thinking make science morally questionable. But I should like to end the discussion of Müller-Hill's findings by considering some remarks he makes about the interpretation of his intentions in writing *Murderous Science*. These remarks come in the preface to the English translation written in 1987, and they comment on the earlier reception of the book:

> Since the German edition first appeared in August 1984, my scientist friends have been concerned that some readers may interpret this book as a condemnation of science and as a denial of rationalism. This would be a complete misinterpretation of my intentions, which are to show that a world in which science flourishes but justice is absent is condemned to the same fate as Sodom. I might add that a world in which justice flourishes and science is absent would be condemned just as surely to a different, but equally horrible, fate.[26]

The claim that a disaster is in store unless science and justice coexist is plausible, but is it correct? One can accept that, as in the period studied by Müller-Hill, it is very dangerous to have science without justice, but must there be a disaster if justice flourishes without science? It is true that in the absence of science people are vulnerable to flood, famine, disease and the rest; but if they meet a bad end as a result of these calamities, is it as much of a horrible fate as the moral disaster of assisting sterilization, mass-execution and the rest in Nazi Germany? The mass-death of people in a flood is bad, but wilful mass-killing is surely much worse: it is the bad will behind the bad outcome that makes the difference. So to say that the fate of the just but scienceless can be as horrible as the fate of the scientific and unjust is, at best, questionable.

The period examined by Müller-Hill shows that, without being directed by unscrupulous but powerful external forces, scientists can perfectly well conceive, and promote, and find ways of implementing, evil ends. But the suggestion that there is something in the nature of science itself, independent of the circumstances of the German scientific community, that made them do what they did or encouraged them to do it, is not very plausible. Or at least, in the formulation we have considered from Müller-Hill, it is not very convincing.

Science and insensitivity

Might not science make it easier to mistreat human beings and other living creatures by allowing them to be conceived as so many machines or so many configurations of cells or genes, or so many organ banks? Might not science make people so preoccupied with ways of producing desired or interesting effects that people begin to be seen as so many sites for these interesting effects? The use of concentration camp prisoners for experimental purposes is only an extreme example of a practice that seems to suggest this utterly clinical conception of people. Another, much less extreme, case is where hospital patients are referred to by their medically interesting condition rather than by name, or where the victim of a fatal accident is looked over for organs that might be useful for transplant. Even the complaint that certain doctors try to treat the disease and ignore the whole person gestures at the sort of objection to a scientific outlook that I am trying to formulate. Science makes its practitioners used to impersonal conceptions of other living beings,[27] and these may interfere with the operation of sympathies associated with prescientific conceptions.

Though the objection has some intuitive appeal, it is not unanswerable. Unless the practice of science, with its impersonal conceptions of other creatures, dominates someone's life, it is not clear that those impersonal conceptions will get the better of others that are required for the rest of life's activities. Moreover, it may be thanks to a scientific conception of other creatures that we learn enough about their make-up to realize that they are capable of feeling pain at certain kinds of treatment, or suffering at certain kinds of interference with their behaviour or habitat. It may be thanks to science that other human beings who strike a prescientific mind as 'vegetables' are revealed as highly intelligent but handicapped fellow beings. Science, in other words, can make us extend sympathetic responses to a wider range of living creatures.

The impersonal nature of some scientific conceptions is only one source of a possible insensitivity caused by science. Another source of insensitivity is the frame of mind that prompts investigation of the nature of a thing for the purpose of manipulation or control. This time the objection is not exactly that science blinds us to the humanity of other people, though this is sometimes how it is put, but that science can encourage us to ask how even others we regard as human can be made use of. Instead of trying to understand others so as to promote friendship or sympathy for their own sake, one may be tempted by a scientific frame of mind to try to discover which psychological levers to press in order to get certain desirable reactions. There is no denying that many people feel and act upon the urge to manipulate others. But it is unclear whether science is to blame. Though the understanding that manipulation requires has something in common with some types of scientific understanding, it seems to me tendentious to say that science is the source of every urge to manipulate, or that scientific understanding is characteristically for the sake of manipulation or control. Sometimes it can be for the sake of relieving curiosity alone, or for solving a puzzle or problem with no technique of control, or any novel prediction, in the offing.[28]

Is there a connection between a scientific frame of mind and a distaste for the unsystematic and disorderly, or for what has evolved by tradition rather than according to a masterplan? If so, cannot science breed another kind of insensitivity, the sort that tells against the traditional, the arbitrary and the quirky, even when these things do no harm?[29] The answer seems to me to be that science can breed this insensitivity but that it need not. It is true that science is a precondition of modernity and perhaps encourages a preference for the new over the old and a taste for progress;[30] all the same, it can acquaint people with phenomena, such as delicately balanced ecosystems, which, if tampered with, can cause the deterioration of life within them; these phenomena can inspire a cautionary approach to large-scale intervention in other areas, e.g. town and country planning, and can even tell against various kinds of so-called social engineering. For better or worse, there is scientific material to support conservatism as much as conscientious innovation. In any case, and as already suggested, it must not be thought that even the chillier scientific frame of mind necessarily cancels out all other non-scientific or prescientific impulses and attractions. It can coexist in people with much else that makes them sentimental, nostalgic and so on.

Science and the conditions of decadence

Science is sometimes thought to do people harm because it makes them soft and lazy. When it is successfully applied, it often enables people to do and get more while expending less effort. It enables people to feed, clothe and shelter themselves efficiently, and so enables them to look beyond the satisfaction of their basic needs. It enables them to save labour, and so gives them leisure to satisfy their questionable native and acquired appetites. The combination of spare time and resources for satisfying desires for things other than the necessities of life, creates a demand for entertainment and eventually the arts. Ultimately, these arts dull the will to work and the will to fight when necessary, making any developed country a target for conquest.

This line of thought is developed at some length by Rousseau in a number of works, but notably in the *Discourse on the Sciences and Arts*, and Kant said in the 'Conjectural Beginning' that there was some truth in it. Rousseau gave the terms 'sciences' and 'arts' a fairly loose interpretation. Under 'science' he seems to have included the body of theoretical subjects taught in the colleges, including physics and mathematics, and by 'arts' he usually means drama, literature, painting, sculpture and music. Occasionally the arts are subjects like history and law, as well as crafts and engineering disciplines. According to Rousseau, the revival of the arts and sciences had encouraged idleness. It had promoted speculation at the expense of useful action. It had encouraged the production of mediocre works that pandered to the taste of the rich, for it grew with the patronage of the rich. Artists of genius were thus reduced to craftsmen. In the sciences, once developed, ideas prospered only if they assisted the accumulation of wealth. Finally, to the extent that the arts and sciences made life comfortable and safe, their growth contributed to the decline of courage and the decay of military skills.

The ill effects of the sciences were not only to be observed in his own day, according to Rousseau. All of the great civilizations of the past had produced advances in geometry and engineering, or had left to posterity admirable works of drama and sculpture; these achievements had not prevented the collapse of standards of public behaviour in Egypt, Athens and Rome. On the contrary, once they had started to be able to support artistic and scientific communities, they already suffered from the prevalence of vices that led to their downfall. The China of Rousseau's day was cited as a further, modern illustration.

Even if Rousseau is right in suggesting that all scientifically advanced cultures are decadent, does he have an argument for the conclusion that the decadence is due to science? Science may be a contributing cause of decadence; for it creates the leisure whose abuse constitutes decadence. But unless there is something intrinsically wrong with leisure, or something intrinsically wrong with what is abusable, science is not enough of a contributing cause to be objectionable. It is true that by creating leisure science presents us with a problem, namely that of how best to spend our time, that we would not have in a life of unremitting toil. It seems to me also to be true that this problem has no scientific solution. But I cannot see how the fact that science creates this problem for us can be turned into a moral criticism of science, or for that matter into any other kind of criticism of science.

A more promising line of attack in the spirit of Rousseau is to do with the way in which, at the same time as it saves labour, science also deskills those whom it benefits. The point is easiest to make in relation to such science-dependent machines as pocket calculators. Someone who can rely on a calculator to add, subtract and multiply does not need to go through the tiresome drills that enable people to calculate quickly unaided. But the fact that the drills are made redundant is both a gain and a loss. It is a gain of convenience at the expense of skill. A child who never learns how to tie shoe-laces because all the fastenings are Velcro may lose something as well. And this is only at one extreme of a range of skills and crafts that can be made redundant by science through technology. When machines are widely available that can print out directly from dictation and read out written text, we will no doubt see sharply increased illiteracy. Not that the loss of skills must result from scientific advance: the leisure created by science can even create an opportunity for relearning the old crafts as pastimes. But skills can be, and quite commonly are, lost.

Science and meaninglessness

Though science can make life easier, it can also acquaint us with facts that put life into a distressing perspective. Facts about our size and longevity compared to the size and longevity of the rest of the universe are familiar sources of unease. In cosmic terms human individuals are infinitesimal and last no time at all. Then there is the way in which the progress of science drives out teleology, including inherent final causes for our species. The loss of authority for a conception of how human beings might turn out if they realized their nature was precisely the loss of authority for a conception that could give meaning to life.[31] To the extent that science has helped to discredit final causes of this kind, as well as final causes derived from a supposed divine plan for us, science might be thought to contribute to our demoralization.

Taken as a criticism of science, however, the point about demoralization is weak. To begin with, science is not the source, but only the medium, of facts about scale that some people find demoralizing. So to criticize science for what may be a dispiriting disclosure is really to blame the messenger for the message. Second, it is unclear how far any of the facts disclosed or how far the banishing of final causes really ought to be taken to be demoralizing. Why should the fact that life is led by small, short-lived creatures mean that human life is meaningless or purposeless? Why should the suggestion that there is no human nature to give our lives a point or a direction, even if the suggestion is accepted, make us depressed if there are other ends, arrived at by individual members of the species, to give lives meaning? Furthermore, even if the scientific basis for being demoralized about life could be unlearnt, would that mean that there was no other basis for being demoralized about life? Why can't the quite unscientific consider-ations that routine and monotony will dominate most lives, that whatever happens most people never get the opportunities to develop the abilities to do something out of the ordinary – why can't entirely humdrum, non-scientific reflection of this kind prove just as sobering or saddening as any finding inspired by science? Finally, *must* the facts made available by science, even when the frame of reference is cosmic, prove disheartening to human beings? There are those who think that the human factor, far from being a parochial feature of a tiny sector of the universe, constrains what is true of the whole universe in important ways, which are captured by various strengths of formulation of a so-called 'anthropic principle' in cosmology.[32]

Conclusion, and a remark about moral objections to the arts

Many of the standard moral objections to science are unconvincing, even though some uses of science are evil. When uses of science are evil, they are not always inspired by unscrupulous non-scientists. Sometimes the unscrupulous come from within the scientific community and their undertakings are made easier for them by frames of mind that science encourages. This is not to say that ways of thinking in science encourage or inspire wrongdoing by themselves, only that they can assist it once it is underway, as perhaps happened in the period studied by Müller-Hill. We have no evidence for the bald claim that science makes people bad or makes them form evil intentions; at most we have reason to believe that bad men can misuse science. We can also conclude that if there is a body of knowledge that tells people the difference between right and wrong and that strengthens their resolve to do only the right, it is the sort of knowledge that is required if science is not to be misused. This agrees with Kant's doctrine, though I do not call that indispensable knowledge of right and wrong a science.

Are moral objections to the arts more persuasive than moral objections to the sciences? The objections that I am aware of do not seem to be more persuasive. Rousseau's idea in the First *Discourse* that the arts indulge the questionable tastes of the idle rich; Plato's idea in *The Republic* that the dramatic arts both pander to base appetites in the audience and make actors proficient at producing the image of virtue rather than genuine virtue; Tolstoy's idea in *What is Art?* that most art is pretentious, degrading, divisive or trivial – all of these ideas seem to me to suffer from the tendency to make the shortcomings of some art into the shortcomings of most art.

There is no reason why all of the branches of the fine arts, or even every specimen of a doubtful branch, must do badly when judged by moral standards, just as, on the whole, there is no reason why science should serve bad ends. The fact that science *can* assist evil, sometimes without its practitioners needing much or any persuasion, shows that whether science does good is a contingent matter. But for it to be contingent is not for it to be untypical. Science can normally have good effects without its being guaranteed to have good effects. And the same, presumably, can be true of the arts, even if some works of art – e.g. the pornographic or the sadistic – are or promote evil.

SECOND THOUGHTS ABOUT THE ENDS OF CULTURE

Suppose that the arts and sciences often are morally unobjectionable. Suppose that they are even morally improving, enlarging our capacity to benefit others and not just ourselves, making us more sensitive to what others want and need. Granted that they promote moral improvement, is this what they ought to promote, or is this purpose somehow limiting? If research into race and intelligence carries the danger of race war or another holocaust, so that there is a moral argument against pursuing it, must such research be forbidden or avoided? Or must the moral arguments against the research compete with arguments about the value of any increase in knowledge? Differently, must art refrain from trying to make the morally forbidden comprehensible? Might there not be a value in the creation that art involves even if what is created is, from a moral point of view, monstrous?

A way of bringing together all of these questions is by asking whether the value of the arts and sciences is really a matter of how well they promote human moral improvement, and, indirectly, how they contribute to some more or less conventional highest good. This is Kant's way of valuing the arts and sciences, but is this way acceptable? An important challenge to Kant's way of thinking is supposed to come from Nietzsche, who connects the worth of culture not with how it helps mankind to be happy in accordance with moral worth, but with how it promotes new kinds of human vitality, new kinds of enhanced life.[33] According to Nietzsche, the arts are better than the sciences at promoting these kinds of vitality, while conventional morality, for its part, is deadening. In the rest of this chapter I shall only consider what is supposed to make vitality a more appropriate end for culture than morality.

Part of Nietzsche's criticism of morality is directed at its pretensions to have a divine source and special divine authority; if its force and content can all be explained in terms of mundane factors, such as the way the conventional virtues encourage a quiescence and tractability that is useful to rulers, and reassuring to a timid mass, then the 'must' of moral precepts becomes a good deal more resistible. Again, Nietzsche complains of the tendency of moral precepts to level and homogenize human beings, to tame and domesticate them, and to ignore or discourage possibilities of enhancement and grandeur. He does not wish human beings to revert to their animal origins and be in the grip of the passions. He wishes human beings to be able to use the passions – including those suppressed or outlawed by conventional morality. Culture consists of broadening the range of affective response that is possible for the will; it is not a matter of stamping out the passions.

In *The Will to Power* Nietzsche writes the following about the task of culture:

> To press everything terrible into *service*, one by one, step by step, experimentally: this is what the task of culture demands; but until it is *strong enough* for this, it must oppose, moderate, veil, even curse all this.
>
> Everywhere that a culture *posits evil*, it gives expression to a relationship of *fear*, thus a *weakness*.
>
> *Thesis*: everything good is the evil of former days made serviceable. *Standard*: the greater and more terrible the passions are that an age, a people, an individual can permit themselves, because they are capable of employing them as *means*, *the higher stands their culture*, the more mediocre, the weaker, the more submissive and cowardly a man is, the more he will posit as *evil*: it is with him that the realm of evil is most comprehensive. The basest man will see the realm of evil (i.e., of that which is forbidden and hostile to him) everywhere.[34]

This is not a complete break from Kant. For Kant culture is the production or enlargement of aptitude, and Nietzsche is speaking of a process that enables human beings to take control of more and more fearful things, including dangerous passions and inclinations. Since this is an enlargement of aptitude, Nietzsche's sense of culture and Kant's overlap. But there is a strong disagreement over the nature of evil, over the kind of strength that enhances character, and over the kind of culture that is highest.

In Kant the highest culture is the kind that consists of the discipline of the inclinations, and that frees the personality to set and try to achieve higher, i.e. moral, ends. It is true that the agency released by this higher culture is other-worldly, while the corresponding result of culture in Nietzsche's conception is not. It is true, too, that the desirability of mastering the inclinations can be reconstructed as a fear or guilt about giving them free rein. The possibility of this reconstruction does not show, however, that evil reduces to whatever we fear or feel guilty about, and problems with the metaphysics of Kant's morals do not show that its dividing line between good and evil is drawn in the wrong place. There may still be objective reasons for refraining from the infliction of pain, even if there is no transcendental faculty of reason for the wrongness of inflicting pain to register with.

As for evil, Kant understands it to be the wilful contravention of duty or the wilful omission of the dutiful action. He thinks that evil in this sense is characteristic of human beings: it is commonplace for them to know what they ought to do and yet do something else. But though evil is characteristic of human beings, according to Kant, it is not necessitated by human nature. Again, though evil often takes the form of succumbing to inclination, it is not equated by Kant with succumbing to inclination; and there are some inclinations, such as the inclination to honour or to act out of sympathy, that produce good (though not morally good) actions. So while morality is always a matter of acting as far as possible independently of inclination and thus of what is animal or pathological, morality is not always a matter of acting *against* inclination or what is animal. At times duty and inclination point in the same direction. There is no simple dichotomy of morality and animality, and so Nietzsche's objection that in conventional morals one's animality is suppressed is not an objection to Kant.

Kant's moral theory *is* open to two other objections of Nietzsche's: the objection that all moral agents are not equal, and the objection that some moral theories do not attach sufficient value to greatness or grandeur. In the *Critique of Practical Reason* Kant shows impatience with taking the great or the grand as moral exemplars (Ak. 5, 157), though he does not deny they are admirable. And he is a moral egalitarian. He says in all of his moral writings that rational human beings are persons, and that persons are equal. Apparently in reply to this latter claim or something like it, Nietzsche says in *The Will to Power* that many human beings lack personality while some have an excess of it.[35] Is this a good objection? What can it mean except that some human beings are ordinary and some extraordinary? Kant does not need Nietzsche to teach him that there is a difference; he is aware of it but he denies its relevance to morality. He denies the moral relevance of grandeur as well. He points out that it distracts people from the requirements of everyday morality. Unless the costs of ignoring everyday morality are negligible or illusory, Kant's objection is to be reckoned with.

Nietzsche may say that being inspired by grandeur has more value for life than the pedestrian fulfilment of common duty, but then the question is why value for life should take precedence over what Kant takes to be moral value. Apparently the answer is that value for life, or, what seems for him to be equivalent, addition to the quantum of power, is a less question-begging measure of value than moral value as interpreted by Kant. It does not carry with it the baggage of transcendental free agency. It does not have pretensions to be incomparably elevated. And it does not come with a background theory so complacent as to assume that certain values with authority for certain people in a given time and place are cosmically authoritative: irresistible to any rational being, no matter where, no matter when.

It cannot be denied that Kant is uncritical of common rational knowledge of morals or common reason. He does not think that it is for moral philosophy to correct the valuations of common reason but only to reveal the principle or principles implicit in them. This is clear from a passage close to the end of the First Section of the *Groundwork*, after he has derived the test for distinguishing moral from immoral maxims:

> Thus within the moral knowledge of common human reason we have attained its principle. To be sure, common human reason does not think of it abstractly in such universal form, but it always has it in view and uses it as a standard of its judgements. It would be easy to show how common human reason, with this compass, knows very well how to distinguish what is good, what is bad, what is consistent or inconsistent with duty. Without in the least teaching common reason anything new, we need only draw its attention to its own principle, in the manner of Socrates, thus showing that neither science nor philosophy is needed in order to know what one has to do in order to be honest and good, and even wise and virtuous. (Ak. 4, 403–4)

Common reason, Kant seems to be saying, is natively capable of making correct moral judgements. Moreover, Kant implies elsewhere, there is something that makes those judgements correct; and this metaphysical basis is objectively valid. Is all of this the expression of an unthinking confidence in conventional moral judgement?

Nietzsche seems to think so, reading an endorsement of conventional morality into all philosophical attempts to provide a rational grounding for morality. In paragraph 186 of *Beyond Good and Evil* he writes,

> What the philosophers called a 'rational foundation for morality' and tried to supply was, seen in the right light, merely a scholarly variation of the common *faith* in the prevalent morality . . . ; indeed, in the last analysis a kind of denial that this morality might ever be considered problematic – certainly the very opposite of an analysis, questioning, and vivisection of this faith.

The objection that the philosophers were only rationalizing conventional morality instead of, as they should have been doing, critically examining it, raises the question of how philosophers are supposed to get outside the prevalent morality. Nietzsche's answer is, roughly, 'by means of anthropology'; by means, that is, of the examination of different peoples, times and their ways of life (ibid.).

Who is to say, however, that this examination of different ways of life will not disclose a substantial agreement between moralities over what is permitted and encouraged on the one hand and what is prohibited on the other? What if it should turn out that, while there were many different supposed 'rational foundations' for different moralities, the actual precepts being justified tended to be the same? This would surely show that from many different perspectives, and not merely the current and local one, it seemed right to do one thing and omit another. And this is not merely a possible outcome of comparing the moral views of a Kant or an English utilitarian or an Aristotle, considered in Nietzsche's way as mouthpieces for the conventional moralities of their time and place; it actually turns out that many of the same types of action are condemned and praised for different reasons by these different outlooks. In this way, contrary to Nietzsche, anthropology may reinforce rather than upset the endorsement of conventional morality.

Nietzsche is too quick to conclude that the examination of different moralities must produce competition for a prevalent morality. He also seems to exaggerate the distance between his own, admittedly unconventional, moral views, and those of the mainstream occupied by 'the philosophers'. As has often been remarked, Nietzsche's views have a lot in common with Aristotle's views,[36] notably in the way Nietzsche's ideal type recalls Aristotle's *megalopsychos*, and in the favourable outlook on aristocratic morality in general. This may show that even Nietzsche had limited success in trying to get purchase on morality from a position entirely outside it.

At various places in his writings Nietzsche tries to subvert the morality of the philosophers from the inside, associating its prohibitions, its catalogues of the virtues and the rest with the immoral motive of wanting revenge against life and with the immoral practice – which he claims runs right through philosophy – of slandering life. A section of *The Will to Power* headed 'Why Philosophers are Slanderers' is all about the ways in which philosophers denigrate the phenomena and impulses which are central to life as it is actually lived. Moral philosophy is an important vehicle for this denigration.

> I fear it is still the Circe of philosophers, morality that has here bewitched them into having to be slanderers forever – They believed in moral 'truths,' they found there the supreme values – what else could they do but deny existence more firmly the more they got to know it? – For this existence is immoral – And this life depends on immoral preconditions: and all morality denies life –.
>
> Let us abolish the real world: and to be able to do this we first have to be able to abolish the supreme value hitherto, morality – It suffices to establish that even morality is immoral, in the sense in which immorality has always been condemned. . . .[37]

What is apparently supposed to establish that morality is immoral is the psychological diagnosis of morality as the instinct of decadence,[38] and the observation that the chief spokesmen for morality, the philosophers, have always been decadent.[39]

Though it is true that philosophers often associate experience or life with appearance rather than reality, with impermanence rather than permanence, in short with the negative sides of the more characteristic philosophical dichotomies, why should this be regarded as a slander or even criticism rather than a simple articulation of the limitations of life or experience? And why is not the effect of the would-be slander cancelled out by the sheer imperviousness of most of life to the findings of philosophy? If the exhausted and flabby really needed propaganda to get their revenge on life and on the vital sections of humanity, it is hard to see why moral philosophy would be thought a good medium for it.

We are still without a good reason for supposing that there is something wrong with morality and hence something wrong with the idea that the arts and science might be valuable because they promote morality.

5

THE TWO CULTURES

Are the arts and sciences badly adapted to promoting our moral improvement? The last chapter suggested that they need not be, and that certain potentially powerful objections to the Kantian account that I favour could be met. One objection was that the arts and sciences are likely to have bad moral effects. Another was that morality is the wrong end for culture to promote. Even if these objections prove to be uncompelling, another remains to be considered – to the effect that the harmony between the arts and sciences depicted by Kant's account is an idealization. Far from working co-operatively toward a common end, the arts and sciences sometimes stake their own, more or less exclusive, claims to be morally improving. These claims can be accompanied by attitudes of mutual disapproval. From the perspective of the arts, scientists sometimes appear to lack a feeling for life and a capacity for moral imagination; while from the standpoint of scientists, novelists and artists sometimes appear not to grasp or care enough about the basic human needs that science provides the means of satisfying. In this chapter I shall argue that despite the existence of these unflattering images, the arts and sciences can be understood to be complementary means of human improvement. After rejecting one account of the way the arts and sciences complement one another, I shall propose another.

THE SNOW–LEAVIS CONTROVERSY

The arts and sciences were not quite what was meant by the phrase 'the two cultures' in C.P. Snow's now famous Rede Lecture for 1959. Snow's two cultures were, on the one hand, the scientific, and, on the other, the 'literary', something narrower than the arts in general and, to judge by Snow's later explanation of his lecture, something that did not include philosophy and some types of social history.[1] Still, while Snow's two cultures do not coincide exactly with the arts and sciences, his lecture does identify and deplore the sort of tension that we are concerned with, embodied in the distorted images that Snow took one 'culture' to have of the other. Here is how these images are described:

> The non–scientists have a rooted impression that the scientists are shallowly optimistic, unaware of man's condition. On the other hand, the scientists believe that the literary intellectuals are totally lacking in foresight, peculiarly unconcerned with their brother men, in a deep sense anti–intellectual, anxious to restrict both art and thought to the existential moment.[2]

Snow believed that these impressions were distorted but not entirely baseless. As he saw things in 1959 some scientists did suffer from an impoverishment of the imagination by refusing to read literature,[3] while others were wrong to think that all literature was as self-absorbed and careless of the future as the worst specimens of the literary culture. For its part, the literary culture was also seriously impoverished, since a deep understanding of nature was unavailable to it. Perhaps, because they had the greater vanity about the culture they possessed, the literary intellectuals were subject to the greater impoverishment.[4]

Though the literary culture was perhaps the poorer of the two, it was not the less influential. Far from it. According to Snow, it was the literary culture, or, as he also describes it, the 'traditional culture', which had managed the Western world for a long time and continued to manage it.[5] He went on to claim that the traditional culture had entirely mishandled one previous revolution – the industrial one – and that if left unreformed and uninfluenced by the scientific culture it would fail to meet the challenge of the scientific revolution. By 'scientific revolution' he meant the 'change that came from the application of real science to industry' and that produced the industrial society of electronics, atomic energy and automation.[6] The challenge of the scientific revolution was that of bringing the benefits of science – improved agriculture, medicine and housing – to the poor of the world. Snow proposed a reform of British education to meet both the problem of mutual incomprehension and the challenge of the scientific revolution. Taking as a working model the educational arrangements in the USSR in the

1950s, Snow recommended far less specialization before university, with a proportion of sciences to arts of 40 per cent to 60 per cent, and a tiered system of higher education to produce first-class pure scientists, supporting professionals, technicians and, finally, politicians and administrators 'who know enough science to have a sense of what the scientists are talking about'.[7]

Snow's idea of the two uncommunicating and mutually uncomprehending cultures got more attention – and criticism – than his proposed reforms of education and his preoccupations with the poor of the world. The most uncompromising of those opposed to Snow's ideas, and the one who was most outraged by their widespread acceptance, was the Cambridge critic and teacher of English literature, F.R. Leavis. Leavis's was no instant response to Snow: his Richmond Lecture was delivered about three years after Snow's, in February 1962. It was published the following month in the London *Spectator* under the title 'The Significance of C.P. Snow'. The lecture was exceptionally hostile. Leavis criticized Snow for letting it be understood that he, Snow, a much published novelist with a scientific training, had a place of eminence in both the scientific and literary worlds. Leavis claimed that Snow was no novelist and that no real knowledge of or feeling for science was conveyed by either his fiction or by the Rede Lecture. He criticized Snow for the superficiality of the suggestion that science could have the status of culture. He wrote with distaste of Snow's heavily Americanized vision of scientifically wrought social hope. And he briefly proposed, in opposition to Snow's proposals for the reform of education, his own answer to specialization in the university, namely a curriculum centred on the study of the literature of one's own language. Leavis's attack provoked outrage in its turn, attracting a large and unfavourable correspondence in the *Spectator*.

Perhaps the best developed of Leavis's objections concerned Snow's use of the concept of culture. In his Rede Lecture Snow had said that

> At one pole, the scientific culture really is a culture, not only in an intellectual but also in an anthropological sense. That is, its members need not, and of course often do not, always completely understand each other; biologists more often than not will have a pretty hazy idea of contemporary physics; but there are common attitudes, common standards and patterns of behaviour, common approaches and assumptions. . . . In

their working, and in much of their emotional, life, their attitudes are closer to other scientists than to non-scientists who in religion or politics or class have the same labels as themselves. If I were to risk a piece of shorthand, I should say that they naturally had the future in their bones. . . . Without thinking about it, they respond alike. That is what a culture means.[8]

Leavis leapt on the last two lines of this passage:

'Without thinking, they respond alike': Snow's habits as an intellectual and as a sage were formed in such a milieu. Thinking is a difficult art and requires training and practice in any given field. It is a pathetic and comic – and menacing – illusion on Snow's part that he is capable of thought on the problems he offers to advise us on. If his lecture has any value for use in schools – or universities – it is as a document for the study of cliché.[9]

Leavis means by cliché here a style of writing and thought that disposes of an issue without really confronting it, a style of writing that he goes on to suggest is essentially journalistic. But the phrase he quotes – 'Without thinking, they respond alike' – is not Snow's, and the point I take Leavis to be criticizing – the point that unthinking response can be dignified with the name of 'culture' – is not Snow's either. Snow is not saying that scientists respond alike without giving thought to their response, he is saying that they respond alike without thinking about responding alike.

Leavis is more accurate and more effective when he criticizes Snow on the significance for culture of rapid industrialization. Taking his examples from the then recent history of the USSR and China, Snow wrote,

These transformations were made with inordinate effort and with great suffering. Much of the suffering was unnecessary: the horror is hard to look at straight, standing in the same decades. Yet they've proved that common men can show astonishing fortitude in chasing jam tomorrow. Jam today, and men aren't at their most exciting; jam tomorrow, and one sees them at their noblest. The transformations have also proved something which only the scientific culture can take in its stride. Yet when we don't take it in our stride, it makes us look silly.[10]

Leavis comments,

> The callously ugly insensitiveness of the mode of expression
> is wholly significant. It gives us Snow, who is wholly
> representative of the world, or culture, to which it belongs.
> . . . It is the world in which the vital inspiration, the creative
> drive, is 'Jam tomorrow' (if you haven't any today) or (if you
> have it today) '*More* jam tomorrow.' It is the world in which,
> even at the level of the intellectual weeklies, 'standard of
> living' is an ultimate criterion, its raising an ultimate aim, a
> matter of wages and salaries and what you can buy with
> them, reduced hours of work and technological resources that
> make your increasing leisure worth having; so that product-
> ivity – the supremely important thing – must be kept on the
> rise, at whatever cost to protecting conservative habit.[11]

Leavis doubts that the increase in the standard of living is by itself
very satisfying, and he thinks that the prospect of more jam 'cannot
be regarded by a fully human mind as a matter for happy
contemplation', bringing with it as it does 'human emptiness and
boredom'.[12] He claims that in respect of being alive an inhabitant
of an advanced industrial society compares unfavourably with
someone who belongs to the Indian peasantry or an African bush
tribe.

Probably Leavis undervalues a rise in the standard of living, just
as he overvalues the vitality of the Indian peasant, the Bushman or
'a member of one of those poignantly surviving primitive peoples'[13]
untouched by technology. Still, one understands what he means.
The transformations that Snow describes, once they bring societies
above subsistence and see to people's basic needs, can start to have
diminishing returns; and the emptiness that is sometimes felt at the
same time as 'the standard of living' is raised is not something that
the scientific culture can take in its stride, unless it is simply blind to
the emptiness or to what forms of life might be preferable to it.

Leavis thinks that the right response to the feeling of emptiness is
a process of questioning, which is where great literature comes in:

> What for – what ultimately for? What ultimately do men live
> by? These questions are in and of the creative drive that
> produces great art in Conrad and Lawrence. . . . But life in
> the civilization of an age for which such creative questioning
> is not done and is not influential on general sensibility tends

characteristically to lack a dimension: it tends to have no depth – no depth against which it doesn't tacitly protect itself by the habit of unawareness (as Snow enjoins us to do our living in the dimension of 'social hope'). In coming to terms with great literature we discover what at bottom we really believe.[14]

And discovering what we believe may be made necessary if we are to make more of the possibilities afforded by leisure than shopping or drinking in our off-hours. Snow does not say explicitly that the future being prepared by science can have only a scientific, not a literary, culture catering for it. But this is implied by his equation of the literary with the traditional culture and by his claim that the traditional culture is utterly unequipped to cope with the scientific revolution. It may well be, as Leavis suggests, that the deep questions about life come into their own with special force once science is doing its work, so that literature is not so much superseded as revived by what science creates – revived, that is, if the habit of not thinking prevents or shortcircuits the questioning that literature is able to engage in.

Instead of speaking of a scientific culture, of the effects on industry of applied science, and 'more jam', Leavis refers to the 'accelerating movement of external civilization'. He contrasts this civilization with the culture that enables mankind 'to be in full intelligent possession of its full humanity',[15] a culture that he thinks the advance of technology makes it urgent to acquire. And he distinguishes between the erection of the scientific edifice and the 'creation of the human world'.[16] He says that the creation of the human world was prior to, and helped to make possible, the erection of the human edifice. And he identifies language as part of the human creation. The human world is kept going, its transmitted culture is enlivened and helped to develop, Leavis says, by a collaborative–creative process that is manifested in one kind of study of literature. The study proceeds by forming judgements on literature that are submitted for correction and amendment to others engaged in the same pursuit. There need be nothing 'traditional' about the literature selected for study, and there need be nothing traditional about the judgements that it elicits. On the contrary, Leavis says, the judgements that he himself arrived at 'in a pioneering book on modern poetry' disturbed the academic received opinion just as much as the intrusion of Sunday trains disturbed the old Master of Jesus College, Cambridge whom Snow took as one of the extreme antagonists of the scientific culture.[17]

THE TWO CULTURES AND ONE-SIDEDNESS

Is Leavis's contrast between external civilization and the culture of the human world to be preferred to Snow's contrast between the literary and the scientific? I think that both contrasts are one-sided: Leavis's gives a clearer sense than Snow's of the ways in which science and technology presuppose and are complemented by a humane culture; but it does not give much sense of mutual dependence, or of how much worse off humane culture would be if there were to be a decline in external civilization. Snow's account suffers from a comparable one-sidedness, but, as might have been expected, on the side of external civilization: we are told why we in the prosperous West, and more importantly, those in poorer parts of the world, cannot get on without the scientific culture, but we are not told that or why it is necessary for the literary culture to be kept fresh, or how, if at all, it complements the scientific culture.

Snow comes close to broaching these questions in 'A Second Look'. Section 7 of the retrospective essay starts with the promising question, 'With the scientific revolution going on around us, what has literature made of it?' But the question is never answered. Snow concentrates on defining a strain of twentieth-century literature as 'modernist', and gives the impression that this literature is not well-suited to absorbing the significance, or sharing the spirit, of the scientific revolution.[18] But he stops well short of identifying writing that does show real understanding of the scientific revolution or that promises to close the gap between the literary and the scientific. For examples of the preferred literature we have to turn to some of the people who decided to defend Snow against Leavis in the pages of the *Spectator*. One of these, the psychiatrist Anthony Storr, named Snow himself as the author of a modern novel – *The Search* – which 'contains an exciting description of the inward experience of making a creative scientific discovery'.[19] Another correspondent, the philosopher of science Stephen Toulmin, cited other writers who were sensitive to the advances of science in their time, though the time he had in mind – a useful corrective to Snow's apparent assumption that no century but the twentieth knew a scientific revolution – was well before the age of electronics. The writers mentioned by Toulmin were Milton and Donne, and, from a later period, Wordsworth, Tennyson and Hardy.[20] Voltaire's name might also have been added to the list. From the twentieth century Brecht's *Galileo* could have been cited. Then there is the whole *genre* of creative writing, namely science fiction, well-known examples of which (e.g. by H.G. Wells or Aldous Huxley) Snow never so much as alluded to. These omissions are evidence, I think, of Snow's not having taken seriously the possibility of literary culture taking science in its stride.

The one-sidedness that I am complaining of in Snow goes beyond the neglect of evidence of a serious literary engagement with science: it comes out also in the tendency to suppose that, while the scientists are narrow and blinkered about literature, they have a more wholesome and positive *moral* outlook than members of the literary culture. For while some literary figures wallow in the tragic condition felt by some human beings with the time and affluence to worry about tragedy, the scientists, according to Snow, are inclined to pay more attention to misfortunes that are more urgent and able to be alleviated, namely famine, homelessness and disease. They are inclined not only to pay attention but also to try to do something:

> [N]early all of [the scientists I have known] – and this is where the colour of hope genuinely comes in – would see no reason why, just because the individual condition is tragic, so must the social condition be. Each of us is solitary; each of us dies alone: all right, that's a fate against which we can't struggle – but there is plenty in our condition which is not fate, and against which we are less than human unless we do struggle.[21]

Is this way of looking at things only available to scientists? Snow does not deny that it is available to others as well, but he thinks those who need to be and can be helped are more likely to welcome scientists as helpers than other people. Why? Because their training helps to free them of paternalism:

> Plenty of Europeans, from St Francis Xavier to Schweitzer, have devoted their lives to Asians and Africans, nobly but paternally. These are not the Europeans whom Asians and Africans are going to welcome now. They want men who will muck in as colleagues, who will pass on what they know, do an honest technical job, and get out. Fortunately, this is an

attitude which comes easily to scientists. They are freer than most people from racial feeling; their own culture is in its human relations a democratic one. In their own internal climate, the breeze of equality hits you in the face, sometimes rather roughly, just as it does in Norway.[22]

Once again, there is the claim that belonging to the scientific culture has moral value, in this case because of the predisposition toward equal treatment that it implants. Though Snow does not spell it out here, he seems to think that this disposition and a spirit of co-operativeness in general are distinctive of the scientific culture, while a marked anti-social tendency can be detected in certain influential literary intellectuals of the twentieth century.

The implication that the scientific culture is morally superior to the literary or that it has a fundamentally different moral outlook from the literary is hard to accept, and commentators on the Leavis–Snow controversy have shown that Snow distorts the message of a number of writers specifically singled out for, for example, their failure to accept the future and think positively about its possibilities. Lionel Trilling demonstrates this in the case of George Orwell.[23] He also rebuts Snow's claim that literary intellectuals were bad custodians of the industrial revolution who tried as far as possible to wish it away. He points out that Coleridge, Carlyle, Dickens, Ruskin, Arnold and others had a beneficial effect on the living conditions of ordinary people badly affected by the factories and slums.[24]

THE ARTS, SCIENCE AND THE MEDIATION OF THE HUMANITIES

Is it possible to arrive at an account of the arts and sciences that overcomes the one-sidedness of Leavis's and Snow's accounts? Is it possible, in other words, to give an account which shows how the arts and sciences are mutually complementary? One account along these lines associates the sciences with an objectifying tendency the alienating effects of which the arts, and especially the fine arts, are needed to counteract. According to this kind of account, science proceeds by presenting us with a conception of the physical world that is less and less dependent on our particular sensory capacities or the concepts that we use to understand the world as sensed, and that is more and more dependent on concepts that could conceivably be shared with a member of any rational species, not necessarily a human being. The mathematization of the study of matter is the principal means of passing from the sense-based to the more objective conception, for mathematical concepts apply to the world as well as sense-based concepts, and yet they could be possessed by creatures who did not have human sensory experience of the world or perhaps any sense-experience.

Because the mathematical conception both fits the world and is available to creatures with many different kinds of sensory purchase on the world, it is more objective than any sense-based conception. But greater objectivity, according to this account, is bought at the price of estrangement. The more objective conception of the physical world acquaints us with a totally unfamiliar reality composed of particles and forces that are impossible for all but a few human beings to conceptualize, and that are extremely remote from the prescientific conception most people share. Not only does the more objective conception make the familiar world appear unfamiliar, the more we find out about the world by means of it, the more we have the feeling that the existence of human beings is utterly contingent and improbable. Although we live here, it is cosmically accidental that there is human life at all. Perhaps even more of a cosmic accident is the fact that we *understand* any of physical reality: certainly we are not biologically constituted to see straight off how things work: most advances in understanding come from ways of conceiving the world that do not come naturally to us. In both these respects science disturbs or perhaps eliminates entirely our sense of being at home in the world. But the artists among us are able to add to natural creation objects that really are designed for human response, namely works of art. Educating oneself to be capable of response to the best of these works of art is the acquisition of one kind of culture, and by forging bonds with the rest of humanity it also helps us to feel at home. Through the arts, then, through culture in general, the edge is taken off the estrangement produced by science.

The sort of account I have been sketching has its roots in German romantic philosophy, but German romantic philosophers do not usually give very clear statements of it. Two recent and relatively clear formulations come from Roger Scruton and Anthony O'Hear. In 'Philosophy and the Neglect of Aesthetics' Scruton emerges as a follower not only of the Germans but of Leavis, who he says 'made mincemeat of C.P. Snow's suggestion that there could be a "culture" of science'. Scruton's quasi–Hegelian and quasi–Leavisite view of the relation between science and culture is easily identifiable as a version of the approach to reconciling the arts and sciences that I have already outlined:

> To possess a culture is not only to possess a body of knowledge or expertise; it is not simply to have accumulated facts, references and theories. It is to possess a sensibility, a response, a way of seeing things, which is in some special way redemptive. Culture is not a matter of academic knowledge but of participation. And participation changes not merely your thoughts and beliefs but your perceptions and emotions. The question therefore unavoidably arises whether scientific knowledge and the habits of curiosity and experiment which engender it, are really the friends or foes of culture? Could it be that the habit of scientific explanation may take over from the habit of emotional response, or in some way undermine the picture of the world upon which our moral life is founded? Could it be that scientific knowledge leads precisely in the opposite direction from a culture – not to the education of feeling, but to its destruction, not to the acceptance and affirmation of the human world, but to a kind of sickness and alienation from it, an overbearing sense of its contingency?[25]

Scruton does not go on to say very much about the distinctive marks of the scientific knowledge or understanding. He says the attempt to explain the world as it is motivates scientific understanding, while 'intentional understanding' aims to describe, justify and criticize the world as it appears. This idea of science explaining the world as it is rather than as it appears is a way of identifying the aim of science with achieving objectivity. And in the passage just quoted Scruton presents science as alienating. As for the suggestion that the arts are a kind of antidote to this alienation, this seems to come out where Scruton says that

> [a] culture . . . is essentially shared; its concepts and images bear the mark of participation, and are intrinsically consoling, in the manner of religious communion, or an act of worship. They close again the gap between subject and object which yawns so frighteningly in the world of science.[26]

Scruton's account, then, runs very much along the lines indicated earlier. Its more distinctive features, however, are questionable. For example, the account implies that the scientific understanding of the world is of no help to us as agents, since science penetrates appearance while 'as agents we belong to the surface of the world'[27] and are subject to 'the priority of appearance'. That is, as agents we are supposed to respond to things as they appear and engage our emotions. But Scruton is here raising to the level of a truth about us as agents something that is at best a truth about us as sympathetic agents. Action takes place not only at the surface and by reference to the appearances of things, but also by reference to the depth of things that science describes. The people who make the particles collide in the CERN accelerator under the Alps are as much agents as (to take Scruton's example) someone who responds to the appearances involved in sexual desire, but they exploit as unsuperficial a conception of the world as it is possible for human beings to acquire. Again contrary to Scruton, it is quite unclear that no pattern of response or sensibility attends scientific activity, or that its practical aspects are exhausted by the habit of curiosity and what Scruton questionably classifies as the 'habit' of experiment. This overlooks the anthropological sense of the scientific culture perfectly properly pointed out by Snow. Related to this oversight is Scruton's false distinction between something's being a matter of academic knowledge and something's being a matter of participation. As if the possession of scientific knowledge were not, among other things, knowing how to participate in and respond sensitively to an extended collaborative activity undertaken by specialists or experts.

Writers other than Scruton have argued that science achieves objectivity at a cost that is reduced by art. Anthony O'Hear has made out this claim at book-length – without falling into the Leavisite trap of denying that science makes any contribution to culture,[28] and without relying on distinctions as crude as that between scientific and intentional understanding. Science, according to O'Hear, not only helps us to live longer and more securely; it is morally improving, since it develops the discipline of seeing things as they are and not as one's desires or fantasies incline us to see them. On the other hand, science neither explains as much as it is sometimes thought to do nor provides all of the knowledge that we require in life. According to O'Hear some of the necessary knowledge is irremediably untheoretical and tacit – in a word unscientific – and yet indispensable. Following Schiller, O'Hear claims that art resolves a number of dualisms which 'permeate our lives' – not only the dualism of feeling and objective rationality but also the dualisms of self and objects and nature and culture. So his claims for art appear to be considerably more general than Scruton's as well as more rigorously defended. Nevertheless, like Scruton's, O'Hear's account has a serious weakness: it exaggerates the divide between art and science by concentrating on the science and the art furthest removed from one another, and so it makes art into an antidote for a kind of objectification that perhaps attends only one kind of science. An account that shows the arts and sciences to be complementary *is* needed, but, as I shall explain, the problem it solves is not one set by the great dualisms on O'Hear's list. Instead, the problem to be solved is the humbler one of the fragmentation and specialization of learning.

The first false step in the Scruton–O'Hear approach is to associate the objective conception that estranges people with science in general rather than with physics. The second is to identify the relation of art to science against the background of the problem caused by objectification. To begin with the first false step, there are many types of science that achieve objectivity without departing as much from everyday thought and everyday response as physics, and of these it is not necessarily true to say that they produce a sense of estrangement from the world. *A fortiori*, the relation of art or the arts to these sciences is not captured by speaking of an antidote to estrangement. The upshot is that the sort of account we have been considering cannot serve to reconcile the sciences in general with the arts in general, but only fine arts with physics – as if there were nothing in between. The approach tried by Scruton and improved upon by O'Hear would be perfectly appropriate if all sciences were aspiring branches of physics or if it were illuminating to see them as varyingly successful imitations of physics, but they aren't and it isn't. Scruton's otherwise forceful claim, 'Estrangement from the world is the poisoned gift of science', is surely false when 'botany' or 'human anatomy' or even 'zoology' is substituted for 'science'. At some points between the extremes, the arts and sciences do not stand in such great need of reconciliation; the divide between the two cultures shrinks.

In his 'Second Look' Snow came close to recognizing the point I am trying to make. The Rede Lecture had proposed as a question to test scientific literacy, 'What do you know of the Second Law of Thermodynamics?' On reflection Snow came to think this the wrong kind of question, since when he had delivered the lecture, the unfamiliar sounding name of the law had raised a laugh – a sure sign, Snow thought, of excessive remoteness from what people could understand. In 'A Second Look' he suggested a substitute:

> I should now put forward a branch of science which ought to be a requisite in the common culture, certainly for anyone now at school. This branch of science at present goes by the name of molecular biology. . . . It is fairly self-contained. It begins with the analysis of crystal structure, itself a subject aesthetically beautiful and easily comprehended. It goes on to the application of these methods to molecules which have literally a vital role to play in our own existence – molecules of proteins, nucleic acids. . . . It includes the leap of genius by which Crick and Watson snatched at the structure of DNA. . . . Unlike thermodynamics, the subject does not involve serious conceptual difficulties. . . . It needs very little mathematics to understand. . . . What [it requires] most of all is a visual and three-dimensional imagination, and it is a study where painters and sculptors could be instantaneously at home.[29]

Snow is not claiming merely that molecular biology is an accessible subject, but that it actually draws on abilities that are useful in the supposedly remote culture of the arts, and that it answers questions that are intrinsically interesting because of their bearing on the nature of human life. Although it has some of the features of the alienating conception of the physical world, acquainting us as it does with microstructure with which we are unlikely to engage emotionally, its claim to be in some clear sense a part of the human world cannot be doubted. Yet if we were to enter into the frame of mind of Scruton, O'Hear and Leavis, we should take it for granted that the concepts of the human and the scientific were antithetical.

Molecular biology, especially when its explanation mentions the things that Snow suggests, is a good example of a science that does not desert humanity and that consequently cannot convincingly be claimed to be alienating. But its humanity does not abolish the divide between some sciences – perhaps most sciences – and some – perhaps most – arts. Even if there is a continuum of arts and sciences rather than a chasm between the fine arts at one extreme and the hardest sciences at the other, even if there is a continuum whose middle region contains the social sciences and the life sciences, a deep gulf, perhaps separating physics and mathematics on the one hand and the rest of learning on the other, may exist. The sheer difficulty of understanding some physics and some mathematics is only part of what divides these parts of learning from the rest, and from common culture. There is also the problem of connecting what the physicist does with, say, what the student of art and literature does, in such a way that all of these pursuits are seen to provide understanding and all are acknowledged to tax the intellect in different ways. The two problems – that of inaccessibility and that of acknowledging the diversity of intellectual problems – call, respectively, for popularization and for mediation between the divided parts of learning. Popularization of even cosmology and quantum mechanics is to be found in a growing number of books, including Weinberg's *The First Three Minutes* and Hawking's *A Brief History of Time*, as well as in increasingly skilful science journalism and television documentary. Mediation, on the other hand, is not a matter merely of explaining so that a lay person can understand: it is a matter of reconciling practitioners of different intellectual disciplines to the reality of different intellectual demands. The physicist who thinks that he needs no training to do historical research, or, as is more often the case, who thinks he needs no training to write philosophy or theology, is as much in need of help (though perhaps not as *much* help) as someone who cannot understand the first thing about the Big Bang. Where, if anywhere, are we to turn for what I am calling mediation?

Perhaps to history and to philosophy. Despite the differences between them, these subjects are able to state connections between the more accessible and the less accessible sciences, connections which are perhaps easier to grasp than the elements of the inaccessible sciences themselves. History is able to show how an earlier and easier to understand stage of physics is related to current stages, and also how very esoteric branches of mathematics developed from the more readily intelligible. History is also able to show how the fragmentation of learning is itself a historical phenomenon, and that subjects from different sides of the supposed divide between the two cultures were once single subjects. Compared to philosophy, history has the advantage of being the more accessible mediator between hard science and the common culture. But philosophy has some uses of its own. It is able to show what method the sciences – inaccessible and accessible alike – might have in common, and how their subject matters might be related to one another and to the humanities. Scientific empiricism is an example of a venture, albeit an unsuccessful venture, in showing how different parts of learning have an underlying unity. There could be others.

Connecting the inaccessible sciences with the common culture is one task that philosophy could help to discharge. Another task it could attempt to carry out, and one which may not be within the competence of history, is that of revealing distortions in the impressions that sciences and the arts have of one another. A respect for science is the sound core of the objectionable scientism of some twentieth-century Anglo-American philosophy, and it is this sound core which suits this kind of philosophy to the task of spreading sympathy for the sciences outside science. Philosophy can also encourage respect for the arts among scientists. In particular, it can encourage respect for literature, e.g. as a medium of moral insight. It can do this, that is, if there is a disrespect for literature in science or an indifference to science in the first place.

The idea that philosophy can act as honest broker between the common culture and the parts of learning that are least accessible to the common culture, or between the arts and sciences in cases where mutual misunderstanding prevails – this idea should not be confused with the idea that the whole purpose or primary purpose of philosophy is to act as honest broker. Everything I have claimed is compatible with holding that philosophy has problems and preoccupations of its own, some with no obvious connection to problems about co-ordinating, or mediating between, the different parts of learning or culture.

Still, when it comes to problems about the different parts of learning, it is primarily in the role of mediator that I am suggesting philosophy plays its part, not in the more exalted role of legitimating other parts of learning. On this point my account disagrees with Kant's. In the late work, *The Contest of the Faculties*, Kant both defended and questioned the division of the faculties of the German university into the three 'higher' ones of law, theology and morals, and the 'lower' faculty of philosophy. He questioned the inferiority of the lower faculty precisely by insisting on a role for philosophy of legitimizing the other sciences, and producing critiques of them. I do not deny that such a role can still make sense with regard to some sciences – psychology or sociology, for example – but it seems to me to be implausible to claim that this should be the primary role of philosophy in regard to the sciences. One of the facts about science which the philosophy of science has both to acknowlege and to explain is the predictive and explanatory success of much of natural science, and this success carries with it a strong claim to legitimacy independent of any provided by philosophy.

I spoke earlier of two false steps in the Scruton–O'Hear account of the relation between the arts and sciences. The first was to exaggerate the alienating effect of scientific objectivity, and this has now been gone into in some detail. The second false step (more evidently taken by Scruton than O'Hear) is to make the relation of art to science depend too much on the alleviation of the alienating effect. This is an inadequate account for more than the reason that not all science is alienating. It is inadequate because it shows how science creates a need for art, but does not consider whether art and science might be mutually dependent. It is also inadequate because it overstresses the consumption as opposed to the production of art. Without denying that one role of the arts, and especially the fine arts, is that of making the objectively conceived world of physics seem human to consumers of art, we can doubt that this role gets to the heart of the relation between the arts and science.

A more promising account of the relation between the arts and science is one that starts from the threefold distinction between discovering causal laws, harnessing observed cause–effect relations for human purposes, and, third, the imaginative production of effects that do not belong to nature – creation. We are not merely passive observers of the world but creatures who can do things to alter the world so that it matches up to our expectations and wishes. This ability to reduce the scope for the unexpected and the undesired helps us to feel at home. Exercising this ability is also morally improving, since some of the unexpected and undesired things harm us, and reducing the scope for them reduces harm. Ironically, in view of the way it can help us to feel at home, the ability to alter the world often depends on the very conception that sometimes produces estrangement. For it is by the acquisition of science that we gain extensive knowledge of how to interfere in the natural order to produce effects we find desirable. Artistic creation has something in common with scientifically informed and beneficial interventions in the natural order: it alters reality. In creation, however, one does more than produce for one's own purposes and in chosen circumstances a type of effect or object that nature produces independently. One produces something that nature, operating impersonally, would not have produced. In artistic creation one produces something that nature would not have produced, something shaped by personal intention and imagination, something having worth and interest partly *because* those forces shaped it and impersonal ones did not. Artistic creation is our way of making our mark on the world and feeling our freedom from natural determination. It is different from our way of making our mark technologically. A device for intervening in nature, like a dam or an irrigation ditch, uses the properties of bodies of water to turn power-generating turbines and make land suitable for agriculture; the properties of the bodies of water are essential to identifying why the artefact is made this way rather than that way, located here rather than there, made out of these materials rather than those; but in a work of art, even one which uses water, like a decorative fountain, these properties can never provide as much of the explanation as the intention, imagination and choices of the artist, the anticipated effects on observers, the tradition of making other decorative fountains. In this way the products of artistic creation take away the sense we may have, even when we intervene technologically, that we are acting vicariously, through natural causes and effects that are there independent of us, and that we can at best redirect or channel, but not add to or transform. The idea is that artistic creation allows for departures from the natural order – i.e. the order constituted by natural law – and that this is at least as important as its humanizing function for distinguishing art from science. It is also important for identifying the moral worth of artistic creation, a worth consisting in a kind of benign exercise of freedom.

Although artistic creation involves departures from the natural order that are not merely interventions or rechannellings, as in science, it can be informed by science, as it was when the laws of perspective started to be used by painters. Again, science can be the subject or the stimulus of imaginative production. Indeed, to the extent that it is desirable for art to be of its time, it is a failing of art if it takes no account of the influence of science on our time. In these ways art can depend on science and not just be compatible with it.

According to the sort of account I have been sketching, creation rather than consolation is the distinctive mark of art in relation to science. Rather than having the function of creating appearances that we can identify with in an allegedly alien world that we are made to conceive by science, art is our way of adding to and altering the real world. In this respect it has something in common with science, for the exploitation of observed cause–effect relations for our own purposes is also a kind of innovative disruption of the natural order. Science enables us to use, and so reduces the extent to which we are used by, nature. The account I am putting forward, then, does not suppose that there must be a tension between the purposes of science and the purposes of art, and it does not imply that only the extra-scientific can be part of the human world and hospitable to human purposes. On the other hand, the account does allow for a distinctive role for the fine arts, and a role related to that of the fine arts for the humanities.

Whereas fine art often involves the imaginative production of effects or things that nature would not have produced independently, the humanities often involve the production of effects – character- istically imaginative responses – that actions and artefacts, especially texts, would not have produced independently. When the humanities are creative, they produce imaginative interpretation, counter- argument and explanation, usually intended to provoke more of the same in their turn. Art-history, philosophy, theology, history and the study of language and literature can all be creative in this way. Is it, however, a kind of creativity that is suitably distinct from scientific creativity? Surely scientific theories are artefacts that are intended by their creators to evoke imaginative interpretation, counterargument or explanation: how, then, are they different from, say, texts, once they have been given creative treatment by a literary critic? This question broaches a large issue, which can only be taken up in earnest, and even then only briefly, in the next section. But two differences between the treatment of a scientific theory and a literary text can be noted in a preliminary way. The first is that the multiplication of imaginative responses to a text is a goal considered to be worth pursuing for its own sake in the humanities, whereas I take it that in science the point of eliciting response is standardly to get others to increase the accuracy and generality of a theory or narrow down the competition for it by proposing experimental tests, not merely to stimulate thought. A second point depends on accepting Kuhn's idea that most science at most times is routine or normal science, science that consists of filling small gaps and resolving minor puzzles, rather than science in the form of innovative theoretical proposals. The reports of 'normal' scientific research are intended to add to the information of their audience, not spur them to imaginative response.

THE DANGER OF DENYING
(OR DECONSTRUCTING) A DIFFERENCE

There are writers who hold, as I do, that philosophy has a role in mediating between the arts and sciences, and yet who either play down unreasonably the differences between the arts and sciences, or assume that the distinction between the arts and sciences expresses a questionable valuation of the arts relative to the sciences, so that the right treatment for the distinction is deconstruction. Feyerabend is a philosopher who comes close to denying the differences while Rorty is a representative of the other approach. In the remainder of this chapter I argue that neither gives a satisfactory treatment.

The new monotony and the value of diversity

The work in which, to my knowledge, Feyerabend comes closest to denying that there is a difference between the arts and sciences is his collection of essays, *Farewell to Reason*.[30] In the Introduction he says that 'treating science as a part of history . . . removes the apparent difference between the sciences and the arts', and in the same place he endorses this treatment of science. *Farewell to Reason* criticizes from many different points of view the growing homogeneity of contemporary culture in the developed countries, the 'new monotony', as Feyerabend calls it, attending the spread throughout the world of Western business and science. Feyerabend claims that the new monotony is both more disturbing and more of a fact of life than the supposed fragmentation of culture complained of by some intellectuals, including Snow.

Discussing some of the ideas that lend respectability to the new monotony, Feyerabend emphasizes concepts that are associated with rationalism, prominent among which are the concepts of objectivity, reason, method and science. He tries to show that, by contrast with the image the rationalists convey, science is not governed in practice by the canons of rationalism, and as a result it does not really discourage diversity. This is despite the rationalist belief in a distinct sector of learning called 'science' and a distinctive practice defined by a so-called 'scientific method':

> [T]he fictitious unit 'science' that is supposed to exclude everything else simply does not exist. Scientists have taken ideas from many different fields, their views have often

clashed with commonsense and established doctrines, and they have always adapted their procedures to the task at hand. There is no one 'scientific method' but there is a great deal of opportunism; anything goes – anything, that is, that is liable to advance knowledge as understood by a particular researcher or research tradition. In practice science often oversteps the boundaries some scientists and philosophers put in its way and becomes a free and unrestricted inquiry.[31]

Opportunism depends upon the availability of a variety of approaches and theories for science to plunder. Opportunism also encourages the growth of more diversity. As soon as one realizes that diversity helps science to progress, Feyerabend says, one need not feel that a cost of rejecting the new monotony is the rejection of science. Science *and* diversity can be embraced simultaneously; what is incompatible with diversity is not science but the apparatus of rationalism.

If anything goes in science, if science is not in practice subject to regulation by scientific method, how different is science from fine art or the humanities? Feyerabend wants to say 'Not really different at all', but without committing himself to the idea that what unifies the arts and sciences are mysterious leaps of individual creativity. Often, he says, what seems to be a creative leap is unconscious adaptation to the self-corrections of the scientific and wider community and the unconscious appropriation of ideas that are 'in the air'. It is opportunism again, but not self-conscious opportunism.

Even if free adaptation and appropriation underlie artistic as well as scientific progress, however, it is hard to accept that they are channelled in similar ways or for similar purposes in both the sciences and the arts. For one thing, even on Feyerabend's showing, the appropriation of ideas and techniques from unusual sources has to appear to the appropriator to advance knowledge; the techniques of the humanities and the arts do not necessarily have this aim: they may be geared to eliciting emotional or imaginative response, or they may simply be a way of letting out what is inside the artist and demands to come out. Again, even as formulated by Feyerabend, the constraints on free adaptation and appropriation in science do not have natural counterparts in the arts. The idea that in science anything goes is dependent on the perspective of the researcher or research tradition. The technique or idea must appear from this perspective to have a chance of advancing knowledge, and who is to say that the researcher or research tradition has not accepted some rationalist lore, so that certain sorts of opportunism seem too risky, however fruitful they would turn out to be? In that case the 'anything goes' slogan would expand into 'anything goes, so long as it meets whatever methodological scruples the researcher happens to have'. This may not be to revert to a recognition of scientific method, but it does allow for a kind of conservatism that would not characteristically be appropriate in the fine arts or the humanities.

There are in fact at least three weaknesses in Feyerabend's account of the way science works against monotony, and how it is thereby of a piece with the arts. There is his use of the 'anything goes' slogan, which on inspection does not necessarily mean that in practice science is open to to ideas and techniques from unusual sources. There are also the widely discussed implausibilities in Feyerabend's views about scientific progress: when one theory supersedes another, according to him, the change can involve the complete reconstrual of terms apparently common to earlier and later theories. Not only is it disputable that scientific progress produces these incompatibilities; it is also disputable that it is good for science to produce these incompatibilities, as if there were no way otherwise of avoiding dogmatism and monotony.[32] Again, and more importantly, Feyerabend seems not to ask the question whether the cultivation of diversity in science, or in high culture on the artistic side, might not be completely compatible with, and not at all subversive of, a more damaging uniformity in the wider culture – the uniformity of television soap opera and pulp fiction, of jeans, fast food outlets, supermarkets, highways and airports. If the answer is 'yes', as I suspect it is, then the explanation may be that the new monotony is not a unitary phenomenon, and that its manifestations in popular culture and mass commercial markets may not have intellectual or theoretical underpinnings, let alone underpinnings in the shape of rationalism. Finally, Feyerabend does not seem to ask whether the promotion of greater diversity in the wider culture does not sometimes have costs that are far worse than monotony, such as nationalist or religious warfare or unjust policies of 'separate development'.

Rorty and 'dedivinization'

It seems that the basis for Feyerabend's denial of the difference between the arts and sciences is unsatisfactory: too many questions surround his would-be dismantling of rationalism and his attack on the new monotony. Rorty takes a different, but not unrelated, approach. In his recent Northcliffe Lectures[33] he is concerned to criticize a kind of philosophy that is overawed by science, and to create sympathy for a kind of philosophy that, instead, is admiring of utopian politics and innovative art, particularly poetry. In promoting this kind of philosophy Rorty is recommending a revaluation upward of poetry and a revaluation downward of science. It is an approach inspired by Nietzsche, as Rorty seems to acknowledge.

Though Rorty 'thinks of himself as [a philosopher who is] auxiliary to the poet rather than to the physicist',[34] he and like-minded philosophers do not denigrate science; they only reject the realism of a certain philosophical interpretation of science, putting something deflationary in its place:

> On this view, great scientists invent descriptions of the world which are useful for purposes of predicting and controlling what happens, just as poets and political thinkers invent other descriptions of it for other purposes. But there is no sense in which *any* of these descriptions is an accurate representation of the way the world is in itself. . . . [T]he very idea of such representation [is] pointless.[35]

Rorty thinks that the alignment of philosophy with poetry is appropriate to a certain stage of evolution of philosophy that is more in tune with our own age than the Enlightenment outlook of the pro-science philosophers. The story of the development of this way of thinking occupies some of the Northcliffe Lectures.

Rorty thinks that he is following Hans Blumenberg in unfolding this story. It begins like this:

> [O]nce upon a time we felt the need to worship something which lay beyond the visible world. Beginning in the 17th century, we tried to substitute a love of truth for a love of God, treating the world described by science as a quasi-divinity.[36]

Rorty has in mind a period in which, as he thinks, the world began to be conceived either as 'the work of someone who had something in mind, who Himself spoke some language in which He described his project' or as itself something with a point of view and preferences about how it is described. Soon this quasi-divinity ceased to be recognized: a stage of what Rorty calls 'dedivinization' is supposed to have taken place: 'Beginning at the end of the 18th century, we tried to substitute a love of ourselves for a love of scientific truth, a worship of our deep spiritual or poetic nature, treated as one more quasi-divinity.'[37] Still, the poetry of the eighteenth century did not get rid of divinities entirely, according to Rorty. It continued the tendency to suppose that there is higher or divine reality not normally available to human beings. Only it said that we have access to it with the priestly mediation of the poet rather than the scientist.[38]

In urging an end to what he calls the 'divinization' of the world and ourselves Rorty is denying that the scientist or the poet has a priestly vocation. Taking up a suggestion he finds in Blumenberg, Nietzsche, Freud and Davidson, he says that we ought to 'try to get to the point where we no longer worship anything, where we treat nothing as a quasi-divinity, where we treat everything – our language, our conscience, our community – as products of time and chance'.[39] To treat language in the way Rorty suggests is to treat it not as some successor to the mind – a medium between self and reality that enables the former to represent the latter – but rather, following Davidson, as a useful pairing of noises and marks between people that enables them to predict one another's behaviour.[40] To treat the self in the way Rorty suggests is, he thinks, to treat it in the style of Freud:

> By associating conscientiousness with cleanliness, and by associating both not only with obsessional neurosis but also . . . with the religious impulse and with the urge to construct philosophical systems, Freud breaks down all the traditional distinctions between higher and lower, the essential and the accidental, the central and the peripheral. He leaves us with a self that is a tissue of contingencies.[41]

As for the community – Rorty considers the community in the form of liberal democracy – the right way of treating it is not to find foundations for the values it embodies, but to provide apologetics. Thus, instead of searching for a non-circular defence of the value of freedom in a liberal democracy, one should grant that 'a circular justification which makes one feature of our culture look good by citing still another, or comparing our culture insidiously with others by reference to our own standards, is the only justification we are going to get'.[42]

Rorty does not exactly argue for the preferred ways of treating language, the self or the community. Instead, as he admits, he emphasizes problems and questions that he thinks will make the preferred treatments look good, and tries to undermine the terms in which criticisms of those treatments would be put. His strategy, he says, is to try to make the objectors' vocabulary look bad.[43] This is the vocabulary of philosophers impressed by science, by objectivity, and by the idea that the truth is discovered rather than created. But it is harder than Rorty thinks to throw doubt on the thesis that truth is created.[44] It is also harder than Rorty thinks to make attractive the rival view that truth is created, the view appropriate to a philosophy that aligns itself with poetry.

In *Philosophy and the Mirror of Nature, Consequences of Pragmatism*[45] and the Northcliffe Lectures, the idea of redescription is central to Rorty's explanation of the view that truth is created. The sense in which we are supposed to be able to make truth is the sense in which we are able to make new bearers of truth-value out of new vocabulary. When one form of description replaces another and is used to express new truths, what happens, according to Rorty, is not that words for appearances are replaced by words for real things; there is not supposed to be some layer of fact that has been waiting to be described in, and that justifies the use of, the new vocabulary. The succession of vocabularies can have a much less involved explanation: users of the old descriptions die or cease to be listened to; something happens which makes a piece of linguistic innovation catch on. Since on this view there is no basis in the world for a given vocabulary's getting the upper hand, and since human art produces the new descriptions, including the true ones, there is a sense in which the truths are made, not found.

The most obvious objection to all of this is that it fits some sorts of intellectual change better than others, and it fits such changes as the shift from Aristotelian to Newtonian physics least well of all. In his discussion of this change Rorty underdescribes the clash between Aristotle and Newton by saying it was a clash of vocabularies, of one jargon with another. It was a clash of theories, of *assertions* of certain explanations of phenomena, phrased in different vocabularies. Between different theories the world sometimes *can* decide, for example, by making the predictions of one true and the other false. Rather than to labour this objection, I want to show that Rorty's account turns out to be unappealing even when it is approached from an angle – a Hegelian angle – that at first seems to show it to advantage.

According to Rorty, Hegelian idealism recognizes an important aspect of cultural change, namely the way in which, in a period of innovation, the language of one innovator seems almost to be designed to lead into the ideas of another innovator. In his second Northcliffe Lecture, Rorty claims that Freud's innovations make people receptive to the ideas of a host of intellectuals. It is unlikely, he says, that

> without Freud's metaphors we should have been able to assimilate Nietzsche's, James's, Wittgenstein's or Heidegger's as easily as we have, or to have read Proust with the relish we did. All of the figures of this period play into each other's hands. They feed each other lines. . . . This is the sort of phenomenon which it is tempting to describe in terms of the march of the World–Spirit towards clearer self-consciousness. . . . [46]

Now Rorty's story is able to accommodate this phenomenon without giving it the portentous interpretation it receives from the Hegelians. The figures of the late nineteenth and the twentieth centuries play into each other's hands because they are all embarked on a similar enterprise, namely that of making literal the metaphors of an earlier age while introducing new metaphors themselves, sometimes in competition with one another. By identifying the process of intellectual change with what happens when old metaphors die and new ones take over, Rorty is able to offer a deflationary account of the development of ideas when compared with Hegel's, but also one that is in keeping with idealism to the extent of not making the development reflect the structure of the world. One person's metaphors make way for the next person's, but not as part of an overall movement toward a fully conscious World–Spirit, still less to some fully accurate representation of reality. Instead, there is only the accumulation of a lot of small contingencies.[47] Individuals who happen to have been born at certain times, who have been driven by certain obsessive states, who happen to have had neurons firing in response to certain random stimulations, happen to invent forms of words that are made public at the right time and place and catch on.

But this account of intellectual change may be too deflationary. If all that happens in the history of culture is that certain metaphors become literalized and replaced by new metaphors, if there is no overall purpose of, for example, revealing more and more of an independent reality or of bringing a World-Spirit to greater and greater self-consciousness, what sort of change counts as progress and why? Rorty plainly thinks that the process of dedivinization has been progress, but when it comes to the question of why, he may be unable to go beyond saying that the metaphors that have contributed to divinization have gone stale. As if the development of culture consisted of so many solutions to a recurring problem of boringness in styles of description. This seems an unsatisfactory account.

Rorty says that in abandoning the vocabulary of accurate representation, intrinsic natures and the rest, he is indicating an allegiance to a poetic as against a scientific culture. This allegiance and Rorty's way of describing it raise two questions with which I should like to conclude. First, how stable is the distinction between poetry and science and the co-ordinate distinction between discovering truth and inventing truth? Second, can Rorty's dedivinized conception of poetry – his conception of poetry as the outcome of time and chance – be squared with his belief that poets are active in the process that results in poetry?

To readers of *Consequences of Pragmatism* Rorty's distinction in the Northcliffe Lectures between poetry and science is familiar as a variation on the distinction between literary and scientific cultures, which he adapts from Snow. Snow's distinction proves useful in the *Consequences of Pragmatism* for classifying different styles of philosophy, and different styles of intellectual work generally. In applying it Rorty tends to mark not just a difference but an antagonism between the scientific and the literary, and he tries to promote an outcome of the antagonism which leaves literature in the dominant, and science in the subservient, position. Why the tension between the two cultures cannot end up in some sort of accommodation – e.g. in good science fiction or a possible genre of literary science (arguably pioneered already by Primo Levi) – is never made clear. It seems that Rorty is so keen to overturn the usual ranking of science over literature that he never wonders whether the antagonism between science and literature is deep after all.

On the other hand, the distinctions that Rorty uses to spell out the antagonism have the unintended effect of weakening it. Thus, the distinction between the practice of redescription (literary) and the practice of revealing the contours of an external reality (scientific), which Rorty evidently takes for a firm distinction, turns out to be frail because redescription can be for the *purpose* of revealing the contours. The redescription in primary-quality vocabulary of facts stated in secondary-quality vocabulary is a case in point. Again, and now ignoring the alleged tension between revealing and redescribing, is it not just a fact that there is a variety of poetry and prose, by no means yet extinct, that is realistic or dedicated to realism, and that tries to reveal reality as it is? If so, is not this further evidence of the softness of the poetry/science distinction or the literature/science distinction?

Rorty takes a dim view of divinizing poetry – poetry that assumes that it is mediating between human beings and their intrinsic nature. He prefers dedivinizing poetry, which knows that intrinsic natures are illusory and which accepts itself as the product of time and chance. In his second Northcliffe Lecture Rorty is trying to give a description of poetry in the spirit of dedivinization when he indicates how slight a dividing line there is between what is called 'fantasy' and what is called 'poetry'. It is a mistake to suppose that poetry reveals something universal and real whereas fantasy reveals something private and unreal. Rather, poetry is a species of fantasy, but one that means something to the whole community in the way that a mere humdrum fantasy means something only to an individual. That a fantasy does mean something to a community – that it catches on – is an accident, according to Rorty, a coincidence of a private obsession with a public need.[48]

One question about this story is whether it only banishes one divinity to introduce another. Even if we accept that poetry is not distinguished from fantasy by getting at or revealing something real and universal – an intrinsic nature of a human being – we may feel dissatisfied with the suggestion that amazing coincidence makes the fantasy answer a public need. If someone is *that* lucky with his fantasy, it might be thought, someone up there has to like him, maybe even use him to speak through. On the other hand, if coincidence is all that it is, and poetry is only fantasy welling up and being expressed at the right time, can the poet really be the figure that makes truth or that makes anything? Might not a fantasy over which someone has no control suggest a metaphor that catches on? If so, then the poet is only a vehicle for a metaphor rather than its inventor. Either the poet's work is inspired – a case of the gods speaking through him – or a case of psychopathology working itself out. Where in all of this is there room for what Rorty so firmly contrasts with discovery, namely making or invention? Rorty has yet to make us see clearly the distinctive characteristics of the poetic culture, let alone its distinctive charms. Until our vision of them is improved, we should not abandon the old divinities.

6

THE NEW SCIENTISM
IN PHILOSOPHY

In the last chapter I suggested that philosophy might have a role to play in reducing the gap between some arts and some sciences. I suggested that philosophy might be able to mediate between different intellectual disciplines, and I distinguished the work of mediation from the work of popularization, i.e. the work of presenting certain parts of learning simplistically so that those with a quite different intellectual training have some idea of them. Though it is necessary to popularize if the divide between certain arts and certain sciences is to be reduced at all, it may be necessary to do more if the divide is to be reduced as far as is desirable. A tolerance of the variety of intellectual work may also have to be created. Sometimes this tolerance must be achieved in the face of the mutual suspicion of those who undertake different kinds of work in the arts and sciences. 'Mediation' seems the right word for the process of reconciling these suspicious parties.

I claim that philosophy *can* undertake the task of mediation, not that philosophers are always happy to do so. There are resources in philosophy for justifying many different uses of the intellect on both sides of the divide between the two cultures, but philosophers have often been uninterested in providing this justification and trying to reconcile the arts and sciences. In an earlier age some philosophers engaged in the criticism of the new science alongside the theologians. In this century, some philosophers have engaged in the criticism of the humanities, including traditional philosophy itself, alongside the scientists. Chapter 1 dealt with the support among the scientific empiricists for an abandonment of metaphysics and an assimilation of the humanities to the sciences; in this chapter we will consider more recent pleas for absorbing traditional philosophy into science. I shall claim that the new assimilations being proposed are no more attractive than the old, and that the recognition of the diversity of intellectual work must start at home, with the acknowledgement that philosophy itself is a distinct subject.

PLURALISM ABOUT PHILOSOPHICAL PROBLEMS

There are philosophers who deny that philosophy is in any important sense a distinct subject, and who suppose that its problems have always been, or have for a long time been, continuous with those of science. This is Quine's view. He thinks that where philosophy does not concern itself with the clarification of scientific concepts and the organization of the sciences into a system, it is concerned with concepts that are related to scientific ones but that are more basic or general.[1] This is a reasonable view to take of some philosophical problems, as I shall indicate in a moment, but it does not apply to others which are at least as characteristic of philosophy. Work on these latter problems is not motivated by the results of the special sciences, nor is the point of taking them up to introduce yet more order or yet more clarity into science as a whole. Examples of what I have in mind are the problem of epistemological scepticism and the problem of free will; there are many others, some at first sight very different from the ones just mentioned. Thus, the 'what is X?' problems of the Socratic dialogues are ostensibly definitional puzzles, but the point of pursuing them to various unsatisfactory conclusions is to give a kind of self-knowledge: the knowledge that we are unable to understand straight off what the nature of courage is, or what justice and knowledge are. In the course of trying and failing to produce the definitions we are alerted to intellectual shortcomings that we, like Socrates' straight men, are at first quite sure we do not have.

Work on the problems I have mentioned adds to a knowledge of what human beings are like and the general facts that constrain human lives. Providing as it does a kind of self-knowledge, it might be said to add to wisdom – wisdom as opposed to science. The knowledge got out of thinking about scepticism or free will is not readily added to the scheme of science, and it is not readily interpreted as clarifying scientific concepts or bringing out the system in science as a whole. Like other problems of philosophy, the problems of scepticism and of free will are perennial: they are very old and are revived and recast again and again. Work on them may be less a matter of finding solutions than of getting a deeper appreciation of their point, which, in the case of epistemological scepticism and free will, may be to reveal some unsuspected limit to a human capacity (e.g. the capacity for science), or something unjustifiable in a widely accepted human practice, like the practice of holding people responsible for what they do. More precisely, the following five conditions seem to be met by the problems I have in mind: (1) they arise from facts that are readily accessible to prephilosophical consciousness, facts that do not require a special training, let alone a scientific training, to recognize; (2) what one learns by working on these problems does not usually lead to their solution; (3) what one learns does not improve anyone's powers of explaining, predicting or controlling natural phenomena, though it may add to an understanding of the limits of those powers and of other human powers; (4) what one learns cannot readily be summarized and communicated to someone else who has not engaged with the problem and arrived at some of the thoughts that constitute progress with the problem; and (5) what one learns may make one more interested in new interpretations of the problem than in would-be solutions or dissolutions of the problem.

Not every philosophical problem meets the conditions just spelled out. On the contrary, many depend for their formulation and point on some understanding of technical apparatus, such as the apparatus of first-order logic. The problem of 'quantifying in' would be an example. This fails to meet condition (1) above. Similarly for the problem of whether there can be incommensurable scientific theories or conceptual schemes. Certain philosophical approaches to the analysis of the concept of reason for action violate condition (3), notably Davidson's excursion into experimental decision theory.[2] The Gettier problem would be an example of a problem that failed to meet condition (4): work on this problem lends itself to very systematic summary. Despite its seeming connection with the problem raised in the *Theatetus*, it is more like a puzzle than the sort of problem I tried to characterize earlier. Now the failure of these problems to meet some of my conditions does not show that they fall outside philosophy: it only shows that not all philosophical problems are alike. The problem of 'quantifying in' and the Gettier problem are philosophical, all right, but they differ in important respects from those of scepticism and free will. Though it is hard to prove, it seems plausible to say that the perennial problems are more central to philosophy than the others, and that understanding their point is necessary and perhaps sufficient for understanding what philosophy is concerned with. The problems, rather than some supposed method or methods of solving them, seem to define the subject.

Philosophers sometimes urge an abandonment of the perennial problems where these take attention away from problems suggested by science or continuous with science. In Chapter 1 I quoted Patricia Churchland, who urges an abandonment of certain traditional problems in the philosophy of mind, and she in turn cites Quine, who has made a similar plea for an abandonment of traditional problems in the theory of knowledge. Whatever the merits of their arguments for pursuing the new problems, neither Quine nor Churchland seems to me to have good reasons for abandoning the old ones.[3]

NATURALIZED EPISTEMOLOGY

Quine's article 'Epistemology Naturalized' was one of the first in the recent literature to set out the case for a scientific approach to the theory of knowledge.[4] Though the article proposes a programme for epistemology that breaks in important ways from the work of Hume, Bentham, Russell and Carnap, in other ways it is strikingly continuous with what it is supposed to supersede: Quine seems to take for granted the soundness of an empiricist approach to knowledge and meaning. I shall not consider his meaning-empiricism, but his approach to knowledge can be briefly summarized. He supposes that the task of epistemology is to show how the body of science can be derived from the sensory evidence for it.[5] He acknowledges the failure of various attempts to capture the derivation by broadly 'logical' means, e.g. by attempting to deduce the body of science from axioms summarizing sensory evidence, or by giving a logical reconstruction of science in a language confined to terms for sense-experience and the resources of the predicate calculus and set theory.[6] He responds to these failures by suggesting that epistemology should focus not on the deduction or logical reconstruction of science from sensory evidence but on the ways that relatively meagre sensory stimulation, taken as input, might issue in the enormous range of posits and hypotheses constituting science, taken as output.[7]

It is noteworthy that this proposal for naturalizing epistemology conceives unreformed epistemology rather narrowly in the first place. Traditional epistemology, Quine tells us, is half conceptual and half doctrinal: on the one hand it clarifies concepts that science uses, such as matter, in terms that mean something in sense-experience; on the other hand it tries to justify by reference to sensory evidence what it claims to be true about nature. This division of epistemology is worked out largely in the abstract – by analogy with the structure of the foundations of mathematics – and whether it recovers much epistemology actually encountered in the history of philosophy is doubtful. Quine thinks that his account fits Hume, and he may be right; but there are many others it does not fit. In Descartes, for example, natural knowledge is not based on sense-experience but on ideas – including mathematical ideas – that the mind possesses and operates with independently of sense-experience. The point is not merely that Quine operates with a fairly selective conception of traditional epistemology, but that he motivates the alternative to it in a way that is likely to appeal only to convinced empiricists.

How does the problem of epistemological scepticism fit into epistemology? Quine gives no answer to this question in 'Epistemology Naturalized'. In the slightly later paper, 'The Nature of Natural Knowledge', he suggests that, wherever it belongs, the problem and responses to it cannot, as in Descartes, constitute the first step in the subject, as if there were some Archimedean point outside science from which to question science. Philosophical doubt, he argues, exploits appearance/reality distinctions, and these are due to science. So philosophical doubt cannot pretend to be prior to science.

Whatever force this argument has, it seems to be relevant only to the project of stating and answering scepticism from a position in first philosophy, not to the project of stating and answering scepticism full stop. A fortiori, it is not an argument against making philosophical doubt the first step in the theory of knowledge. The problem of scepticism can be posed even if it is assumed that doubt prior to science is impossible. The problem arises as soon as an example is presented of incompatible hypotheses that make equally good sense of the evidence. For one way of formulating scepticism is by asking whether there might not be, for any hypothesis, an equally credible but incompatible hypothesis purporting to explain the same thing. If this is a possibility, then to commit oneself more than tentatively to any one hypothesis can be regarded as dogmatic.

Better, then, to keep one's allegiances to hypotheses loose. Better, in other words, to remain noncommittal. This is a clear echo of the line of argument leading to the more general sceptical advice that we suspend judgement, and yet it does not depend on any extra-scientific vantage point.

The problem of our dogmatically holding things true does not seem to be closely related to the problem of how so elaborate a scheme as science – such 'torrential output', in Quine's phrase – should be derived from so meagre a basis as sensory stimulation; yet Quine thinks that this latter problem, which he makes the focal point of a reformed epistemology, is a version of the problem which has always stood at the centre of the theory of knowledge. In *The Roots of Reference*, he speaks of an 'enlightened persistence in the original epistemological problem'.[8] Unfortunately, he does not bother to spell out what he takes the 'original' problem to be. To go by 'Epistemology Naturalized' it seems to be the Humean problem of justifying a science whose content seems to overreach the evidence. How do we feel justified in holding beliefs about nature whose scope goes well beyond what we have past and present experience of, if the only basis for any belief is current and past sensory experience? Is this intelligible, however, as a variation on the worry about the meagre and the torrential? The problem proposed by Hume is surely not, as Quine suggests, concerned only with how we are able to *arrive* at an inclusive science on the basis of meagre evidence; it is about the reasonableness of believing the inclusive theory on the basis of the evidence available to us, evidence which is supposed to be extremely ephemeral and local. It would have to be about reasonableness or justification if it were to qualify even prima facie as the 'original' epistemological problem. And for Quine's problem about the meagre and the torrential to count as a reincarnation of an old epistemological problem, it, too, would have to be a problem about reasonableness or justification, and so be related to scepticism.

It does not seem to be such a problem. Hence work on it does not really make a breakthrough with an old problem or show us that what was formerly taken to be a problem is not really one. It simply changes the subject without disposing of it. Naturalized epistemology turns attention away from scepticism, but without silencing the sceptic or even forcing him to reformulate very much of the traditional case for doubt. Quine's naturalized epistemology puts in the place of trying to justify science by reference to conscious sensory evidence, a programme of explaining how science can be generated from conscious *and* unconscious information, information that empirical psychology reveals to be a byproduct of sensory bombardment. In trying to answer the sceptic the naturalistic epistemologist is no longer constrained to regard conscious sensory evidence as the only basis for science. He no longer has to construct all knowledge of physical reality from things like clear and distinct perceptions. He can, instead, refer to any mechanisms for the formation of belief, and any hypothesis about the source of belief in sensory evidence, that science makes credible. Naturalized epistemology, then, is likely to give both a more elaborate and a less speculative theory of sense-based belief than one finds in traditional epistemology.

But the greater elaborateness and the stronger support by empirical evidence do not stifle questions about whether the mechanisms for forming belief can be counted upon to produce true belief. In other words, the benefits of naturalized epistemology do not stifle questions traditionally associated with scepticism. Naturalized epistemology does not even force one to detach sceptical questions from the perspective of consciousness adopted by Descartes. For even if it is conceded that not all beliefs considered by epistemology are conscious beliefs and that not all mechanisms for forming beliefs are conscious mechanisms or governed by a method that a subject can deliberately apply and defend against sceptical questioning, it is hard to believe that no beliefs are conscious and that no beliefs can be formed deliberately, so that the traditional sceptical criticism and the traditional defence against it never make sense. Naturalized epistemology enables us to acknowledge sources of belief and mechanisms for forming belief that are inaccessible to consciousness; it does not force us to deny that some beliefs, some sources of belief, and some mechanisms for forming beliefs are conscious and able to be subjected to first-person criticism. The upshot is that naturalized epistemology does not only leave open questions *like* traditional sceptical ones, about whether our ways of forming belief tell in favour of their truth, but also traditional questions themselves.[9]

Variations on a 'replacement' thesis

It is hard to see how the question that Quine places before naturalized epistemology has much in common with questions that have been at the centre of traditional epistemology. It seems more likely that Quine wishes to replace the old questions with new ones. As we have seen, however, the new questions do not in fact deprive the old ones of their point; they do not even seem to make redundant the perspective of consciousness in every case. Is there no other account of naturalized epistemology and its relation to traditional epistemology that is more defensible than Quine's?

In a useful introduction to his collection on naturalized epistemology,[10] Hilary Kornblith presents a framework for understanding different forms of naturalized epistemology, Quine's included. Naturalized epistemology, he suggests, is best expressed as a view about the relation between answers to these three questions about the formation of belief:

(1) How ought we to arrive at our beliefs?
(2) How do we arrive at our beliefs?
(3) Are the processes by which we do arrive at our beliefs the ones by which we ought to arrive at our beliefs?

Naturalized epistemology is the view that question (1) cannot be answered independently of question (2). Now the 'cannot be answered independently' is open to a number of interpretations, and Kornblith thinks that for Quine, in the papers we have been considering, question (1) cannot be answered independently of question (2) in that question (2) is supposed to replace question (1). This is to attribute to Quine what Kornblith calls the 'replacement' thesis, and is in line with what was suggested in the last section. Kornblith, however, considers at least two arguments for the replacement thesis that I have not yet discussed, and also formulates a weaker version of the replacement thesis, which he suggests is more credible than the unqualified replacement thesis. I shall argue that the two further arguments do not really strengthen the case for the replacement thesis, and that even when it is weakened the replacement thesis is uncompelling.

The first of the further arguments is inspired by considerations from evolutionary theory, and can be stated as follows: 'Human beings would not have survived to reproduce their kind if their beliefs were regularly false. Whatever mechanisms are responsible for forming human beliefs, then, they must for the most part produce true beliefs. Truth is what our beliefs enjoy when they are formed as they ought to be. So human beings would not have survived to reproduce their kind if the means by which they form beliefs were not the means by which they ought to form beliefs. To study how human beings do form beliefs, then, is as good as studying how we ought to form them, and answers to question (2) will serve as answers to question (1).' This argument for the replacement thesis is too general to be credible. It is implausible to hold that all or most of our beliefs have survival value, and hence hard to believe that our survival attests to the truth of very many of our beliefs. Take a belief about the outcome of the next local horse race or, very differently, a belief about the soundness of a proof of a theorem in set theory, or, differently again, beliefs about the outcome of a collision in a particle accelerator. These beliefs are standardly too far removed from threats to life and limb, sources of food and shelter, and occasions for copulation, to receive the support of an argument from survival value. Again, it seems that beliefs which do have an unquestioned bearing on survival or reproduction do not have to be true invariably, and do not have to be precisely true, in order to have survival value. Perhaps their being true in general or their always being approximately true is enough. If so, the survival value of beliefs is not a conclusive reason for supposing that they are formed as they ought to be: one could require that in the ideal case beliefs be precise and also true without qualification. That it be 'no accident' that they are true might be a further requirement.

The final argument for the replacement thesis that Kornblith sketches is to do with our ability to interpret other people's behaviour. According to this argument, the assumption that there could be widespread error or irrationality is incompatible with the fact that we are successful in making sense of other people's speech and non-linguistic behaviour. Sometimes the necessity of assuming that people are mostly rational and mostly right is argued for in defending methodological principles for translation or interpretation, notably the principle of charity.[11] Apparently, however, weaker principles than the principle of charity, which calls for maximizing the truth of attributed belief or maximizing agreement in beliefs between the subject and the interpreter, are serviceable for the purposes of interpretation.[12] And, in any case, there is too much straight-forward evidence in the psychological literature of irrationality coexisting with intelligence for the a priori argument to be credible.[13]

The additional arguments for the replacement thesis look weak: is the right response a retreat to what Kornblith calls 'the weak replacement thesis'? The weak replacement thesis holds that question (1) can be replaced by question (2) because answers to questions (1) and (2) will eventually converge: the processes by which we ought to form beliefs, which traditional epistemology tries to identify, will turn out to coincide with the processes by which we do form beliefs, which psychology tries to identify. Why anyone should believe that epistemology and psychology will converge in this way is never made clear by Kornblith, and there are further problems with his explanation of the weak replacement thesis. To begin with, Kornblith claims that the thesis allows for the genuine distinctness of epistemology and psychology. The genuine distinctness, even the independence, of the two subjects is strongly suggested where Kornblith says that weak replacement is a matter of epistemology and psychology arriving at the same place in two ways.[14] If the talk of the 'two ways' is taken seriously, and a passage from Kornblith to be quoted in a moment shows that it should be, then it is hard to see how the weak replacement thesis even expresses naturalized epistemology. For as we have already seen, naturalized epistemology is supposed to be a matter of pursuing question (1) subject to the answer to question (2), and talk of two ways of getting to the same place suggests that questions (1) and (2) are pursued independently. Again, it is hard to see how talk of reaching the same identifications from two different starting points is compatible with the idea of one subject replacing another. Kornblith says that if the weak replacement thesis is true, 'then psychology of belief acquisition and epistemology are two different fields, which ask different but equally legitimate questions and have different methodologies'.[15] According to Kornblith these subjects could converge in their answers to their different questions. But even if they did, in what sense could epistemology replace the psychology of belief acquisition or vice versa; in what sense, as Kornblith claims, could psychologists be subject to replacement by epistemologists or epistemologists by psychologists?[16] Even on the assumption of convergence there is no reason to think that one subject can replace the other: the distinctness of their questions and methodologies prevents it. If the same processes have relevance to each field, then the most that can be said is that the two subjects have an overlapping subject matter, not that they are able to replace one another. A parallel from the recent history of logic and linguistics may help to clarify this point. In the early 1970s it was believed that what Chomskyan linguistics called 'deep structure' and what logicians called 'logical form' might prove to be one and the same thing.[17] It was surely no consequence of the conjecture that even a part of logic might replace a part of linguistics or vice versa. The motivation for recognizing logical form – the structure in sentences relevant to the validity of arguments – would always have remained distinct from the motivation for recognizing deep structure, which is posited not to distinguish valid from invalid arguments but for the sake of explaining different kinds of linguistic competence, like the ability to recognize the equivalence of certain active and passive forms of sentence. Similarly, the motivation for identifying certain processes as the sort that ought to produce belief keeps epistemology distinct from psychology – even if epistemology and psychology are concerned with the same processes. The upshot is that it is unclear how the thesis that Kornblith presents can be regarded as a replacement thesis. This fact, together with Kornblith's failure to explain why we should believe it, even if it *is* a replacement thesis, makes one reluctant to suppose that the weak replacement thesis makes much of an advance on Quine's.

Unassimilated epistemology

Philosophers who recoil at the idea of naturalized epistemology, and who oppose the abandonment of the theory of knowledge for psychology,[18] sometimes explain themselves by saying that if the old questions about the justification of our beliefs and the validation of our knowledge are dispensed with, then philosophy itself is being forsaken. Thus, it is sometimes held that

> the dignity of philosophy, its own special importance, is that its task is to provide the foundation for all other intellectual disciplines, for science, taken broadly in the sense of the German term *Wissenschaft*. This means that philosophy must be self-critical. Philosophy must contain a metaphilosophy or philosophy of philosophy to justify the fundamental concepts and principles of philosophy itself.[19]

Though there is something right in saying that by naturalizing epistemology one ignores certain philosophical questions that make sense and have a strong claim to be answered even after the lessons of psychology are in, it is another matter to suggest that turning one's back on these questions is turning one's back on philosophy; this claim is plausible only if philosophy is identified with traditional epistemology, and such an identification seems unwarranted.

I recommend a more moderate reaction to the replacement thesis. It can be put by saying that answers to questions in traditional epistemology must be consistent with, and hence had better not be answered in ignorance of, any compelling results of the psychology of belief acquisition. Since on this view it is prudent but not strictly necessary to examine the findings of empirical psychology – answers to traditional questions could conceivably be consistent with psychology without such examination being undertaken – the approach that I favour may not qualify as naturalistic on Kornblith's criterion. As for the traditional questions of epistemology that have to be pursued, I would not think of Kornblith's 'How ought we to arrive at our beliefs?' as the central one, since it seems to prejudge the question of whether we should form beliefs at all. In other words, the formulation seems to prejudge the question that motivates the oldest form of scepticism – the form that tells us to try to stop holding true or making judgements. A better choice of central question from traditional epistemology is: 'What, if anything, can we have reason to believe?' Not only is this a genuine expression of philosophical scepticism historically speaking; it need not be pursued on the understanding that epistemology is the focal point of philosophy, or that the main task of epistemology is the vindication of the sciences.

There is a further advantage to making this question central: its form helps us to drop the assumption, which seems highly suspect to me, that the dividing line between traditional and naturalized epistemology neatly coincides with some supposed dividing line between normative and descriptive questions in epistemology.[20] The question of what we have reason to believe is not ultimately a normative question. It does not arise from the ethics of belief but from a realistic interpretation of beliefs, i.e. an interpretation according to which their conditions of truth transcend their grounds. To believe something – in at any rate many cases – is to represent certain truth conditions as fulfilled on the basis of evidence that does not rule out the non-fulfilment of some of those conditions. It is to represent something as true while being unable to rule out possibilities incompatible with the truth of that thing. There is no need to invoke counterpossibilities like Descartes's Dream or Demon Hypotheses in order to bear out the thought that what is held true often goes beyond what one's evidence shows to be true. There are quite humdrum possibilities that subjects do not bother to rule out when they hold things true. Take the belief that

Wittgenstein wrote the *Tractatus*. One of the truth conditions of the belief is that there was such a person as Wittgenstein. Another condition is that that person and no other wrote the *Tractatus*. Suppose that there never was such a person as Wittgenstein and that a committee of people wrote the *Tractatus*. These are possibilities that many holders of the belief – especially undergraduate takers of philosophy courses with only a hazy idea of who Wittgenstein was or when he lived – are unable to rule out. Probably they believe that Wittgenstein wrote the *Tractatus* because their philosophy teachers told them so, or because they read it in a book. Even if they have good reasons for trusting their teachers or the books, the reasons may not be relevant enough to the counterpossibilities mentioned to rule them out. With respect to many other beliefs we are all in a similar fix. And with respect to all of our beliefs there are probably some counterpossibilities of the humdrum kind, and some of the metaphysical kind made use of by Descartes, that we are unable to rule out. This is the basis for the sceptic's suggestion that we hold our beliefs dogmatically, and that where life and our constitution permit, we should try to adopt a more noncommittal attitude toward propositions, perhaps closer to entertainment than outright belief.

Placing the issue raised by the sceptic at the centre of epistemology does not prejudge other traditional issues, such as whether knowledge is a kind of belief, or whether we can have reasonable beliefs about the future and the past, about other minds and the material world. It does not even prevent one from taking an interest in the psychology of belief acquisition or the survival value of beliefs. It may even be that by taking an interest in the latter topics one will be able to pose scientifically informed versions of the problems confronted by a priori epistemology.[21]

According to the view of epistemology that I am arguing for, traditional philosophical questions occupy the centre of the field, and there is room for questions continuous with these that have been suggested by empirical psychology or evolutionary theory. The view entails that epistemology and empirical psychology can influence one another, but it stops short of implying that epistemology contains or is contained by empirical psychology, and it carries no suggestion that work on any unresolved issue from traditional epistemology should be stopped. On my view epistemology remains a distinctly philosophical enterprise, though one that can be pursued in co-operation with psychology. Epistemology remains philosophical not because it uses philosophical methods in what is otherwise a branch of psychology,[22] but because its central problem is one of those that help to define philosophy itself. On the other hand, the epistemology described is not purist: its questions and answers do not have to be arrived at a priori, and it is not only or primarily to do with defining or delimiting epistemic concepts, so that it leads to results with a modal status supposedly quite different from the results of science.[23] It is exposed to science without being part of science.

PHILOSOPHY WITHOUT FOLK PSYCHOLOGY?

Quine urges the renovation of the theory of knowledge, but he does not declare the traditionally central problems of epistemology to be obsolete; on the contrary, he holds (not altogether convincingly, as we have seen) that naturalized epistemology keeps 'the original problem' in view. Patricia Churchland seems to lack any comparable attachment to the traditional problems of epistemology, and she is hostile to the framework for the traditional problems of the philosophy of mind, namely 'folk psychology'. In a paper entitled 'Epistemology in the Age of Neuroscience',[24] she claims that 'the grand old paradigm' in epistemology, a set of assumptions, problems and results generated by logical empiricism and earlier empiricism, has more or less lapsed, and that now is the time to have one's preoccupations in the theory of knowledge shaped by neuroscience.

Churchland thinks that the concepts that are accepted uncritically for analysis in the traditional philosophy of mind probably need radical revision. These concepts belong to 'folk psychology' – the set of intuitions and generalizations that constitute common sense about the mind. In her *Neurophilosophy*[25] and elsewhere, Churchland claims that this common sense is too low in explanatory power and too much at odds with empirical evidence to be worth retaining by philosophers as a theory of the mind. Instead, philosophy ought to be informed by two interacting empirical theories: cognitive psychology and neuroscience, the former eventually evolving into a form that permits it to be reduced to the latter. The boldness of Churchland's agenda is not always made entirely evident: the conclusion officially reached in *Neurophilosophy* is the modest one that neuroscience matters to philosophy. As will emerge, however, Churchland sometimes gives the impression that so far as the theory of the mind is concerned empirical neuroscience supersedes philosophy. It is true that she maintains that philosophy matters to neuroscience,[26] but what she means is philosophy of science rather than the philosophy of mind.

The philosophical thesis that is crucial to her case for embarking on neuroscience is that folk psychology is open to a certain kind of inter-theoretic reduction, and that the usual reasons for thinking that psychology is irreducible are not objections, or at least are not compelling objections, to this kind of reduction. Churchland's argument for this thesis depends on analogies between the would-be reduction of folk psychology and the already successful reduction of folk physics and other folk disciplines. While her argument has consequences for a number of different traditional solutions to the traditional mind–body problem, it is not really inspired by any of these problems and solutions. On the contrary, Churchland locates many aspects of her approach in the tradition of positivist philosophy of science, albeit with a more flexible and historically sensitive understanding of reduction. Her argument, then, does not extend the traditional philosophy of mind; rather, it applies and extends certain arguments from the philosophy of science to various forms of psychology. So far as it contributes to an acceptable theory of the mind, philosophy seems to have the sole task for Churchland of demonstrating the reducibility of psychology and the viability of neuroscience. As a byproduct of the demonstration, philosophy is supposed to help neuroscience to orient itself in the scheme of the sciences as a whole. But the two tasks of founding the new science and providing the synoptic view are the only ones Churchland seems to regard as distinctively philosophical in this area:[27] once the case for neurophilosophy is made the philosophy of mind appears to be made redundant.

I shall argue that as explained by Churchland the analogy between folk psychology and other folk disciplines is forced, mainly because 'folk psychology' refers to a range of theories, only some of which have the kind of explanatory and predictive pretensions that would make them analogous to folk physics. Even if explanatory folk psychology were reduced to neuroscience, there would still be a use for the remaining non-explanatory folk psychology, and traditional problems in the philosophy of mind, such as the problems of weakness of the will and self-deception, as well as the problem of whether privacy is a mark of the mental, would still have a point.

Folk psychologies

'Once folk psychology is held at arm's length and evaluated in the way that any theory is evaluated', Churchland writes, 'the more folkishly inept, soft, and narrow it seems to be.'[28] Being inadequate, folk psychology requires first revision, and ultimately elimination in favour of 'the conceptual framework of a matured neuroscience'.[29] What, then, is folk psychology?

> [B]y folk psychology I mean that rough-hewn set of concepts, generalizations, and rules of thumb we all standardly use in explaining and predicting human behaviour. Folk psychology is commonsense psychology – the psychological lore in virtue of which we explain behaviour as the outcome of beliefs, desires, perceptions, expectations, goals, sensations and so forth. It is a theory whose generalizations connect mental states to other mental states, to perceptions, and to actions. These homey generalizations are what provide the characterization of the mental states and processes referred to; they are what delimit the 'facts' of mental life and define the explananda. Folk psychology is 'intuitive psychology', and it shapes our conceptions of ourselves.[30]

Folk psychology not only aims at being explanatory and predictive in the way any scientific theory tries to be; its content is also supposed to be expressible, in conformity with the deductive–nomological model of scientific theories, as some set of generalizations and observation sentences. As in the case of other folk theories, it is hard to say how exactly its theoretical concepts – belief, desire, perception and so on – developed; it is even hard at first to regard something so familiar and second nature to us as a theory. Nevertheless, the fact that its origins are obscure is no more to its discredit than the fact that the origins of almost all theories are obscure, and the fact that it is used for prediction and explanation makes it into a theory, however natural and untheoretical it seems.[31]

According to Churchland the difference between folk psychology and scientific psychology is largely a matter of differences between the generalizations of the two theories. The generalizations of folk psychology are imprecise, often unsubtle and oversimple. An example of such a generalization would be, 'If someone x has normal hearing, and someone else y says "p" in a normal speaking voice in x's vicinity, and x knows the language, then x hears that p.'[32] Another would be, 'Seeing that a is F is a normal cause of believing that a is F.'[33] Churchland claims that it is the generalizations of folk psychology that 'delimit the "facts" of mental life'. By this she means, I think, that we commit ourselves to the existence of perceptions, beliefs, pains and so on because our background generalizations commit us to them, and not, for example, because the introspectible contents of our minds present themselves to mental observation as different mental kinds. If this is what Churchland means it suggests that our concepts for different types of mental states are primarily theoretical concepts, concepts we apply for the sake of explanation. This is plausible enough for uses of the concepts in third-person psychological descriptions, and even for some unusual first-person descriptions, as when we posit some unconscious belief or desire to explain behaviour of our own that is puzzling to us. But it seems inadequate as an account of the use of, for example, the concept of belief in standard first-person belief sentences or the use of the concept of pain in 'I am in pain'. To make a point that is very familiar in this area, when I say I am in pain I am probably doing something closer to expressing pain than explaining any pain behaviour, and when I say I believe something I am not standardly attributing a belief to myself for the purpose of explaining my behaviour. If this is right, neither belief nor pain are exclusively explanatory concepts; by the same token some of the facts one describes using these concepts are not delimited by explanatory generalizations. Perhaps the attribution to myself of pain on occasions on which I am in pain is due not to a regularity read off nature but to my having been conditioned to replace one sort of expression of pain with another. In that case the mental facts corresponding to first-person sentences about pain, or perhaps sensation generally, would be delimited by the convention that the training makes me follow. Another sort of convention might apply in the case of the facts corresponding to some first-person belief sentences.

When psychological concepts are applied outside the context of explaining behaviour, do the applications belong to folk psychology? If the answer is that they do not, then there must be roles for psychological concepts outside what Churchland is calling a theory, or at least a predictive theory; roles that, contrary to her, are undetermined by generalizations. On the other hand, if folk psychology does extend to these uses of the concepts – and some of Churchland's more permissive glosses on 'folk psychology', e.g. 'commonsense framework for understanding mental states and processes', suggest that it can – the framework for understanding is not exclusively explanatory and predictive. If that is so, however, no purely explanatory and predictive successor to folk psychology, no matter how much better at predicting and explaining it is, and no matter how much freer of error, can be the same sort of theory as folk psychology.

Now my own view is that a number of different things qualify as folk psychology. Certain claims that Churchland makes commit her to a similar view. Her criticism of folk psychology, however, and her case for its elimination, bear on just one of the things that folk psychology can be. The elimination of this part of folk psychology, supposing it were possible, would not be the elimination of all of folk psychology. What would be left over would be enough for the traditional philosophy of mind and for psychologically penetrating art, like novels or film.

Among the different elements of folk psychology that tend to be obscured by Churchland's emphasis on homey psychological generalizations are (1) common-sense canons of interpretation; (2) the understanding that would enable a novelist to create a particular character or that would enable an actor to behave in character; and (3) certain beliefs elicited in psychological investigations of common sense about scientific psychology.

(1) Attributions of belief to others, and, more generally, theories of the beliefs of others, depend in part on interpretations of the utterances of others. For the purpose of interpretation speakers are often assumed to be reasonably well-informed, consistent and sincere, and their remarks are taken to meet certain standards of coherence and relevance. These are common-sense canons of interpretation, and following them sometimes makes the difference between, on the one hand, knowing or having some idea of what someone believes, and, on the other hand, being in the dark. Do we adopt these canons because we subscribe to their corresponding empirical generalizations? That is, do we decide to take a given speaker as consistent and well-informed because observation has shown that, as a rule, speakers *are* consistent and well-informed? Do we even decide to take a given speaker as consistent and well-informed because we believe that not to do so will frustrate our aim of arriving at interpretations of speakers? In both cases the answer

seems to be 'no'. The canons of interpretation seem to be assumed rather than based on observed regularities, and they seem to be too deeply embedded in our way of thinking about other people, or in a non-theoretical skill of interpreting them,[34] to be described as things that we adopt in an experimental spirit for the sake of improving our chances of arriving at interpretations. So while using the canons is a way of elaborating a common-sense theory of other people's beliefs, and therefore a contribution to folk psychology, the theory that results does not make quite the use of generalizations that Churchland's picture of folk psychology suggests.[35]

Do the canons of interpretation even belong to a predictive theory? In one sense they do: conjectures made on one occasion about what a speaker believes or means are relevant to our expectations about his speech, non-linguistic action and beliefs in the future. But like the canons that govern the explanation of non-linguistic action by reference to belief and desire, the canons of linguistic interpretation recognize the rationality of the agent whose behaviour is being explained, and so exploit the agent's point of view in forming those expectations. The interpreter assumes that the agent is reasonable in forming beliefs and effective in expressing them, and so arrives at hypotheses about what the speaker believes by asking what a rational person in those circumstances would say, and want to be taken to say. The stance adopted toward the other agent does not maintain a strict detachment of theorist from subject, but rather calls upon the theorist to attribute as little of what the theorist would regard as wrong, irrelevant or incoherent to the subject in his circumstances, as is required to get an interpretation. The theorist is thus got to operate with a conception of the subject not only as a rational being, but as a fellow rational being largely in agreement with the theorist. Even when the interpreter and his subject already speak the same language there is a sense in which the interpreter goes native, constructing a point of view he can share with the subject. This is not exactly empathy or stepping into the other's shoes; at most it is lending the other shoes that one also wears oneself. Nevertheless, in interpretation, the expectations one forms are expectations that would help one to interact as a fellow interpreter or agent with the subject, not merely predictions about what effects will be observable next in the subject. It is even possible that the canons of interpretation and the canons for the explanation of action by reference to reason and desire allow for a more substantial interaction as equals, one in which the subject is as active as the theorist in forming the theorist's expectations. That is, the canons may allow the theorist to recognize that the agent (a) realizes that a construction will be placed on a given action by other agents and (b) has himself a preferred construction which he wishes the other agents to adopt as well.[36] Whether or not interaction between agent and interpreter is as co-operative as this, interpretation usually proceeds as if the predictions it generated were meant to be useful for communing with the subjects of interpretation, and this distinguishes the predictions arising from interpretation from those of a more standard predictive theory.

(2) Canons of interpretation, I have been suggesting, belong to folk psychology, and yet they do not seem to play a theoretical role that Churchland recognizes, or to belong to the sort of theory that she thinks folk psychology is. Other material from folk psychology proves difficult to fit into her picture of folk psychology. Take the folk-psychological theories that we can suppose certain novelists draw upon in their narratives. Churchland recognizes that different novelists use different networks of generalizations in their work, and that, despite differences, they share 'many general beliefs about why human beings behave as they do'.[37] I wonder, however, whether it is generalizations about human beings alone that contribute to novelists' work. I wonder whether there might not be much more of a role for thoughts about individual character, thoughts which might not be general, and which might not play the same role in the psychology of writing as generalizations about human beings.

Novelists who describe the process of composition often speak of characters beginning to take on a life of their own. As the writing progresses it becomes clearer what the character would and would not do. At times characters are modelled on real-life originals and then the author's knowledge of a particular personality guides such things as choices about plotting and dialogue. At other times the characters are more like genuine creations. In either case, the theories about these personalities that determine the novelist's choices do not seem to consist of generalizations about human behaviour, which for Churchland typify the folk psychology that neuroscience would replace; instead, where the theories contain generalizations at all, it is more probable that they would be generalizations about a particular individual:[38] 'X always grovels in the company of rich people'; 'Y would never think about anyone else long enough to consider the effects of not repaying his debts.' I suppose that it is generalizations of this kind that also inform acting in character on the stage.

Considerations about the creation of characters not only seem to show that Churchland's account of the types of generalization in folk psychology is oversimplified; it also reveals a connection with canons of interpretation and all of the trouble that they make for Churchland's claim that the use of folk psychology is predictive in exactly the way that folk physics is. Once again the phenomenon that is important is that of a character beginning to have a life of its own. When this happens the novelist's relation toward the character seems to me to become comparable to that of an interpreter of another person in real life. Instead of feeling free simply to decree what the character will do, the novelist forms expectations about what the character will do, given the personality with which the character is endowed. As in the explanation and anticipation of the actions of real people, these expectations can be disappointed or confounded. The reason this is possible is not that the characters really do have lives of their own, but that certain twists of event and plot can unexpectedly occur to the novelist and appear consistent with what has been created earlier.

(3) A third basis for unease about Churchland's account is its implication that there is a sharp distinction between folk psychology and scientific psychology. This is the implication given where she contrasts some of the generalizations of scientific psychology with some of the generalizations of folk psychology.[39] Not only does this contrast disappear in certain cases, as Churchland admits, but more than differences between generalizations are relevant to deciding how folk and scientific psychology are related. Other factors have a bearing, and these include the results of empirical studies which Churchland (for once!) does not appear to take into account. In a fascinating book that reports the results of many studies of the ways in which common sense anticipates findings in the social sciences, Adrian Furnham cites work by Mischel and Mischel indicating that '9- and 11-year-old children were able correctly to predict the outcome of nearly two-thirds of the famous experiments presented to them'.[40] Studies by J. Houston mentioned by Furnham point in a similar direction: testing for a common-sense grasp of principles of learning and memory in classical experimental psychology, and using a jargon-free questionnaire,

Houston found that, of fifty volunteer adults recruited in a Los Angeles park on a Sunday afternoon, '76% of the questions were answered correctly more often than by chance'.[41]

Churchland does not hold that the separation of folk from scientific psychology is always total. In *Neurophilosophy* she acknowledges in passing that two branches of scientific psychology, namely cognitive psychology and social psychology, contain generalizations that use propositional attitude concepts like belief and inference, and theses about the use of representations.[42] In other words, she acknowledges that at the moment these sectors of scientific psychology contain elements of folk psychology. Yet she does not seem to allow for the possibility that these elements could continue to survive in scientific psychology for as long as it co-evolves with brain science: her adherence to eliminative materialism, a materialism emptied of folk psychology, precludes this. Surely, however, it is a possibility that the co-evolution of a neuroscience and a scientific psychology tainted by folk elements will be eternal. Indeed, it is unclear that when folk-psychological generalizations are employed in the context of scientific psychological theories they are open to quite the objections they attract in their homelier settings.[43]

The upshot of the preceding discussion for Churchland's account is quickly stated: 'folk psychology' refers to more than a theory for predicting behaviour impersonally, and so it is not strongly analogous to folk physics. It refers to a theory that helps human beings to interact as equals, that enables us to get a deeper appreciation of human character. As for the elements of folk psychology that do contribute to prediction, these are not confined to crude generalizations whose only use is a prescientific one. Some of the generalizations of folk psychology take on a scientific role when properly embedded in scientific psychology, while some of the principles of scientific psychology seem independently to be latent in psychological common sense. All of these points tell against the abandonment of folk psychology. Even if folk psychology were a hopelessly defective predictive theory, that would not be a reason for doing away with it, since more than the purpose of prediction is served by folk psychology. In any case, and as things are, not all of folk psychology is useless for prediction.

The reasons that have emerged for not eliminating folk psychology are of course compatible with the claim that folk psychology needs revision and that its concepts of belief, perception, consciousness and so on do not provide the most useful taxonomy of psychological states and processes for the purposes of predicting behaviour. Folk psychology may well have to be revised and different concepts used for prediction–generating taxonomy, and Churchland is right to point this out. Her mistake is to jump from this correct point to the conclusion that unrevised folk psychology must be scrapped, as if the only use for psychological concepts was taxonomic, and as if the only setting for folk-psychological generalizations was the prescientific predictive theory.

Churchland's reasons for doing away with folk psychology were supposed to act at the same time as reasons for abandoning philosophical work geared to folk psychology. Since the reasons have proved uncompelling, we seem to be without much of a case for abandoning the traditional philosophical work. Indeed, the case for abandoning such work seemed uncompelling anyway. Partly this is because Churchland seems to approach the traditional philosophy of mind from the angle of her concern with reduction. The alleged subjectivity of the mental and the representational character of the mental matter to her because they have often been presented as obstacles to identifying mental processes with brain processes or reducing folk psychology to something better. But traditionally these topics have also been taken up outside the context of the main-brain identity theory and concerns with reduction. The subjectivity of the mental has been problematic because the notions of privileged access and private languages have been; mental representation has been of interest philosophically because the study of linguistic representation has become so sophisticated. Not only have these topics been philosophically important apart from the mind–body problem; when they *have* been pursued in relation to that problem it has not always been anti-scientifically or on the assumption that folk psychology is unrevisable. It is possible to ask what subjectivity consists in *given* what we know about the brain, and not only to ask what subjectivity consists in on the assumption that the brain can have nothing to do with it. It is possible to ask what mental representation can be, given that the representations are the work of the brain, and not only to ask what can account for mental representation given that no physical object can be a source of representations. Again, it is possible to ask whether the mind really does have unity, given a natural interpretation of the data from split-brain cases. It is the same in the area of the philosophy of mind occupied by considerations about rationality. The fact that experiments show that intelligence can coexist with quite a lot of irrationality does not mean that irrationality in the form of weakness of will and self-deception cannot be philosophically interesting. These problems can be pursued without disregarding or refusing to take seriously scientific findings. In general, it seems, versions of traditional problems in the philosophy of mind can be scientifically informed and not necessarily pursued as if science were irrelevant to them. That being so, it is unclear why there cannot be a co-evolution of neurobiology, scientific psychology *and* traditional philosophy.

7

NATURALISMS IN THE MORAL SCIENCES

Philosophy may be informed by science, but it is not a part of science: it has problems and preoccupations of its own, including, as we saw in the last chapter, problems and preoccupations that keep alive the traditional theory of knowledge and the traditional philosophy of mind. There are other non-scientific subjects. Theology falls outside science because it tries to go beyond science. Either it is concerned with a metaphysically ultimate sort of explanation, which conditions scientific explanation itself, or else it tries to reach an accommodation between scientific explanations and ways of understanding made possible by faith. Another extra-scientific subject is aesthetics – not because there are no standards of taste, but because a body of criticism using these standards is not strongly comparable to a scientific theory making use of laws. In this chapter, however, I consider morals and social studies.

These, too, have strong claims to be non-sciences. In part they inherit these claims from philosophy, for in part they are philosophical subjects – in social studies 'political theory' very evidently has a philosophical character, for example. Morals and social studies are also unscientific in the sense that they are not entirely concerned with the explanation of phenomena: they are also concerned with what ought to be done, that is, with irreducibly practical or normative questions. In what follows I am once again going to criticize approaches to these subjects which are strongly 'naturalistic'. I begin with the thinking behind a certain kind of naturalistic reduction of moral facts to facts about emotional response. Then I describe and criticize a related attempt to reconstruct morality on Darwinian principles. I argue that these approaches are unsatisfactory. Their shortcomings give us reasons for supposing that normative ethics is an autonomous subject. I go

151

on to consider a consequence of this conclusion for the social sciences. Without denying that these sciences sometimes succeed in being explanatory and predictive in ways that make them resemble natural sciences, I hold that they share concerns with normative ethics and philosophy, concerns which prevent their outright assimilation to the natural sciences. I therefore disagree with the naturalistic thesis that says flatly that the sciences of man and society are natural sciences.[1]

ETHICS, OBJECTIVITY AND NATURALISM

An important naturalistic argument about ethics starts from a question about the relation of specific moral judgements to moral principles: the principles to some extent explain the judgements, while the judgements are to some extent used to assess or test the principles; so are not particular moral judgements similar to observations in natural science? Gilbert Harman, who makes this question the starting point for his introduction to moral philosophy, gives the following answer, using 'moral observation' to mean 'unreflective moral judgement':

> [O]bservation plays a role in science that it does not seem to play in ethics. The difference is that you need to make assumptions about certain physical facts to explain the occurrence of the observations that support a scientific theory, but you do not seem to need to make assumptions about any moral facts to explain the occurrence of the so-called moral observations I have been talking about. In the moral case, it would seem that you need only make assumptions about the psychology or moral sensibility of the person making the moral observation. In the scientific case, theory is tested against the world.[2]

Harman illustrates his point. If one's reaction to seeing children set a cat on fire is that it is wrong, one does not have to posit, independent of oneself, a moral fact of the wrongness of setting fire to the cat to explain one's reaction; while if one sees a trail of vapour in a cloud chamber and concludes, 'There goes a photon', the presence in the cloud chamber of a travelling proton may well have been necessary to produce the observation. In this way the photon has an objective existence that the wrongness of igniting the cat does not.

In Harman's account and in accounts like it, objectivity is a matter of being causally explanatory. Moral facts either exist in nature to account for moral observation, or else they have a supernatural character. Believers in the objectivity of value must either recognize occult entities – a Platonic Form of the Good, Moorean non-natural qualities, eternal fitnesses or unfitnesses – or else they must do without distinctively moral features of reality, drawing only on the value-free ontology of the best going theory of nature.[3] A corresponding dilemma is supposed to confront an objectivist moral psychology. Either ethical perception and motivation have a transcendental source, and so a mysterious basis, or else naturalism prevails, in which case there is no distinctively ethical perception and no distinctively ethical motivation: no distinctively ethical perception because there is no Good to be apprehended, or because what is apprehended is open to naturalistic reduction; no distinctively ethical motivation because there is no Good to act in accordance with or no irreducible Good to act in accordance with.

Harman puts all of that more briefly.[4] 'Naturalists', he says, 'must be either ethical nihilists or ethical naturalists.' They must either 'deny that there are any moral facts at all' or show how moral facts reduce to natural ones. The reductive option is not easily distinguished from the nihilistic one: instead of saying that there aren't any moral facts one says that there aren't really any, that moral facts are just constructions out of natural ones. Either way the objectivity of value is compromised, for the objectivist claims that there are moral truths and that some are irreducible.[5] If Harman is right the objectivist must forgo that claim or eschew naturalism.

Naturalism would be an acceptable option if it had the resources to show that values were not objective while explaining why they seem to be. How would the supposedly false objectification be accounted for? Mackie has remarked on the parallel between an 'error theory' of the secondary qualities, specifically colours, and a would-be 'error theory' of value.[6] Some of the modern philosophers tried to establish that material things are not intrinsically coloured though they seem to be, and perhaps something similar can be done for the apparently intrinsic good or evil in persons, and rightness and wrongness in actions. So Mackie seems to suggest. Harman entertains a similar proposal.[7]

The model account of the secondary qualities does not seem to me to be properly regarded as an error theory, and the seeming objectivity of the secondary qualities is unlike the seeming objectivity of value. The upshot is that false objectification in the one area is a bad model for alleged false objectification in the other. Both the strengths and the shortcomings of the parallel between secondary qualities and values emerge by way of the psychology of ethics – the theory of moral perception and motivation – so that is where I will lay the stress. The breakdown of the parallel tells against one kind of naturalism in morals and in favour of one kind of objectivism.

Values and secondary qualities compared

My claim is that secondary qualities are not similar enough to values to undercut objectivism in morals. I do not say that secondary qualities and values cannot interestingly be compared. On the contrary, once the comparison is made, many otherwise miscellaneous features of moral experience start to assume a sort of unity.

There is the fact that we sometimes 'detect the moral aspects of a situation . . . by looking and seeing'.[8] Not that, as talk of detection might suggest, one need always bring to bear a kind of acumen: discernment only sometimes plays a part,[9] and conscious inference only occasionally operates. As Harman puts it,

> if you round a corner and see a group of young hoodlums pour gasoline on a cat and ignite it, you do not need to *conclude* that what they are doing is wrong; you do not need to figure anything out; you can *see* that it is wrong.[10]

It ties these points together to say that value-judgement can be non-trivially observational. The same can be said, of course, of secondary quality judgement, and in both cases there is a prima facie connection between the phenomenology of observation – what it is like – and the objectification of observational content.

To begin with, it is sometimes as if we are *subject* to moral observation: part of what it is like to see that the cat's being set on fire is wrong, is for the wrongness of the action to be borne in on one. Seeing that the thing is wrong is in some respect involuntary, and the content of the observation seems to be supplied wholly by an event external to the observer. The corresponding elements of passivity and adventitiousness in secondary quality experience have

154

often been taken by philosophers to encourage the naïve objectification of the secondary qualities, and perhaps it is the same with values. If there is a tendency to locate the wrongness of an act of torture *in* the act, then perhaps that only recapitulates the tendency to locate in a material thing, and so outside the mind, what is passively experienced in observing it, like the smell the thing gives off, or its colour.[11]

The passivity and adventitiousness of some moral observation may be one source of the naïve objectification of value. The seamlessness of observational content may be another. In Harman's example the observed wrongness of the ignition of the cat does not come apart from the observed ignition of the cat. So there is nothing in the observation to set apart what is objective (the action) from what is arguably objectified (its wrongness). In disputes over the objectivity of the secondary qualities much has been held to depend on the corresponding seamlessness of the connection between experienced secondary qualities and experienced primary qualities. Berkeley confessed that he was unable to form an image of a thing's shape without forming an image of a thing's colour, and he claimed that the inseparability in images counted toward the inconceivability of a thing objectively devoid of secondary qualities.[12] The corresponding inability of someone to think of certain kinds of action without thinking of their value or disvalue, might similarly be taken to count toward objective seamlessness, and so toward the equally objective standing of an act and its wrongness.

A model for the subjectivity of value?

Passivity, adventitiousness and seamlessness appear to be the objectifying pressures that impressed the empiricists among the modern philosophers. They tended to identify the objective with what 'existed without the mind', and the subjective with the mind's contents. Accordingly, an error of objectification consisted in a confusion of the mind's contents with extra-mental things. And the cause of the confusion would be a faulty inference from what a kind of observation was like to what things observed were like. If an idea arose unbidden (felt passivity and adventitiousness), or if an association of ideas seemed irresistible (conscious seamlessness), that would be a ground for the naïve thought that what the unbidden idea was *of*, was an external thing, or that what were irresistibly associated were properties of things independently connected to one another. These naïve inferences a scientific conception of the secondary qualities would either bear out or confute. In particular, a scientific conception of the secondary qualities would confute erroneous inferences from secondary quality observation. Which erroneous inferences exactly? Is the distinction between being external to the mind and being internal to the mind the key to the subjectivity of the secondary qualities, let alone the subjectivity of value?

The first thing to clear up is the subjectivity of the secondary qualities. To keep to the type of secondary quality favoured by Mackie and Harman, in what sense might colours be said to be subjective? In this sense: ascriptions of colours to objects are conditional for their truth on how it is with *subjects* of colour experience. More specifically, colour ascriptions are true in virtue of facts about the experiences a normal perceiver would have if his sense organs were affected by objects with certain types of surface in standard conditions of illumination. Thus, for something to be red is for it to produce experiences of red in someone with normally functioning sense organs in normal conditions of illumination. Being red is irreducibly a relational property, and one of the relevant relata is a conscious subject, physiologically constituted in a certain way.

Now if values were subjective in the way that secondary qualities were, then ascriptions of rightness and wrongness would similarly depend for their truth on the sensitivities of the normal human constitution. To go back to Harman's example, the wrongness of setting the cat on fire would consist in the power of that act to elicit in normally constituted observers feelings of outrage or horror or disapproval. More generally, and with values modelled on colours, one might put it as Harman does, expounding Hume:

> . . . colours are dispositional properties, and so are moral properties. A dispositional property is to be defined in terms of the corresponding occurrent property. . . . The occurrent property for colours is an object's looking a certain colour. We might speak of colour sensations. An object is red if it conveys the colour sensation of red to observers – just as something is warm if it gives the sensation of heat to observers. And, something is wrong if it gives 'disapproval sensations' to observers. Wrongness is a disposition to cause disapproval.[13]

As Harman would concede, that formulation masks a disanalogy between redness and wrongness, because it speaks undiscriminatingly about observers and observation. Moral observation is dependent on the prior adoption by the observer of what Harman calls 'a completely disinterested and impartial point of view'. More, the attitude of disapproval prompted by the observation of wrongness is constrained not to depend on mistaken beliefs. Neither proviso has a counterpart in the experience of colour.

Furthermore, both provisos count against unqualified talk of 'disapproval sensations'. The sensory or experiential content of moral disapproval at best accompanies or results from but does not constitute the disapproval. Or, to put it another way, if the observation of certain morally wrong actions produces certain feelings, that is by way of the thoughts the observer has about the actions. The feelings derive from how he conceives it, not the conceptions from how he feels it. For suppose that moral disapproval were purely or primarily a sensory affair, so that what made the ignition of the cat seem wrong was the feeling of revulsion it produced. Then, to echo an objection that Hume put to himself in the *Treatise*, would not too many actions count as morally wrong and too many things count as morally bad? Would not 'any object, whether animate or inanimate, rational or irrational, . . . become morally good or evil, provided it can excite a satisfaction or uneasiness?'[14]

Evidently, a distinction is needed between moral uneasiness and uneasiness in general. To count as moral, the uneasiness must not only arise in someone who conceives the 'object' impartially: that is only one of the necessary conditions Hume recognizes;[15] there must also be something about the object, viewed impartially, that causes uneasiness or disapproval. Hume claims that once the reason for disapproval is given, no further explanation is required of our calling something vicious.[16] Thus, no further explanation is needed if what inspires abhorrence is a 'cruel and treacherous' action.[17] And in the corresponding case of ascriptions of virtue no further explanation is needed if what gives rise to the ascription is pleasure at the spectacle of a 'noble and generous' action.[18] In both cases the reason for the pleasure or the abhorrence is written into the description of its object. But then, presumably, the pleasure or abhorrence is inspired by the *thought* that the action is noble or generous, cruel or treacherous. So if wrongness is 'a disposition to cause disapproval sensations' in an impartial observer, then the disapproval has a sensory aspect only derivatively, by way of thoughts or conceptions of what is observed. It is the other way round with colour. There it is sensations or experiences that would be caused, and only derivatively conceptions or judgements.

The asymmetry developed

We have come to an asymmetry between values, considered as dispositional, observational properties, and colours considered in the same way. Though it is plausible to say that each kind of observation has a sensational and a conceptual component, it seems that they combine in different ways in the two cases. In the moral case how an action is 'felt' depends on how it is conceived; in the colour case how it is conceived depends on how it is experienced. The disanalogy becomes clearer when one investigates the suggestion that disagreement in secondary quality judgement might be a model for disagreement in moral judgement.[19]

When the colour-blind man disagrees with the standard observer the disagreement does not merely consist in conflicting judgements. It is not just that the colour-blind man thinks that the pillar-box is brown and that the standard observer thinks it is red. There is also the sensory difference between them. The standard observer is affected by an experience as of a red thing when the colour-blind man is affected by an experience as of a brown thing. In a straightforward sense the sensory difference is the basis for the conflict in their judgements. It is the other way round with moral judgement. There a sensory difference ('disapproval sensations' in one man, 'approval sensations' in the other) has a basis in conflicting judgements.

What makes the colour-blind man wrong and the standard observer right? What counts as right is determined by what the majority of observers would experience and judge the colour of the pillar-box to be, and the standard observer's experiences and judgements are by definition representative of those of the majority. But what if it came about that sensory reactions now characteristic of colour-blindness were as common as those of what now pass for standard observers? In that case there would *be* no standard observers, and the question of who was right about the colour of the pillar-box would become an open question.

Could moral judgements be thrown into comparable disarray? If it came about that setting cats on fire elicited feelings of disapproval in impartial observers only non–standardly, would that mean that there was no fact of the matter concerning the moral value of the action? It is hard to agree that it would: we know too much about cats to unlearn the fact that setting fire to them causes them agony. And if we have any hold on the concept of agony, the connection between agony and the wrongness of causing it can hardly escape us. So even if there ceased to be a standardly sentimental reaction to setting cats on fire, the connection between agony and wrongness would remain to lend substance to the view that setting fire to cats is wrong.

Once again it seems inappropriate to view value and its alleged subjectivity on the model of colour. The reason the one sort of subjectivity seems to be the model for the other is that both are connected, but as will shortly emerge, very differently connected, to observation or perception.

According to objectivism in morals there are reasons for bene-fiting others, and for not harming others, that can only be ignored on pain of irrationality, and these reasons are generally perceivable. Thus, to labour Harman's example, there is a generally perceivable reason for not setting fire to a cat, and it consists in the badness of pain or agony. Someone who denies the objectivist line in the case of the cat must take issue with at least one of the following claims: that pain is bad; that the badness of pain can generally be perceived; that the cat can suffer pain; or that the badness of pain is a reason for not setting fire to the cat, a reason that cannot be shrugged off. Those who think that values are subjective on the model of secondary qualities try to cast doubt on the first two of these claims by querying the relation between them.

Without quite denying that pain is bad, or that the badness of pain is generally perceivable, they ask whether it has to be a fact that pain is bad in order for the badness of the pain, or the wrongness of inflicting it, to be generally perceivable. Their answer is 'No', on the ground that no moral facts have to be posited in order to explain moral observation.[20] Similarly in the case of colours. To explain the making of colour observations there is no need to assume that there are distinctive colour-facts. We need only assume that someone is perceptually constituted in a certain way, and that on account of this and the way a local surface reflects light to his retina, he has an experience as of something being a certain colour.

Of course, as the previous discussion has shown, the parallel holds only up to a point. Moral principles that one accepts explain moral observation, but no comparable principles are required to count for colour experiences, or even colour judgements. So why could not moral principles serve as the moral facts which explained moral observation? Harman concedes that in a sense they can fill this role. 'Certain moral principles might help to explain why it was *wrong* of the children to set the cat on fire, but moral principles seem to be no help in explaining *your thinking* that that is wrong.'[21] Moral principles, Harman is saying, help to explain the *content* of an observation of wrongness. What they cannot explain, and what they have to explain if their status as facts is to be as unquestionable as the factual standing of scientific principles, is the occurrence of *an event of observing* something to be wrong. Only if they explain an event of observing can the observing be evidence for the truth of the principles.

I agree that the truth of moral principles is not evidenced by observation in the same way as the truth of scientific principles, but this is an asymmetry one should expect, given that moral observations have a place in practical as against theoretical reasoning. Moral observations function primarily as reasons for action and only derivatively as reasons for belief; scientific observations function primarily as reasons for belief and only derivatively as reasons for action. There is a corresponding difference in the relation between moral observations and moral principles. It is true that moral principles can be inferred from moral observations, but the inference involved is not inference to the best *explanation* of why the observations occur, but rather inference to a practical principle that ties the observer's reason for action in certain circumstances, to a reason for action anyone might have in a wider range of circumstances, or in any circumstances. It is when moral observation and secondary quality observation are taken to contribute to the same kind of inference to principles that the parallel between values and secondary qualities becomes persuasive.

When moral observation is located in the context of practical reasoning, the natural question about it is not, 'What explains its occurrence?' but 'What gives it its authority?' In other words, how, if at all, can a reason for action that someone perceives be a reason for action that he cannot shrug off? Kant located the inescapability of the relevant reasons or maxims in their relation to an overarching principle of conduct of the good will: 'To act only according to that maxim by which I can at the same time will that it become a universal law.' More recently, Nagel[22] has tried to ground the inescapability of the reasons not in the autonomy of a certain kind of will, but in the conception of oneself as one person among others. Neither objectivist position is easy to argue for, but the work of mounting a defence is made no harder by an alleged analogy between values and secondary qualities. The analogy is unstable, and the model of inference that is needed to give the analogy its point is itself beside the point.

'DARWINIAN ETHICS'

There is another strain of naturalistic argument about ethics that is supposed to bear out subjectivism, only without the aid of an analogy between values and secondary qualities. This time the idea is not that ascriptions of value depend for their truth on how it is with an idealized impartial subject or observer, but rather that 'morality is a function of human nature, and that without it there is no right and wrong'. This formulation, and the argument from evolutionary theory that is used to enlarge upon it, are due to Michael Ruse.

In *Taking Darwin Seriously*,[23] Ruse argues that morality – an internalized sense of what we are obliged to do for others with no expectation of return – is an evolutionary mechanism whose effect is to direct most help to those who share most genetic material with us, those who must survive to reproduce if copies of our genes are to be passed on (219–23). Though morality is in some sense indiscriminate, getting us to help those who are not genetically related to us as well as those who are, acting according to it is simpler and less demanding on our brains than acting in the light of the complex calculations we would need to make to direct help only to those who were most likely to maximize the distribution of our genes.

Three terms from E.O. Wilson's writings on sociobiology are important to bringing out the connection between Ruse's position and evolutionary theory: 'epigenetic rule', 'hard-core altruism' and 'soft-core altruism'. An epigenetic rule is 'a constraint which obtains on some facet of human development, having its origin in evolutionary needs, and channelling the way in which the growing or grown human thinks and acts' (143). An epigenetic rule is followed in the widely uniform human classification of colours. Hard-core altruism is the disposition to help without expecting anything in return, and it operates only between close relatives

– people with most in common genetically. Soft-core altruism is the disposition to help others where help in return seems a possibility: it operates between agents who are not genetically related. These biological altruisms promote such harmony between people as is required for reproductive ends; but they also prepare the ground for altruism in the non-biological sense, or, as Ruse puts it, altruism 'in the literal sense, demanding genuine sentiments about right and wrong' (221).

Ruse thinks that biological altruisms are among the causal conditions of altruism in the literal sense, and of morality in general: what does he take to be the nature of altruism in the literal sense and of morality in general? Ruse speaks of

> that prescriptive force which is distinctly characteristic of morality. As in the case of sibling incest, our feelings are backed by a (likewise innate) sense that approved actions are 'right' and disapproved actions are 'wrong'.
>
> It is not just that we do not want to go to bed with our siblings. We feel that we *ought* not to have intercourse with them. We have such a strong drive to copulate, particularly with any member of the opposite sex who is almost literally thrown at us, that (biologically) we need something really strong to steer us away. Morality does the trick. Similarly, in the face of our general inclination to serve ourselves, because it is biologically advantageous to us to help and co-operate, morality (as mediated through the epigenetic rules) has evolved to guide and stiffen our will. We are moved by genuine, non-metaphorical altruism. (222)

The 'ought' of morality is described as a force strong enough to overcome or limit potentially harmful dispositions. But this seems simply wrong. Very often the force of the 'ought' (or more often the 'ought not') is felt and yet the agent goes ahead and steals or commits adultery or lies. The fact that the precept does not get one to act in accordance with it or against some contrary inclination does not keep it from being moral. Surely what makes a precept moral is not the strength of its grip on one but the source of its grip on one, namely its content, and, with that, the type of reason for action it is. A moral precept usually gets its force from the clarity of the good it seeks to promote or the clarity of the bad it seeks to prevent, and the fact that it is addressed to people in virtue of conditions they almost all satisfy – being sane or adult or moderately rational, for example. These things often make it irrational (rather than psychologically hard or impossible) to ignore them. Ruse compares moral to pre-moral inclinations in the wrong terms when he only mentions their felt force and ignores their content.

Other passages reinforce the suspicion that Ruse has a defective theoretical conception of the moral. Comparing the sentiments that our biological nature is supposed to make us develop with the attitudes required by a utilitarian normative ethical theory, Ruse finds a certain prima facie discrepancy, which he tries to explain away. Our biologically evolved sentiments make us give more weight to our nearest and dearest than to other human beings; yet utilitarianism (in common with other ethical theories) requires us to act so as to make the maximum difference to human welfare impersonally conceived. If more lives would be saved or more pain alleviated by helping strangers and ignoring one's children in certain circumstances, then that is what we are morally obliged to do.

Ruse claims that, by Rawls's test of reflective equilibrium, Darwinism is correct to ask less of us than utilitarianism. When we take into account everything we know and feel about human beings, he says, we get the most satisfactory mix of principle and intuition by accepting a theory that makes moral obligations to strangers and foreigners weaker than moral obligations to friends and neighbours (242). But this is a question-begging answer and a misleading use of the test of reflective equilibrium. It may be that the feelings and intuitions that Ruse congratulates Darwinism for agreeing with are morally suspect for not being impartial; unless this possibility is ruled out they can hardly be used to counter the objection that Darwinism is not impartial enough. Rawls himself requires the test to be applied to principles chosen from behind a veil of ignorance, a veil that enforces impartiality by keeping us in the dark about the identities and well-being of those whom a choice of principles would affect.

Does Ruse offer Darwinism as an explanation of the actual sentiments we typically have about the well-being of others, whether or not these are the sentiments we ought to have, or is he saying that the actual sentiments we have are the only ones that a moral theory ought to require of us, so that utilitarianism, which requires something else, is unreasonable? If it is the former, then Darwinism is credible; if it is the latter, it is not. The fact that we tend to care more about family and friends than strangers, and more about compatriots than foreigners, may well be due in part to factors captured by evolutionary theory; but standard normative ethics says that others have a right to our concern, and sometimes that their plight can require us to divert resources that would benefit those close to us: it is unclear whether Darwinism agrees – indeed, how it *can* agree. Darwinism may be able to explain feelings of concern for the interests of completely unrelated foreigners if these feelings exist: they may be the byproduct of a not entirely discriminating mechanism that produces the greatest advantage to those who are related to us. But Darwinism does not seem to say that these feelings about agents unrelated to us ought to exist, that it is biologically advantageous for them to exist. On the contrary, it seems to say that these feelings are a kind of accidental byproduct of an evolutionary arrangement for helping those who are related to us. If a mechanism evolved that directed our help *only* to those most likely to reproduce our genes, and if this mechanism did not take up too much of our energy and brain power, Darwinism could not avoid saying that it would be biologically better for this mechanism to replace the one that is supposed to move us as things are, the one that is not discriminating enough to screen out help to those of no use to the replication of our genes. Yet though Darwinism would have to applaud the evolution of this mechanism, it makes sense to ask whether a world in which it operated would be morally better than the actual one. The intelligibility of this question by itself shows that the Darwinist apparatus and the concept of the moral come apart.

Ruse's account is questionable where he thinks Darwinism and conventional normative ethics agree, as well as where he thinks they disagree. We have already seen in outline his unsatisfactory handling of a disagreement between Darwinism and utilitarianism; we can now consider a point of agreement he thinks there is between Darwinism and Kantianism:

> From the biological viewpoint, we are all persons in society, interacting in such a way that aims to maximize our share of society's goods. But, for each and every one of us, there must be a point beyond which the acquisition of society's goods becomes too high. It is just not worth the cost. And the bottom line clearly is where we are used merely for the benefit of others. Thus, as Darwinians, we want to stop this

happening to us. The most obvious way to prevent this
happening, particularly where the chief underlying mechanism
for social functioning is reciprocal altruism, is to agree that
we will not use others as a means either. But how is this
'ideal' to be enforced? Natural selection serves it up under
the guise of morality. We have the categorical imperative,
or something very much like it, embedded in an epigenetic
rule. We feel we ought to treat others as ends. They feel the
same about us. Hence, Darwinism and Kantianism are each
satisfied. (244)

It is hard to believe that in this story about a quid pro quo we have
the categorical imperative or anything like it. To the extent that the
categorical imperative can be interpreted as an order to treat every
other person as a member of the realm of ends, it is a categorical
order to do so. It is not, as Ruse's account suggests, the order to
treat other people as ends so that they will reciprocate, or the order
to treat people as ends if one wants to be spared treatment as a
means: these interpretations make the imperative not categorical
but hypothetical. What the categorical imperative tells one to do is
to treat other people as ends – full stop. One is to do so whether
one likes it or not, whether people reciprocate or not, whether it is
convenient or not, just because it is right to do so.

There is a pattern in Ruse's failure to get Darwinian ethics to
square with Kantian ethics and his failure to get Darwinian ethics to
seem superior to utilitarianism on the ground that it corresponds
better to what we feel and think in advance. In downplaying the
impartiality of ethics and the categorical nature of its precepts, Ruse
misses the respects in which morality is addressed to us as reasons
for action. He seems to think that morality acts through us as a
natural compulsion to behave in certain ways that turn out to
increase the well-being of others, sometimes in the face of impulses
that incline us to put our own well-being first. How morality
involves the weighing of different options in practical deliberation;
how some reasons can be understood in theory and recognized in
practice to be better than others – these matters are left dark.

To object that Ruse gives us an inadequate conception of the
moral is not to say that it is inadequate because it mentions
biological fact and theory. On the contrary, it is no part of my case
against his treatment that biological fact and theory are irrelevant to
moral theory. The fact that human sympathies tend to be limited is

a morally relevant fact about us, and to the extent that evolutionary theory illustrates and explains this fact, it can complement moral theory. So if Ruse were only insisting that biological theory was relevant to moral theory, there would be no dispute between us. But he claims more. He claims that 'on the basis of [a Darwinian] factual theory about the nature and process of evolution, you can provide a total explanation of morality' (256). We have seen that with his 'total explanation' he does not explain why (and indeed doubts that) morality involves a high degree of impartiality; and he does not seem to acknowledge, let alone account for, the fact that morality requires us to do some things categorically. Worse, he does not even explain how what he regards as moral sentiments differ in kind from 'mere feelings', as he repeatedly insists they do (e.g. 221, 267). Merely to say that they differ from 'mere feelings' by involving 'a sense of obligation' or by having a 'prescriptive force' is to label rather than to explain the difference.

These are more than small gaps in an explanation that is otherwise complete: impartiality and categorical content are among the defining characteristics of the moral. I suspect that Ruse does not really distinguish the moral from the factors that make human beings, in common with other species, sociable, and that when he claims that Darwinism can provide a total explanation of the moral, he is better taken as making a claim about the power of Darwinism to explain sociability.

Sociability is the ability to get along with others. It is the ability to get on with others whether or not one gives weight to their interests or their well-being. Some of the requirements of living in groups – such as the requirement that fighting be kept under control or that food be distributed widely enough to keep going more than the few – may call for things that would also be required by the well-being of others, but this does not make the requirements moral, unless the requirements make the well-being of others the motive for complying with them. Sometimes, as in his discussion of studies of the behaviour of chimpanzees at Arnhem zoo, Ruse seems to set aside motivation and identify moral behaviour with behaviour that regularly turns out to be beneficial to others (228). The fact that it is a mistake to ignore motivation in giving a criterion of moral behaviour may not matter, however, if what is really at issue is fitness for society. It is plausible that the chimpanzees at Arnhem zoo are sensitive to the organization of their group and to the age and identities of creatures within it. It is plausible that some of the sensitivity manifests itself in behaviour that is naturally described as deferential or commanding. In particular the youngest chimpanzees seem to defer most to one or two of the oldest females, who appear to be called upon by younger adult females to stop fighting when their own interventions do not have that effect. This behaviour could well pay biological dividends, and is part of the sociability that evolution could help to explain. Interpreted in this way, Darwinism could be claimed to throw light on a condition of human morality rather than all of morality or its central features. It would leave untouched the question of the nature of moral impartiality, of the weight to be given to morals in practical reasoning, of the relation between individual morality and political organization, and, in normative ethics, all of the justifications of familiar moral prescriptions and prohibitions that do not depend on survival value – which is to say most such justifications.

FROM MORALS TO THE MORAL SCIENCES

In taking issue with naturalism about morals I have been criticizing two theses. One is reductionist. It says that the truth of evaluative statements consists of the truth of certain psychological statements. The other is a thesis about the comprehensiveness of Darwinian theory. According to this thesis, socially beneficial behaviour which might be explained by reference to distinctively moral motivations is more economically and more clearly explained by reference to mechanisms which promote the replication of one's genes. Both naturalisms are supposed to counteract the metaphysical excess of other accounts of value. Thus, accounts like Mackie's and Ruse's are supposed to show that, rather than having an abstract existence in a Platonic heaven, objective values are embedded in our behaviour and therefore exist naturally.[24]

Naturalism in the social sciences does not typically have this anti-metaphysical motivation, though perhaps it once did. Marx's historical materialism was explained by Engels in terms of the priority of nature over spirit, any alternative to this position being assumed to bring with it commitment to the supernatural agency of God.[25] But in our own day naturalistic and non-naturalistic theories alike can be atheistic. Naturalistic theories say that methods of explaining natural phenomena transfer to the study of society, while non-naturalistic theories – such as those of hermeneuticists

– aim at a different sort of understanding, but one that is nevertheless still of this world. A characteristic motivation for naturalism is that the methods of the natural sciences have been outstandingly successful at producing accurate explanations and predictions, and these methods are even held to define what it is for a theory to be scientific, so that if there is to be a social *science* in the strict sense, it will have to incorporate these methods as well. This is broadly the sort of motivation for the naturalism that one finds in Mill, and in some of the members of the unity of science movement who were mentioned in Chapter 1.

Other ways of defining naturalism do not seem to require that the practice of the social sciences be consciously modelled on that of the natural sciences. Instead, social sciences are counted naturalistic if they are open to an interpretation in the philosophy of science that fits the natural sciences, or that was devised with the natural sciences in mind. On this view,[26] social science is naturalistic if actual theories in the social sciences have approximately the same structures as theories in the natural sciences, if they have laws, or informative generalizations, if they aim at prediction, if they are subject to some kind of falsifiability and so on.

Naturalism in this second, weaker sense, covers theories that are deliberately constructed to emphasize their use of quantitative techniques and their concern with formulating generalizations, but it also covers theories which leave generalizations and predictions implicit and which do not explicitly or systematically amass evidence, theories which need to be given new presentations if their findings and the justifications for them are to be made clear and orderly. Marx's theory in *Capital* may be a case in point.[27] For the purposes of this chapter, nothing important hangs on the difference between social science that sets out to resemble natural science, and social science that, once reorganized and clarified, comes to resemble a natural science. Taking naturalism to cover either sort of social science, I shall ask whether it must conflict with hermeneutical or interpretive approaches to social studies. At least one philosopher of social science, Roy Bhaskar, thinks that an accommodation between the two approaches is possible in the form of 'critical naturalism'. But this form of naturalism may prove unsatisfactory as well.

Social studies, science and interpretation

A demand among English-speaking social theorists for approaches modelled on, or simply appropriated from, natural science began to be heard often in the 1950s and 1960s, primarily in the United States. Quentin Skinner associates the demand with a dislike of 'grand theory', a theory giving a comprehensive theory of human nature and society, and usually worked out more or less a priori.[28] Peter Manicas dates the development in America of self-consciously scientific human sciences – politics, economics, sociology and anthropology – to the early decades of the century. He suggests that, by defining their subjects as sciences, German-trained American academics were able to adjust to the influence of big business and its technocratic concerns on the American university. They were able to Americanize their disciplines, a development that seemed particularly appropriate in the anti-German atmosphere that followed the First World War.[29] Whatever its cause, the enthusiasm for scientific social studies – studies with a heavy emphasis on statistical surveys and exact generalizations – was clearly visible in 'political science' and scientific textbooks by the middle of the century. Representatives of this approach in politics included Easton, Lipset, Almond and Verba.[30]

The idea that politics, sociology or anthropology might resemble a mature natural science has provoked scepticism on many grounds, some of which motivate the interpretive approach which is customarily presented as the alternative to naturalism in the social sciences. To begin with, the role of a social scientist is often that of a participant in what he is studying rather than, as in most of natural science, that of a detached observer. Another objection is that, unlike the objects studied by the natural sciences, people have their own understandings of themselves which may constrain social scientific theories and compromise their pretensions to objectivity. Again, human subjects are able to take in the theories of social scientists and make their behaviour conform to theoretical expectations, even when the behaviour would not otherwise have done so. The common theme of these objections, and of many others put forward by hermeneutics, is that there is a possible, or even an unavoidable, influence of theory and theorist on the subject matter of theory, and that since natural scientific method always tries to exclude this influence, natural scientific method is not cut out for social studies. Instead, a method of understanding

169

should be adopted that does not seek detachment in the first place – hermeneutics.

Like the naturalistic approach with which it is supposed to be in competition, hermeneutics or the theory of interpretation is supposed to apply primarily to subject matter outside the social sciences. Its primary application is in the humanities and to written texts: actions, the data of the social sciences, are text-analogues, and a hermeneutical approach to the social sciences tries to capture their meaning by means that are broadly comparable to methods of interpreting texts. Since the assignment of meaning is a significantly different enterprise from conjecturing the causes of appearance, and since the formulation of laws and generalizations in natural science aims precisely at the identification of causes, the hermeneutical and the naturalistic approaches to the social sciences are often taken to stand in opposition to one another. Indeed, factors which are supposed to make interpretation appropriate, and naturalistic approaches utterly inappropriate in the humanities – philology, aesthetics, literary criticism and so on – have sometimes been thought – e.g. by Dilthey – to show that a naturalistic approach is inappropriate in the social sciences as well. Crudely, Dilthey held that hermeneutics was made for the humanities because the humanities are concerned with conscious subjects and lived experience, and the understanding of lived experience is a matter of entering into it rather than finding its external causal conditions. Formulations after Dilthey by such hermeneuticists as Gadamer concede a role to interpretation in the natural sciences as well, but nevertheless insist on a different relation between interpretation and things interpreted in the natural sciences on the one hand and in the humanities on the other, with social sciences in an intermediate position.[31]

Gadamer's account goes some way in the direction of removing the tension between the social and natural sciences. Habermas's (in *Knowledge and Human Interests*) goes further. As Giddens summarizes it, rather more clearly than Habermas himself:

One of Habermas's most interesting contributions to philosophy is his attempt to reconcile hermeneutics and positivism and therefore overcome the division between them. There *are* circumstances in which human social life is conditioned by factors of which those involved know little – in which social forces resemble forces of nature. To that degree, the advocates of a natural science model are correct. But they are wrong to suppose that such social forces are immutable, like laws of nature. The more human beings understand about the springs of their own behaviour, and the social institutions in which that behaviour is involved, the more they are likely to escape from constraints to which previously they were subject.[32]

In this respect, according to Habermas, social science is a bit like psychoanalytic explanation, in which an interpretation that the patient himself could see the application of, sometimes has to be supplemented by reference to mechanisms for repressing material that is not exposed to interpretation.

An account that agrees with Habermas's in holding that interpretation and causal explanation can complement one another, has been put forward by Roy Bhaskar in *Scientific Realism and Human Emancipation*.[33] I am going to consider this account of social science rather than Habermas's because it operates with a concept of naturalism akin to the one we have already introduced. Bhaskar calls his way of reconciling interpretation and causal explanation 'critical naturalism': I shall ask whether, as opposed to the other naturalisms we have rejected in this chapter and the last, it is accommodating enough to be acceptable.

'Critical naturalism'

Bhaskar's account is extremely elaborate and often obscure, but at least the following ideas seem to be central. First, the things studied by the social sciences depend for their existence on natural objects, but the converse is not the case. Social objects are the complex products of human beings. They result, directly or indirectly, from action upon things that are not themselves the product of human activity – natural objects (122). The activity takes time and occurs in space, and has an impact on a natural environment (130). In all of these ways human activity is enmeshed in nature, and, more specifically, dependent on matter (113). But human activity cannot be explained in the terms afforded by the sciences of matter (the natural sciences). Its transformational character is essential to it, and the way in which it transforms matter is captured by descriptions that have no place in natural science, at least as natural science is at present (113). Eliminate the descriptions and one loses human activity.

171

What is the relation between human activity and society? Bhaskar writes (123) as if each presupposes the other. Certain kinds of activity, such as the communication of meaning or the exercise of power, are essentially social, while interaction with others is characteristically intentional and active. Interdependent as they are, human activity and society are apparently distinguishable, and are the subject matter of distinct sciences, at least in principle (124). Thus, a distinct science of sociology would be concerned 'with the social relations within which any human action or social effect must occur' (124), while individual social sciences would be concerned with 'the structure of reproducible outcomes' that actions have at places and times, or with enduring practices and the mechanisms that generate them.

Bhaskar thinks that the subject matter of the social sciences is social structures and that, like the causal mechanisms that produce natural phenomena, social structures produce social phenomena. However, to the crucial question of whether social phenomena are analogous enough to natural phenomena to admit of strongly comparable explanations, he returns a largely negative answer, sympathizing with the claim that some social objects are 'typically differentiated from natural objects in that they are internally complex, pre-interpreted and transient' (108). The sciences of social objects, Bhaskar says, are, up to a point, 'concrete (in the sense of Husserl), hermeneutical (in the sense of Dilthey) and historical (in the sense of Marx)' (ibid.). Though he goes on to disentangle his own account in some respects from those of Husserl, Dilthey and Marx, I do not detect any real retreat from the position that a science of social objects must be significantly different from a science of natural objects. Indeed, Bhaskar goes on to say that a science of social objects must be *sui generis* (122).

How, then, does his account differ from that of hermeneuticists? Bhaskar answers that at the same time as he accepts that social reality is 'linguistically mediated' and 'conceptually dependent', and therefore specially suited to an interpretive approach, he denies that any interpretations arrived at are 'incorrigible, insusceptible to scientific explanation or exhaustive of the subject matter of the social sciences' (121). Causal structures underlie social as well as natural phenomena. They produce events or conjunctures and other social phenomena as well as beliefs about social arrangements (134–5). Contrary to the hermeneuticist presumption of incorrigibility in interpretations and independence from causal explanation, the causal structures can imply that interpretations are false, and explain, in a sense of 'causally explain' familiar from the philosophy of natural science, how the interpretations are produced. In both these ways, then, Bhaskar's account is supposed to be at odds with hermeneutics. But is this really so? The most that Bhaskar seems to establish is that, when described at a very high level of generality, the explanations of social and natural phenomena have something in common. Why should this fact tell in favour of naturalism – the thesis that social science somehow conforms to a pattern set by natural science – rather than in favour of the thesis that natural and social explanation are both scientific? It is plain that the two theses are not equivalent. Bhaskar, however, simply asserts that the second is a version of naturalism (118).

I think that a similar objection confronts any version of naturalism about social science which attempts to do justice to the interpretive approach and accommodate what is correct in it. And since the alternative to this naturalism appears to be one which simply ignores the ground for hermeneuticist doubts about modelling of the social sciences directly on the natural ones, the objection seems to be important. Its force may perhaps be brought out more clearly in the form of the following dilemma. Either naturalism is too understated, merely to the effect that the social and natural sciences have significant features in common, which is not obviously a naturalistic conclusion,[34] i.e. a conclusion in keeping with the thought that nature or the sciences of nature should determine the form of social science; or else naturalism is too overstated, taking such forms as we saw in Chapter 1 were advocated by Clark Hull, or such forms as were outlined by Mill in *A System of Logic*.[35] Either way, naturalism seems an unsatisfactory approach to social science, or at any rate all of social science.

In the case of Bhaskar's naturalism, the trouble is not confined to its understatedness. Another area of difficulty can be approached by asking what his account implies is the relationship between explanatory social theory and practice. 'On the thesis advocated here', Bhaskar writes, 'social science is neutral in a double respect: it always consists in a *practical intervention* in social life and it sometimes *logically entails* value and practical judgements' (169). Enlarging on this second respect in which social science is non-neutral, Bhaskar says that the possibility of a scientific *critique* of lay (and proto-scientific) ideas . . . affords to the human sciences an essentially emancipatory impulse. Such a *conatus* does not license an unmediated transition from factual appraisals to practical imperatives in particular situations. But mediated by the explanatory power of theory and subject to the operation of various *ceteris paribus* clauses, we do nevertheless pass securely from statements of fact to practice. (ibid.)

The way in which explanatory theory emancipates people is by showing that the forces that they think determine their actions are not the ones that really do, and by showing that the interests that their actions promote are not their real interests; the forces that really do determine their actions are ones that people neither want nor need in order to attain goals in keeping with their interests. This revelation, once it engages the feelings and desires that are bound to be felt whenever social theory is formulated and listened to, motivates changed behaviour, behaviour which really does serve the real interests of agents, and which helps people to emancipate themselves in Bhaskar's sense (170).

In stressing feelings and the like, and the way in which their presence, independently of theory, is required for theory to work its emancipatory effect, Bhaskar thinks he is avoiding the mistake of what he calls 'theoreticism', 'which conceives social science as immediately efficacious in practice' (170). His account does not imply, as a 'theoreticist' account would, that theory by itself will get us to free ourselves; it implies, to the contrary, that certain extra-theoretical facts and impulses may be necessary for us to act on what the theory tells us. The mistake of theoreticism sounds like a cross between two mistakes that Hume identified: that of deriving 'ought' from 'is' and the other of supposing that passion and action could be in the control of fact and reason. But Hume may be wrong to say that these are mistakes, and naturalistic accounts, which tend to agree with Hume in this area, may be wrong as well. Thus, Bhaskar may avoid theoreticism at the cost of missing the difference between the practical character of social theory and the practical character of other sorts of explanatory theory. There is a difference between the sort of practical upshot of theory that emancipation is, and such practical upshots of theory as improved food production, quicker rail travel or more durable housing. The difference is that emancipation comes closer to something people could want unconditionally. If that is right, however, and social theory is understood to improve the chances of getting emancipation, there is no need to posit extra-theoretical feelings to explain how the theory gives people particularly forceful reasons for action, or how it motivates people. The kind of good it promotes explains it. This is not to say that a theory promising emancipation will always get people to act; it is to say that a theory promising emancipation gives people a strong reason to act. If this claim expresses theoreticism, then, in the case of emancipatory social theory, theoreticism is no mistake.[36]

Not only does Bhaskar seem to miss the way in which a value like emancipation makes social theory practical; he does not seem to see to what extent the distinction between natural and social sciences needs to be referred to the distinction between the practical and the theoretical. Natural sciences presuppose some goods – like the good of discovering the truth – and lend themselves to the pursuit of other goods – like increased food production – but natural science does not identify these things as goods, nor say which goods are to be subordinated to others. Social theory does identify some goods as goods, and it is sensitive to judgements about the relative values of goods, which are formulated in another practical theory – ethics. In this way the practical character of social theory distinguishes it from natural science. The different roles of causality and interpretation in the two are not all there is to it, though these are the things that naturalism emphasizes. In view of this one-sidedness; in view also of the dilemma I have claimed naturalism faces, the dilemma of claiming too little kinship between social and natural science to amount to naturalism, or of claiming too much kinship to be credible, I conclude that it is an unpromising approach to social science, as it is to morals.

CONCLUSION

There are old and new forms of scientism in philosophy, and in different degrees all are unsavoury. One old form of scientism is conveyed by Bacon's classification of learning: poesy and history are second-class subjects with limited scope; natural science is both incomparably more inclusive and, in principle, incomparably more valuable. Another old form of scientism is close to the surface in D'Alembert's and Diderot's *Encyclopaedia*: the reason one gives an exhaustive presentation of the sciences is to make people more knowledgeable and thereby more virtuous: religion is not the way to inculcate moral knowledge, and the really elevating arts are the ones that enable human beings to do more, not to feel more: they are the science-based mechanical arts, not the fine arts. The scientific empiricists in our century were not the immediate successors of Bacon and the Encyclopaedists, but they were propagandists for the success of science, and they renewed an interest in the unity of science. They did more, calling into question the worth of sectors of culture that were anti-scientific, and undertaking the scientific reform or reinterpretation of sectors that were merely prescientific. The scientific empiricists thus continued the old form of scientism.

To confront this form of scientism more is required than a catalogue of its errors and omissions. One needs a way of thinking about the principal parts of learning or culture all at once. One needs a way of thinking about them while keeping under control the philosophical tendency to overvalue the purely rational and systematic parts of learning or culture. This way of thinking can, I believe, be found in Kant's *Critiques*, and in Chapters 3 to 5 I tried first to expound it, and then to defend some of its more important implications.

The *new* scientism in philosophy is a kind of naturalism. It is not the dogma of an organized movement, with concerns extending to the whole of culture. It is a set of responses to a supposedly outmoded and supposedly presumptuous kind of academic philosophy. Either it is a reaction against the presumption of a priori investigation of questions on which empirical evidence has a clear bearing (Churchland), or else it is a reaction against the presumption of invoking the metaphysical to make sense of things that science is perfectly capable of explaining (Quine, Ruse, Harman, Mackie). In this second form the new scientism has an attractively deflationary air, while the philosophy to which it is an antidote is made to seem extravagant and fanciful. The right way of answering the new scientism is by showing that there are legitimate questions it does not touch and others that it answers badly. Some of the legitimate questions turn out to be familiar from the traditional philosophy that it tries to supersede, just as, in the older form of scientism, some of the things left out turn out to define whole areas of the supposedly prescientific culture.

A response to the new form of scientism does not have to draw on a framework as comprehensive as the Kantian one, for the task is not to show that much of culture apart from science is valuable, but only that much remains for *philosophy* to do when some of its central questions are cut down to the size of scientific ones. In trying to establish this, I drew in Chapter 6 on some (pretty standard) ideas about what philosophical questions are, as well as on the pretensions of the naturalized departments of philosophy. A broadly similar approach was taken in the first part of Chapter 7, and naturalism in a slightly different sense was taken up after that.

It will be clear that according to me scientism in philosophy is something to be combated; at one time I should have said the same thing about scientism outside philosophy as well. But in the wider world, critics of scientism run the risk of helping those who are simply anti-science, or who peddle supposed 'alternative' science, such as 'creation science'. It may be that with all this to contend with, genuine science needs the support of scientistic rhetoric to keep it ahead of the competition. If so, scientism may have its uses in the wider world. In philosophy, at any rate in the English-speaking world, something else is needed: the problem is not to create respect for science but to dissuade people from worshipping it.

NOTES

1 SCIENTISM AND 'SCIENTIFIC EMPIRICISM'

1 W. Gallie, in a careful article on the concept of the 'scientific' as applied to a wide variety of disciplines, says that probably in its central application the term is honorific. See p. 120 of his 'What Makes a Subject Scientific?', *British Journal for the Philosophy of Science* 8 (1957–8), pp. 118–39.

2 As my mention of Kant should already have made clear, I will not confine myself to twentieth-century philosophy, although I shall start there in this chapter. Earlier views are also considered, with an emphasis, before Kant, on those of Bacon and Descartes. The distance between these seventeenth-century writers and those writing today is considerable. No one conception of science has lasted from Descartes's day to our own, and no one kind of scientism either. Though I shall not try to hide the differences, I believe that, outside the Hegelian tradition at least, philosophers have worked with a fairly stable core conception of science. Since the appearance of writings by Hanson, Feyerabend, Kuhn and others this core conception has been questioned and revised, but it has not yet been superseded.

Science has been thought to consist of three components: a set of laws or lawlike statements that purport to explain phenomena, a set of true descriptions of phenomena, and methods of inferring descriptions from laws and laws from descriptions. The precepts for moving to and from the laws are not confined to those of a recognized formal logic, or to those of formal logic plus those of such mature mathematical sciences as geometry. Usually extra-mathematical or extra-logical means of reaching conclusions are recognized as well. These include techniques for designing and conducting experiments and communicating their outcomes, standards for recording observations, standards for accepting someone as a qualified observer and so on. Features of both the extra-logical and logical means of reaching conclusions are characteristically cited to explain the objectivity, explanatory power and usefulness of the laws reached by means of them.

3 Jawaharlal Nehru, *Proceedings of the National Institute of Science of India* 27 (1960), p. 564. Quoted in the epigraph of Max Perutz, *Is Science*

Necessary? (London: Barrie & Jenkins, 1989).

4 Anatole Rapaport, 'A Scientific Approach to Ethics', *Science* (1957), pp. 796–9. For a classification of this paper as scientistic by a criterion different from mine, see S. Richards, *Philosophy and Sociology of Science*, second edition (Oxford: Blackwell, 1987), pp. 137–8.

5 For a brief (but partisan) introduction to creationism as a threat to science, see J. W. Grove, *In Defence of Science* (Toronto: University of Toronto Press, 1989), Ch. 6.

6 Hilary Putnam, *Meaning and the Moral Sciences* (London: Routledge & Kegan Paul, 1978), p. 20.

7 Patricia Churchland, 'Epistemology in the Age of Neuroscience', *Journal of Philosophy* 84 (1987), p. 546.

8 ibid.

9 Carnap's list in his article on scientific empiricism in D. Runes's *Dictionary of Philosophy* (New York: Philosophical Library, 1960), pp. 285–6, includes Hempel, Gomperz, Ayer, von Mises, as well as the anti-positivist Popper. The list might also have included Russell, *circa* 1914. The title of a book he published that year, usually given as *Our Knowledge of the External World*, goes on 'As a Field for Scientific Method in Philosophy'. Russell's tendency to blur the boundary between philosophy and science was a source of some disagreements with Wittgenstein both before 1920 and much later. Another figure in tune with scientific empiricism was Hans Kelsen, who tried to place the interpretation and application of law on a scientific footing.

10 For a very full and extremely clear account of the relevant view, see the long 'critical introduction' in F. Suppe (ed.), *The Structure of Scientific Theories* (Urbana, Ill.: University of Illinois Press, 1977), pp. 3–233; also useful, but more elementary and on a much smaller scale, is C. Dilworth, *Scientific Progress* (Dordrecht: Reidel, 1986), Chs 1–5.

11 Following Putnam's usage in 'What Theories are Not', reprinted in volume 1 of his philosophical papers, *Mathematics, Matter and Method* (Cambridge: Cambridge University Press, 1979).

12 See R. von Mises, *Positivism: A Study in Human Understanding* (Cambridge, Mass.: Harvard University Press, 1951).

13 O. Neurath, 'The New Encyclopaedia', in B. McGuinness (ed.), *Unified Science* (Dordrecht: Reidel, 1987). There are strange echoes of the belief in a unified science – albeit a very different, interpretive science – in R. Barthes. See his *Elements of Semiology*, trans. A. Lawes and C. Smith (New York: Hill & Wang, 1968).

14 Italics in original. R. Carnap, *The Logical Structure of the World*, trans. R. George (Berkeley, Calif.: University of California Press, 1967), p. 290.

15 Von Mises, op. cit., p. 273.

16 In Runes, op. cit., p. 285.

17 C. Hempel, *Aspects of Scientific Explanation* (New York: Free Press, 1965), p. 81.

18 See the 'autobiography' in P. Schilpp, *The Philosophy of Rudolf Carnap* (La Salle, Ill.: Open Court, 1963), p. 21.

19 Hans Reichenbach, *Experience and Prediction* (Chicago: University of

Chicago Press, 1938), pp. 6–7.
20 Von Mises, op. cit., p. 273.
21 See Carnap's 'autobiography', where he reports Neurath's opposition to supernaturalism in and out of religion. Schilpp, op. cit., pp. 22, 23.
22 Hempel, op. cit., p. 81. For a more recent account in this vein, see the title essay in Max Perutz, *Is Science Necessary?* (London: Barrie & Jenkins, 1989).
23 The autobiography, Schilpp, op. cit., p. 21.
24 O. Neurath, 'Unified Science and Psychology', in McGuinness, op. cit., p. 9.
25 ibid., p. 8.
26 ibid., p. 9.
27 McGuinness, op. cit., p. 22.
28 C. Morris, *Logical Positivism, Pragmatism and Scientific Empiricism* (Paris: Hermann, 1937), p. 14.
29 ibid.
30 McGuinness, op. cit., p. 6.
31 ibid., pp. 13ff.
32 Egon Brunswik, 'The Incorporation of Psychology into the Exact Sciences', in McGuinness, op. cit., p. 145.
33 C. Hull, 'Logical Positivism as a Constructive Methodology in the Social Sciences', in McGuinness, op. cit., p. 159.
34 ibid., p. 161.
35 ibid.
36 ibid., pp. 161–2.
37 McGuinness, op. cit., pp. 74ff.
38 H. Gomperz, 'Interpretation: Logical Analysis of a Method of Historical Research', in McGuinness, op. cit., pp. 191–272.
39 C. Hempel, 'The Function of General Laws in History', reprinted in *Aspects of Scientific Explanation*, op. cit., pp. 231–43.
40 ibid., p. 243.
41 ibid., pp. 239–40.
42 Schilpp, op. cit., p. 23.
43 ibid., p. 867.
44 ibid., pp. 23–4.
45 O. Neurath, *Empirical Sociology* (Dordrecht: Reidel, 1973). Originally published as *Empirische Soziologie* (Vienna, 1931).
46 R. von Mises, *Positivism*, op. cit., p. 253.
47 On this point see Alastaire MacIntyre, *Marxism and Christianity* (London: Duckworth, 1983), pp. 88ff, and H. Uchida, *Marx's Grundrisse and Hegel's Logic* (London: Routledge, 1988).
48 O. Neurath, 'The New Encyclopaedia', in McGuinness, op. cit., pp. 140–1.
49 Althusser's hermetic theory of science revives the approach von Mises brushes aside. See *For Marx* (London: New Left Books, 1969).
50 The Russian formalist school had pretensions to putting art criticism on a scientific footing. Their views seem to me to have something in common with von Mises's.
51 McGuinness, op. cit., p. 140.

2 THE ROOTS OF SCIENTISM?

1 The scientific empiricists themselves identified seventeenth-century philosophers among their more important forerunners. Neurath, for example, was conscious of the continuity between Bacon's ideas about the organization of learning and his own idea of a unified science through Bacon's influence on the work of D'Alembert, Diderot and Holbach, the eighteenth-century French Encyclopaedists. See O. Neurath, 'The New Encyclopaedia', in B. McGuinness (ed.), *Unified Science* (Dordrecht: Reidel, 1987), pp. 133, 134. Charles Morris (*Logical Positivism, Pragmatism and Scientific Empiricism* (Paris: Hermann, 1937), pp. 56–64) recognized four major periods of empiricism in Western philosophy, the last two of the four having most in common with the unity of science movement.

It was the third period of empiricism that was really important, according to Morris:

> The third period of combined empirical–semiotic interest is the best known and most influential, that of English empiricism of the 17th to the 19th centuries. From Bacon through Mill opposition to rationalistic metaphysics is supported by the analysis of the nature and limitations of language. . . . [M]odern science had taken on its distinctive and typical features, and the new empiricism was oriented around science. But science itself had found certain features of the Pythagorean–Platonic–Augustinian tradition useful in its attempt to free itself from the scholasticized Aristotle, to carve out a domain of investigation restricted enough to be manageable, and to buttress up its confidence in its mathematical quantitative methods. (60)

It was not until Hume, Morris claims, that the need for ridding science and philosophy of metaphysics came to be acted upon. Morris thinks that Hume's significance 'lay in the fact that he wiped the slate clean again' (60), or wiped it almost clean – he and succeeding British empiricists, according to Morris, had a defective theory of mind.

Auguste Comte is credited with inaugurating 'the fourth or contemporary period of empiricism'. In Comte Morris finds the beginning of the modern appreciation of the pre-eminent place of mathematics among the sciences, as well as a break from the individualism of previous philosophies of science. The social and co-operative character of science, as well as the relation between objectivity and agreement among experts, begins to be stressed properly. On the other hand, according to Morris, Comte did not really anticipate the importance of logic to methods of philosophy or the naturalization of the theory of mind.

Von Mises's account of the history of the positivist outlook (*Positivism: A Study in Human Understanding* (Cambridge, Mass.: Harvard University Press, 1951), Ch. 28) is broadly similar to Morris's. Like Morris, von Mises names Comte as the founder of the 'newer development of positivism' (359), and he agrees to a large extent with Morris in his view of

181

the earlier high points of positivism. The English empiricists of the thirteenth and fourteenth centuries are again mentioned, and their work is said to be 'continued by Francis Bacon, Thomas Hobbes, John Locke and Bishop Berkeley', the same figures singled out by Morris.

2 P. Feyerabend, *Against Method* (London: Verso, 1978).

3 T. Kuhn, *The Structure of Scientific Revolutions* (Chicago: Chicago University Press, 1959).

4 R. Rorty, *Philosophy and the Mirror of Nature* (Oxford: Blackwell, 1980). Subsequently abbreviated P&MN.

5 For a still sound but ageing account of the sixteenth-century belief in the decay of nature and the inferiority of the modern intellect, see R. F. Jones, *Ancients and Moderns* (New York: Dover, 1961), Ch. 2. For Bacon's effect, see Ch. 3.

6 Page references to these works (abbreviated to W) are by volume and page of the Spedding and Ellis edition of Bacon's *Works* (London: Longman, 1858).

7 Maurice Cranston, *Philosophers and Pamphleteers* (Oxford: Oxford University Press, 1985), p. 48. Passmore comes close to claiming that both Descartes and Bacon are scientistic in Chapter 1 of his *Science and its Critics* (London: Duckworth, 1978).

8 Fontenelle ascribed to these scientists not only the pastoral virtues of simplicity, humility, austerity and disinterested love of nature, but also the Stoic excellences of courage, strength and knowledge of duty. See T. Hankins, *Science and the Enlightenment* (Cambridge: Cambridge University Press, 1985), p. 7.

9 See Thomas Hobbes, *De Corpore*, Ch. 1, vi.

10 See my *Hobbes* (London: Routledge & Kegan Paul, 1986), pp. 33ff and 124.

3 REASON, SCIENCE AND THE WIDER CULTURE

1 References are by volume and page of the Akademie edition of Kant's works. The following abbreviations are used: CB: 'Conjectural Beginning of Human History', trans. E. Fackenheim, in L.W. Beck (ed.), *Kant on History* (Indianapolis, Ind.: Bobbs-Merrill, 1963); CJ: *The Critique of Judgement*, trans. J.C. Meredith (Oxford: Oxford University Press, 1969); CPR: *The Critique of Pure Reason*, trans. N. Kemp Smith (London: St Martin's Press, 1978); CPrR: *The Critique of Practical Reason*, trans. L.W. Beck (Indianapolis, Ind.: Bobbs-Merrill, 1956); MM: *Metaphysics of Morals*, Part I ('Metaphysical Elements of Justice'), trans. J. Ladd (Indianapolis, Ind.: Bobbs-Merrill, 1965), Part II ('The Doctrine of Virtue'), trans. M. Gregor (New York: Harper & Row, 1964); Rel.: *Religion Within the Limits of Reason Alone*, trans. T.M. Green and H.M. Hudson (Chicago: Open Court, 1934).

2 CSM: *The Philosophical Writings of Descartes*, trans. J. Cottingham, R. Stoothoff and D. Murdoch (Cambridge: Cambridge University Press, 1985); AT: Adam and Tannery edition of Descartes's works.

3 In what follows I am indebted to Emil Fackenheim, 'Kant's Concept of History', *Kant-Studien* 48 (1957), pp. 381–98.

4 See Ernst Cassirer, *Kant's Life and Work*, trans. J. Haden (New Haven, Conn.: Yale University Press, 1981), pp. 66ff.

5 ibid., p. 127.

6 T. Nagel, *The Possibility of Altruism* (Oxford: Clarendon Press, 1970).

7 See Fackenheim, op. cit., and L.W. Beck's Introduction to *Kant on History*, op. cit.

8 In what follows I am indebted to Allen Wood, *Kant's Moral Religion* (Ithaca, NY: Cornell University Press, 1970), Ch. 5.

9 ibid., p. 204.

4 MORAL CRITICISMS OF THE ARTS AND SCIENCES

1 J.-J. Rousseau, *Discourse on the Sciences and Arts* (DSA), ed. and trans. V. Gourevitch (New York: Harper & Row, 1986). References beginning 'OC' give the corresponding pages in the Pléiade volume of Rousseau's *Oeuvres complètes*.

2 Michel de Montaigne, *In Defence of Raymond Sebond*, trans. A.H. Beattie (New York: Frederick Ungar, 1965).

3 E. Haeckel, *Die Welträtsel*, pp. 365–6; quoted in N. Rescher, *The Limits of Science* (Berkeley, Calif.: University of California Press, 1984), p. 116.

4 This is not far from the position of the Nobel prize winner, Peter Medawar, in the title essay of his *The Limits of Science* (Oxford: Oxford University Press, 1984). Though I think the position is correct, I would not base it, as Medawar does, on an argument from a so-called Law of the Conservation of Information (78ff). According to Medawar, science has limits because its conclusions can only have as much content as the hypotheses and observations which give rise to them. Since the observations and hypotheses are empirical, they cannot help with questions about 'first and last things'. Even apart from the unclarity of 'empirical', this argument is weak. It is possible, and commonplace in philosophy, to infer grounds of hypotheses as well as consequences, and since the grounds must only be consistent with the hypotheses, not draw their content exclusively from them, no limitation of the kind Medawar envisages seems to be encountered. On the other hand, the difference between an interest in finding grounds for things – the conditions that make them possible – and an interest in finding causes, seems to be a difference between an extra-scientific and a scientific interest, and the existence of questions and answers corresponding to the interest in grounds creates a presumption in favour of limits to science.

5 In Chapter 8 of his *The Limits of Science* Rescher, op. cit., argues against the existence of scientific insolubilia, and tries to show that various alleged examples of insolubilia are not in fact insolubilia at all. I accept his point that the existence of unanswered questions at any stage of scientific development does not show that there are unanswerable questions in science, and I agree that it is risky to identify those questions that are supposed permanently to defy science. All of this, however, is compatible with the existence of insolubilia. Indeed, for all

Rescher shows, the traditional examples of insolubilia could well be what they purport to be. Rescher takes the traditional 'riddle of existence': why is there anything rather than nothing? Why are there physical things at all? Why does anything exist? He holds (correctly, I think) that the questions that express the riddle cannot simply be dismissed as improper or meaningless (121). And he even proposes a form that an answer to the riddle of existence could take: the answer would ground the existence of things in a 'hylarchic' principle to the effect that it is for the best that they exist (124). But faced with the question of whether this principle gives a *scientific* solution to the riddle of existence, Rescher gives a notably touchy response: 'To the objection that such an explanation strategy is inherently unscientific one must coolly reply: "Do tell! From what mountain did your theoreticians' Moses descend with the tablets that say just what sorts of explanatory mechanisms are or are not scientific?" ' (124). A parallel version of this 'cool' reply is presumably available to someone who insists in the face of Rescher's objections to the contrary that the hylarchic principle belongs to a metaphysical explanation of existence, so that the riddle of existence is, even if soluble, beyond the powers of science.

6 Bruno Müller-Hill, *Murderous Science*, trans. George Fraser (Oxford: Oxford University Press, 1988).
7 Quoted in Müller-Hill, op. cit., p. 7.
8 Quoted in Müller-Hill, op. cit., p. 9.
9 ibid., pp. 77–8.
10 Quoted in Müller-Hill, op. cit., p. 18.
11 Quoted in Müller-Hill, op. cit., p. 80.
12 Quoted in Müller-Hill, op. cit., p. 79.
13 ibid., p. 11.
14 ibid., p. 12.
15 Quoted in Müller-Hill, op. cit., p. 10.
16 Quoted in Müller-Hill, op. cit., p. 11.
17 ibid., p. 13.
18 ibid., p. 14.
19 ibid., p. 13.
20 Quoted in Müller-Hill, op. cit., p. 67.
21 For an account of Mengele's scientific research in Auschwitz, see Müller-Hill, op. cit., pp. 71ff.
22 ibid., p. 89.
23 ibid., pp. 52–3.
24 ibid., pp. 45–6.
25 ibid., p. 88.
26 ibid., p. vii.
27 For the way that the scientific frame of mind is supposed to blind scientists to animal consciousness and animal pain, see Bernard Rollin, *The Unheeded Cry* (Oxford: Oxford University Press, 1989).
28 Here I think I am in disagreement with J. Habermas (*Knowledge and Human Interests*, trans. J. Shapiro (Boston, Mass.: Beacon Press, 1971)), who seems to me to take an unduly narrow view of the constitutive interest associated with science.

29 Anthony O'Hear associates science with a fondness for the utopian in *The Element of Fire* (London: Routledge, 1988).

30 For scepticism about the value of progress in the 'age of science and technology', see the remarks of Wittgenstein's collected as *Culture and Value*, trans. P. Winch (Oxford: Blackwell, 1979), p. 56.

31 Alasdaire MacIntyre has suggested that the demise of final causes gave a point to, but also doomed, 'the Enlightenment Project' of justifying morality. See his *After Virtue* (London: Duckworth, 1981).

32 For a brief, sober, readable discussion of the question of whether it is accidental or necessary that (human) life has evolved, see David Park, *The How and the Why: An Essay on the Origins and Development of Physical Theory* (Princeton, NJ: Princeton University Press, 1988), Ch. 18. For a formulation of the weak and strong anthropic principles, see Brandon Carter's discussion in M.S. Longair (ed.), *Confrontation of Cosmological Theories with Observational Data* (Dordrecht: Reidel, 1974).

33 See, for example, F. Nietzsche, *Beyond Good and Evil*, trans. W. Kaufmann (New York: Vintage Books, 1966), para. 19, whose closing words seem to organize morals around the concept of life.

34 F. Nietzsche, *The Will to Power*, trans. W. Kaufmann and R.J. Hollingdale (New York: Vintage Books, 1968), para. 1025.

35 ibid., para. 886.

36 See, for example, Philippa Foot's 'Nietzsche: The Revaluation of Values', reprinted in *Virtues and Vices* (Oxford: Blackwell, 1978), pp. 81–95, esp. p. 92.

37 Nietzsche, *The Will to Power*, op. cit., para. 461.

38 ibid.

39 ibid.

5 THE TWO CULTURES

1 See C.P. Snow, 'The Two Cultures: A Second Look', in *The Two Cultures and a Second Look* (Cambridge: Cambridge University Press, 1964). Philosophy is referred to as a non-literary discipline on p. 95. Social history is one of a range of subjects that Snow thinks make up a 'third' culture – neither straightforwardly literary nor scientific. See ibid., p. 70.

2 ibid., p. 5.

3 ibid., p. 14.

4 ibid.

5 ibid., p. 11. An impression not shared by Beatrice Webb. In *My Apprenticeship* (Harmondsworth: Penguin, 1938), p. 153, she writes that in her youth it was the men of science 'who were routing the theologians, confounding the mystics, imposing theories on philosophers, their inventions on capitalists, and their discoveries on the medical men'.

6 Snow, op. cit., pp. 29–30.

7 ibid., p. 38.

8 ibid., pp. 9–10.

9 F.R. Leavis, 'The Significance of C.P. Snow', *Spectator*, 9 March 1962, p. 300, col. 1.

10 Snow, op. cit., p. 44.
11 Leavis, op. cit., p. 302, col. 3.
12 ibid.
13 ibid., p. 303, col. 1.
14 ibid., p. 302, col. 3.
15 ibid., p. 303, col. 1.
16 ibid., p. 303, col. 2.
17 ibid., p. 303, col. 3.
18 Officially Snow is neither pro- nor anti-modernist.
19 Anthony Storr, *Spectator*, 16 March 1962, p. 332, col. 3.
20 Stephen Toulmin, *Spectator*, 16 March 1962, p. 332, col. 3.
21 Snow, op. cit., p. 6.
22 ibid., p. 8.
23 See Lionel Trilling, 'The Leavis–Snow Controversy', in *Beyond Culture* (Oxford: Oxford University Press, 1967), pp. 134ff. Trilling notes an important parallel between the Leavis–Snow controversy and a controversy in the nineteenth century between Matthew Arnold (whose *Culture and Anarchy* (1869) falls on the Leavisite side of the controversy) and Thomas Huxley.
24 ibid., pp. 136ff.
25 Roger Scruton, 'Philosophy and the Neglect of Aesthetics', *Times Literary Supplement*, 5 June 1987, p. 616, col. 1.
26 ibid., p. 616, col. 2.
27 ibid., p. 616, col. 3.
28 Anthony O'Hear, *The Element of Fire* (London: Routledge, 1988).
29 Snow, op. cit., p. 73.
30 P. Feyerabend, *Farewell to Reason* (London: Verso, 1987).
31 ibid., p. 36.
32 For details, see F. Suppe (ed.), *The Structure of Scientific Theories*, (Urbana, Ill.: University of Illinois Press, 1977), pp. 170–80 and 636ff.
33 R. Rorty's three lectures, under the titles 'The Contingency of Language', 'The Contingency of Selfhood' and 'The Contingency of Community', were published in the *London Review of Books*, vol. 8, on 17 April, 8 May and 24 July 1986 respectively.
34 Rorty, 'The Contingency of Language', op. cit., p. 3, col. 4.
35 ibid., p. 3.
36 ibid., p. 6.
37 ibid.
38 ibid.
39 ibid.
40 ibid., p. 5
41 Rorty, 'The Contingency of Selfhood', op. cit., p. 12.
42 Rorty, 'The Contingency of Community', op. cit., p. 13.
43 ibid., p. 10.
44 See my 'The World from its Own Point of View', in A. Malachowski (ed.), *Reading Rorty* (Oxford: Blackwell, 1989).
45 R. Rorty, *Philosophy and the Mirror of Nature* (Oxford: Blackwell, 1980); R. Rorty, *Consequences of Pragmatism* (Brighton: Harvester, 1982).
46 Rorty, 'The Contingency of Selfhood', op. cit., p. 14.

47 Rorty, 'The Contingency of Language', op. cit., p. 6.
48 Rorty, 'The Contingency of Selfhood', op. cit., p. 14.

6 THE NEW SCIENTISM IN PHILOSOPHY

1 See W.V.O. Quine, 'Has Philosophy Lost Contact with People?', originally published in 1979, reprinted in *Theories and Things* (Cambridge, Mass.: Harvard University Press, 1981), p. 191. In *Word and Object* (Cambridge, Mass.: MIT Press, 1960), Quine was already putting forward much the same view. See pp. 3, 275–6.
2 See the digression on this matter in D. Davidson's 'Psychology as Philosophy', reprinted in Davidson's *Essays on Actions and Events* (Oxford: Oxford University Press, 1980), pp. 233ff.
3 It is possible for someone to hold that a traditional philosophical problem is distinct from a scientific one and also that scientific progress makes the philosophical answer straightforward. This is the view J. Searle takes of the mind–body problem in some of its aspects. See his Reith Lectures for 1984, *Minds, Brains and Science* (Harmondsworth: Penguin, 1989). Though I am broadly in sympathy with many things Searle says in this book, especially things he says about science, his treatment of the mind–body problem seems casual to me.
4 'Epistemology Naturalized', in W.V.O. Quine, *Ontological Relativity and Other Essays* (New York: Columbia University Press, 1969), pp. 69–90. Essentially the same ideas are put forward in Quine's 'The Nature of Natural Knowledge', in S. Guttenplan (ed.), *Mind and Language* (Oxford: Oxford University Press, 1975).
5 Quine, 'The Nature of Natural Knowledge', op. cit., p. 71.
6 ibid., pp. 72–82.
7 Quine, 'Epistemology Naturalized', op. cit., p. 83.
8 W.V.O. Quine, *The Roots of Reference* (La Salle, Ill.: Open Court, 1974), p. 3.
9 For a much more involved and subtle discussion of how Quine's programme not only permits but positively invites scepticism, see Barry Stroud, *The Significance of Philosophical Scepticism* (Oxford: Clarendon Press, 1984), Ch. 6.
10 Hilary Kornblith (ed.), *Naturalizing Epistemology* (Cambridge, Mass.: MIT Press, 1985), pp. 1–15.
11 See Quine, *Word and Object*, op. cit., Ch. 2, and Davidson, 'Thought and Talk', in Guttenplan (ed.), op. cit., p. 21. A related view is defended by Dennett in 'Intentional Systems', reprinted in *Brainstorms* (Hassocks: Harvester, 1978), p. 17.
12 A principle that one should minimize the attribution of inexplicable error, rather than error full stop, is defensible, for example. For scepticism about the principle of charity in the form defended by Davidson, see Colin McGinn, 'Charity, Belief and Interpretation', *Journal of Philosophy* 74 (1977).
13 See Stephen Stich, 'Could Man be an Irrational Animal?', in Kornblith (ed.), op. cit., pp. 249–69.
14 Kornblith, op. cit., p. 6.

15 ibid., p. 7.

16 ibid.

17 See G. Harman, 'Deep Structure as Logical Form', in G. Harman and D. Davidson (eds), *The Semantics of Natural Language* (Dordrecht: Reidel, 1972), pp. 25–47.

18 These include Putnam, and R. Rorty in *Philosophy and the Mirror of Nature* (Oxford: Blackwell, 1980).

19 Paul T. Sagal, 'Naturalistic Epistemology and the Harikiri of Philosophy', in A. Shimony and D. Nails (eds), *Naturalized Epistemology* (Dordrecht: Reidel, 1987), pp. 322–3.

20 This is clearly implied by Kornblith. In the same vein, see the introduction to Alvin Goldman's *Epistemology and Cognition* (Cambridge, Mass.: Harvard University Press, 1986), p. 3.

21 See A.J. Clark, 'The Philosophical Significance of Evolutionary Epistemology', in W. Callebaut and R. Pinxten (eds), *Evolutionary Epistemology* (Dordrecht: Reidel, 1987), pp. 228ff.

22 A. Shimony, 'Integral Epistemology', in Shimony and Nails (eds), op. cit., p. 300.

23 See the abstract of George Bealer's 'The Boundary Between Philosophy and Cognitive Science', *Journal of Philosophy* 84 (1987), pp. 553–5.

24 P. Churchland, 'Epistemology in the Age of Neuroscience', *Journal of Philosophy* 84 (1987), pp. 544–53.

25 P. Churchland, *Neurophilosophy* (Cambridge, Mass.: MIT Press, 1986).

26 ibid., p. 482. See also Churchland's letter in the *Times Literary Supplement* for 13 March 1986, p. 271, cols 2–3. This is a comment on a review of *Neurophilosophy* by Colin McGinn.

27 See Churchland, letter, op. cit.

28 Churchland, *Neurophilosophy*, op. cit., p. 395.

29 ibid., p. 396.

30 ibid., p. 299.

31 ibid., p. 303.

32 ibid., p. 301.

33 ibid.

34 See Hilary Putnam, *Meaning and the Moral Sciences* (London: Routledge & Kegan Paul, 1978), pp. 70ff.

35 Churchland does not consider this argument against her claim that generalizations fix the range of the mental. What she discusses (*Neurophilosophy*, op. cit., p. 305ff) is the objection that one's access to some mental facts is 'immediate' and therefore pre-theoretical. Nothing like this is entailed by my argument.

36 The point is developed in P. Pettit, 'Rational Man Theory', in C. Hookway and P. Pettit (eds), *Action and Interpretation* (Cambridge: Cambridge University Press, 1978), pp. 43–64.

37 Churchland, *Neurophilosophy*, op. cit., p. 301.

38 Or perhaps a type of individual – a Pickwickian figure, another Casaubon or whatever. However, the generalizations would not be as general as those that Churchland seems to have in mind and still be serviceable for choices about plotting and so on. That further, more inclusive generalizations might explain those that novelists use, so that

there is a link between the folk psychology I am discussing here and folk psychology about human beings in general, I do not deny. I only deny that these more inclusive generalizations could guide the novelist's choices under discussion.

39 Churchland, *Neurophilosophy*, op. cit., p. 310.
40 A. Furnham, *Lay Theories: Everyday Understanding of Problems in the Social Sciences* (Oxford: Pergamon Press, 1988), p. 51. Furnham refers to W. Mischel and H. Mischel, 'Children's Knowledge of Psychological Principles', Stanford University, unpublished, 1980.
41 Furnham, op. cit., p. 55, citing J. Houston, 'Untutored Lay Knowledge of the Principles of Psychology: Do We Know Anything They Don't?', *Psychological Reports* 57 (1985), pp. 567–70.
42 Churchland, *Neurophilosophy*, op. cit., p. 311.
43 Owen Flanagan substantiates this point very well by reference to experiments in scientific psychology. In his *The Science of the Mind* (Cambridge, Mass.: MIT Press, 1984), p. 220, he writes,

> [F]olk psychological concepts function differently in the hands of cognitive psychologists than in the hands of the person in the street. In large part this is because folk psychological concepts are being deployed in experimental settings in which enrichment as well as revision of our commonsense understanding is the goal. Furthermore, it is simply not true that in accepting the basic conceptual scheme of folk psychology, intentional-stance psychology also accepts the generalizations of folk psychology. Many of the experiments I have discussed here completely undermine folk psychological wisdom, for example, the view that people have privileged access to their own minds, or that the mind is a simple unity, or that we are by nature completely rational animals.

7 NATURALISMS IN THE MORAL SCIENCES

1 For a very different line of criticism of the scientific pretensions of the social sciences, this time focusing on the scientism in 'scientific' justifications of social planning and social engineering, see F.A. Hayek, *The Counter-Revolution of Science: Studies on the Abuse of Reason* (Glencoe, Ill.: Free Press, 1952).
2 G. Harman, *The Nature of Morality* (New York: Oxford University Press, 1977), p. 6.
3 I take this to be an amplification of part of Mackie's 'argument from queerness'. See his *Ethics: Inventing Right and Wrong* (Harmondsworth: Penguin, 1977), p. 38.
4 In Chapter 2 of *The Nature of Morality*, op. cit. The quotations in this paragraph come from p. 17.
5 For a bald statement of the position, see M. Platts, *Ways of Meaning* (London: Routledge & Kegan Paul, 1979), Ch. 10, esp. p. 244.
6 Mackie, op. cit., pp. 19–20.
7 Harman, op. cit., Ch. 4.

8 Platts, op. cit., p. 247.

9 Though an important part, often understressed. For the proper emphasis, see Iris Murdoch, *The Sovereignty of Good* (London: Routledge & Kegan Paul, 1970), pp. 38 and 56.

10 Harman, op. cit., p. 4.

11 These remarks may (I am unsure) enlarge on what Wiggins calls the 'externality' values share with secondary qualities. See his 'Truth, Invention and the Meaning of Life', *Proceedings of the British Academy* 62 (1976), p. 349.

12 G. Berkeley, *A Treatise Concerning Principles of Human Knowledge* (1710), I, x.

13 Harman, op. cit., p. 44.

14 D. Hume, *A Treatise of Human Nature*, Bk III, Pt ii, s. 2 (Selby-Bigge edn (Oxford: Clarendon Press, 1888), p. 471).

15 ibid. (Selby-Bigge: p. 472).

16 ibid. (Selby-Bigge: p. 471).

17 ibid. (Selby-Bigge: p. 470).

18 ibid.

19 Harman, op. cit., pp. 45–6.

20 ibid., p. 7.

21 ibid., p. 8.

22 T. Nagel, *The Possibility of Altruism* (Oxford: Clarendon Press, 1970).

23 M. Ruse, *Taking Darwin Seriously* (Oxford: Blackwell, 1986). Page references to Ruse are in parentheses until the end of the section.

24 It is hard to see why objectivism cannot be centred on values that are clearly of this world, like the badness of pain, or the goodness of being able to pursue one's goals. For objectivism without an objectionable metaphysical realism about values, see Chapters 8 and 9 of Nagel's *The View from Nowhere* (Oxford: Oxford University Press, 1986).

25 For a careful and extremely clear discussion of this matter, see Chapter 11 ('Materialist Naturalism') in Allen Wood, *Karl Marx* (London: Routledge & Kegan Paul, 1981), pp. 159–73.

26 See David Thomas, *Naturalism and Social Science* (Cambridge: Cambridge University Press, 1979).

27 See David Little, *The Scientific Marx* (Minneapolis, Minn.: University of Minnesota Press, 1986).

28 See Quentin Skinner's editor's introduction to *The Return of Grand Theory in the Human Sciences* (Cambridge: Cambridge University Press, 1985), p. 1.

29 P. Manicas, *A History and Philosophy of the Social Sciences* (Oxford: Blackwell, 1987), pp. 213–40.

30 Charles Taylor considers a number of relevant writings in a now famous paper taking issue with the claim of scientific social studies to be reasonably value-free. See his 'Neutrality in Political Science', reprinted in A. Ryan (ed.), *The Philosophy of Social Explanation* (Oxford: Oxford University Press, 1973), pp. 139–70.

31 For details, clearly presented, see W. Outhwaite's essay on Gadamer in Skinner, op. cit., pp. 30ff.

32 A. Giddens, 'Jurgen Habermas', in Skinner, op. cit., p. 126.

33 Roy Bhaskar, *Scientific Realism and Human Emancipation* (London: Verso Books, 1986).

34 Thomas, op. cit., is another source of a too understated naturalism.

35 For an extended examination of the overstated naturalism in Mill's plans for social science, see Alan Ryan, *The Philosophy of John Stuart Mill*, second edition (London: Macmillan, 1987), esp. Chs 8–10.

36 The difference between the goods of emancipation and, for example, improved food production extends to their respective relations to theory. Social theory does not just *lend* itself to promoting the value of emancipation, as natural scientific theory lends itself to improved food production. Social theory – or at least a certain kind of social theory: what might be called German social theory in view of the influence of Kant, Hegel and Marx – is premissed on the assumption that freedom is the ideal of social organization and that how to achieve it is *the* question of social theory. In this sense, *pace* Thomas, another defender of naturalism in social science, value and theory can be internally related. See Thomas's handling of his sense (b) of value-ladenness, op. cit., pp. 120 and 126.

BIBLIOGRAPHY

Arnold, M., *Culture and Anarchy* (London, 1869).

Bacon, F., *Works*, ed. J. Spedding and R. Ellis (London: Longman, 1858).

Barthes, R., *Elements of Semiology*, trans. A. Lawes and C. Smith (New York: Hill & Wang, 1968).

Bealer, G., 'The Boundary Between Philosophy and Cognitive Science', *Journal of Philosophy* 84 (1987), 553–5.

Beck, L.W. (ed.), *Kant on History* (Indianapolis, Ind.: Bobbs-Merrill, 1963).

Berkeley, G., *A Treatise Concerning Principles of Human Knowledge* (1710).

Bhaskar, R., *Scientific Realism and Human Emancipation* (London: Verso Books, 1986).

Brunswik, E., 'The Incorporation of Psychology into the Exact Sciences', in B. McGuinness (ed.), *Unified Science* (Dordrecht: Reidel, 1987), 142–58.

Callebaut, W. and Pinxten, R. (eds), *Evolutionary Epistemology* (Dordrecht: Reidel, 1987).

Carnap, R., *The Logical Structure of the World*, trans. R. George (Berkeley, Calif.: University of California Press, 1967).

Cassirer, E., *Kant's Life and Work*, trans. J. Haden (New Haven, Conn.: Yale University Press, 1981).

Churchland, P., 'Epistemology in the Age of Neuroscience', *Journal of Philosophy* 84 (1987), 544–53.

Churchland, P., *Neurophilosophy* (Cambridge, Mass.: MIT Press, 1986).

Clark, A.J., 'The Philosophical Significance of Evolutionary Epistemology', in W. Callebaut and R. Pinxten (eds), *Evolutionary Epistemology* (Dordrecht: Reidel, 1987), 223–31.

Cranston, M., *Philosophers and Pamphleteers* (Oxford: Oxford University Press, 1985).

Davidson, D., *Essays on Actions and Events* (Oxford: Oxford University Press, 1980).

Dennett, D., *Brainstorms* (Hassocks: Harvester, 1978).

Fackenheim, E., 'Kant's Concept of History', *Kant-Studien* 48 (1957), 381–98.

Feyerabend, P., *Against Method* (London: Verso, 1978).

Feyerabend, P., *Farewell to Reason* (London: Verso Books, 1987).

Flanagan, O., *The Science of the Mind* (Cambridge, Mass.: MIT Press, 1984).

Foot, P., *Virtues and Vices* (Oxford: Blackwell, 1978).

Furnham, A., *Lay Theories: Everyday Understanding of Problems in the Social Sciences* (Oxford: Pergamon, 1988).

Gallie, W., 'What Makes a Subject Scientific?', *British Journal of the Philosophy of Science* 8 (1957–8), 118–39.

Goldman, A., *Epistemology and Cognition* (Cambridge, Mass.: Harvard University Press, 1986).

Gomperz, H., 'Interpretation: Logical Analysis of a Method of Historical Research', in B. McGuinness (ed.), *Unified Science* (Dordrecht: Reidel, 1987), 191–272.

Grove, J.W., *In Defence of Science* (Toronto: University of Toronto Press, 1989).

Guttenplan, S. (ed.), *Mind and Language* (Oxford: Oxford University Press, 1975).

Habermas, J., *Knowledge and Human Interests*, trans. J. Shapiro (Boston, Mass.: Beacon Press, 1971).

Haeckel, E., *Die Welträtsel* (Bonn, 1889).

Hankins, T., *Science and the Enlightenment* (Cambridge: Cambridge University Press, 1985).

Harman, G., 'Deep Structure as Logical Form', in G. Harman and D. Davidson (eds), *The Semantics of Natural Language* (Dordrecht: Reidel, 1972), 25–47.

Harman, G., *The Nature of Morality* (New York: Oxford University Press, 1977).

Hayek, F., *The Counter-Revolution of Science: Studies on the Abuse of Reason* (Glencoe, Ill.: Free Press, 1952).

Hempel, C., *Aspects of Scientific Explanation* (New York: Free Press, 1965).

Hempel, C., 'The Function of General Laws in History', in C. Hempel, *Aspects of Scientific Explanation* (New York: Free Press, 1965), 231–44.

Hobbes, T., *English Works*, ed. Sir W. Molesworth (London, 1839).

Hookway, C. and Pettit, P. (eds), *Action and Interpretation* (Cambridge: Cambridge University Press, 1978).

Hull, C., 'Logical Positivism as a Constructive Methodology in the Social Sciences', in B. McGuinness (ed.), *Unified Science* (Dordrecht: Reidel, 1987), 159–62.

Hume, D., *A Treatise of Human Nature* (1739).

Jones, R.F., *Ancients and Moderns* (New York: Dover, 1961).

Kant, I., *The Critique of Judgement*, trans. J.C. Meredith (Oxford: Oxford University Press, 1969).

Kant, I., *The Critique of Practical Reason*, trans. L.W. Beck (Indianapolis, Ind.: Bobbs-Merrill, 1956).

Kant, I., *The Critique of Pure Reason*, trans. N. Kemp Smith (London: St Martin's Press, 1978).

Kant, I., *Foundations of the Metaphysics of Morals*, trans. L.W. Beck (Indianapolis, Ind.: Bobbs-Merrill, 1969).

Kant, I., *Metaphysics of Morals*, Part I, trans. J. Ladd (Indianapolis, Ind.:

Bobbs-Merrill, 1965).

Kant, I., *Metaphysics of Morals*, Part II ('The Doctrine of Virtue'), trans. M. Gregor (New York: Harper & Row, 1964).

Kornblith, H. (ed.), *Naturalizing Epistemology* (Cambridge, Mass.: MIT Press, 1985).

Kuhn, T., *The Structure of Scientific Revolutions* (Chicago: Chicago University Press, 1959).

Leavis, F.R., 'The Significance of C.P. Snow', *Spectator* (9 March 1962).

Little, D., *The Scientific Marx* (Minneapolis, Minn.: University of Minnesota Press, 1986).

Longair, M. (ed.), *Confrontation of Cosmological Theories with Observational Data* (Dordrecht: Reidel, 1974).

McGinn, C., 'Charity, Belief and Interpretation', *Journal of Philosophy* 74 (1977), 252–35.

McGuinness, B. (ed.), *Unified Science* (Dordrecht: Reidel, 1987).

MacIntyre, A., *After Virtue* (London: Duckworth, 1981).

MacIntyre, A., *Marxism and Christianity* (London: Duckworth, 1983).

Mackie, J., *Ethics: Inventing Right and Wrong* (Harmondsworth: Penguin, 1977).

Manicas, P., *A History and Philosophy of the Social Sciences* (Oxford: Blackwell, 1987).

Medawar, P., *The Limits of Science* (Oxford: Oxford University Press, 1984).

Morris, C., *Logical Positivism, Pragmatism and Scientific Empiricism* (Paris: Hermann, 1937).

Müller-Hill, B., *Murderous Science*, trans. G. Fraser (Oxford: Oxford University Press, 1988).

Murdoch, I., *The Sovereignty of Good* (London: Routledge & Kegan Paul, 1970).

Nagel, T., *The Possibility of Altruism* (Oxford: Clarendon Press, 1970).

Nagel, T., *The View from Nowhere* (Oxford: Oxford University Press, 1986).

Neurath, O., *Empirical Sociology* (Dordrecht: Reidel, 1973).

Neurath, O., 'The New Encyclopaedia', in B. McGuinness (ed.), *Unified Science* (Dordrecht: Reidel, 1987), 132–41.

Neurath, O., 'Unified Science and Psychology', in B. McGuinness (ed.), *Unified Science* (Dordrecht: Reidel, 1987), 1–23.

Nietzsche, F., *Beyond Good and Evil*, trans. W. Kaufmann (New York: Vintage Books, 1966).

Nietzsche, F., *The Will to Power*, trans. W. Kaufmann and R.J. Hollingdale (New York: Vintage Books, 1968).

O'Hear, A., *The Element of Fire* (London: Routledge, 1988).

Park, D., *The How and the Why: An Essay on the Origins and Development of Physical Theory* (Princeton, NJ: Princeton University Press, 1988).

Passmore, J., *Science and its Critics* (London: Duckworth, 1978).

Perutz, M., *Is Science Necessary?* (London: Barrie & Jenkins, 1989).

Pettit, P., 'Rational Man Theory', in C. Hookway and P. Pettit (eds), *Action and Interpretation* (Cambridge: Cambridge University Press, 1978), 43–64.

Platts, M., *Ways of Meaning* (London: Routledge & Kegan Paul, 1979).

Putnam, H., *Meaning and the Moral Sciences* (London: Routledge & Kegan Paul, 1978).

Putnam, H., 'What Theories are Not', in H. Putnam, *Mathematics, Matter and Method* (Cambridge: Cambridge University Press, 1979), 215–27.

Quine, W.V.O., *Ontological Relativity and Other Essays* (New York: Columbia University Press, 1969).

Quine, W.V.O., *The Roots of Reference* (La Salle, Ill.: Open Court, 1974).

Quine, W.V.O., *Theories and Things* (Cambridge, Mass.: Harvard University Press, 1981).

Quine, W.V.O., *Word and Object* (Cambridge, Mass.: MIT Press, 1960).

Rapaport, H., 'A Scientific Approach to Ethics', *Science* (1957), 796–9.

Rescher, N., *The Limits of Science* (Berkeley, Calif.: University of California Press, 1984).

Richards, S., *Philosophy and Sociology of Science* (Oxford: Blackwell, 1987).

Rollin, B., *The Unheeded Cry* (Oxford: Oxford University Press, 1989).

Rorty, R., 'The Contingency of Community', *London Review of Books* (24 July 1986).

Rorty, R., 'The Contingency of Language', *London Review of Books* (17 April 1986).

Rorty, R., 'The Contingency of Selfhood', *London Review of Books* (8 May 1986).

Rorty, R., *Philosophy and the Mirror of Nature* (Oxford: Blackwell, 1980).

Rousseau, J.-J., *Discourse on the Sciences and Arts* (1750).

Runes, D., *Dictionary of Philosophy* (New York: Philosophical Library, 1960).

Ruse, Michael, *Taking Darwin Seriously* (Oxford: Blackwell, 1986).

Russell, B., *Our Knowledge of the External World* (London: Allen & Unwin, 1914).

Ryan, A., *The Philosophy of John Stuart Mill* (London: Macmillan, 1987).

Ryan, A. (ed.), *The Philosophy of Social Explanation* (Oxford: Oxford University Press, 1973).

Sagal, P., 'Naturalistic Epistemology and the Harikiri of Philosophy', in A. Shimony and D. Nails (eds), *Naturalized Epistemology* (Dordrecht: Reidel, 1987), 321–32.

Schilpp, P. (ed.), *The Philosophy of Rudolph Carnap* (La Salle, Ill.: Open Court, 1963).

Searle, J., *Mind, Brains and Science* (Harmondsworth: Penguin, 1989).

Shimony, A., 'Integral Epistemology', in A. Shimony and D. Nails (eds), *Naturalized Epistemology* (Dordrecht: Reidel, 1987), 299–320.

Shimony, A. and Nails, D. (eds), *Naturalized Epistemology* (Dordrecht: Reidel, 1987).

Skinner, Q. (ed.), *The Return of Grand Theory in the Human Sciences* (Cambridge: Cambridge University Press, 1985).

Snow, C.P., *The Two Cultures and a Second Look* (Cambridge: Cambridge University Press, 1964).

Sorell, T., *Hobbes* (London: Routledge, 1986).

Stich, S., 'Could Man be an Irrational Animal?', in H. Kornblith (ed.), *Naturalizing Epistemology* (Cambridge, Mass.: MIT Press, 1985), 249–68.

Stroud, B., *The Significance of Philosophical Scepticism* (Oxford: Clarendon Press, 1984).

Suppe, F., *The Structure of Scientific Theories* (Urbana, Ill.: University of Illinois Press, 1977).

Taylor, C., 'Neutrality in Political Science', reprinted in A. Ryan (ed.), *The Philosophy of Social Explanation* (Oxford: Oxford University Press, 1973), 139–70.

Thomas, D., *Naturalism and Social Science* (Cambridge: Cambridge University Press, 1979).

Trilling, L., *Beyond Culture* (Oxford: Oxford University Press, 1967).

Uchida, H., *Marx's* Grundrisse *and Hegel's* Logic (London: Routledge, 1988).

von Mises, R., *Positivism: A Study in Human Understanding* (Cambridge, Mass.: Harvard University Press, 1951).

Webb, B., *My Apprenticeship* (Harmondsworth: Penguin, 1938).

Wiggins, D., 'Truth, Invention and the Meaning of Life', *Proceedings of the British Academy* 62 (1976), 331–78.

Wittgenstein, L., *Culture and Value*, trans. P. Winch (Oxford: Blackwell, 1979).

Wood, A., *Kant's Moral Religion* (Ithaca, NY: Cornell University Press, 1970).

Wood, A., *Karl Marx* (London: Routledge & Kegan Paul, 1981).

INDEX

Habermas, J., *Knowledge and Human Interests* 170–1
Haeckel, Ernst 76–7
Hallervorden, Professor J. 81
Hals, Franz 21
happiness, unattainability of 53; and worthiness 47–8
hard-core altruism 161–2
Hardy, Thomas 105
Harman, Gilbert 152–3, 154, 155, 156–7, 160, 177
Hawking, Professor Stephen, *A Brief History of Time* 112
Hegel, Georg 14, 15, 17, 123
Heidegger, Martin 26, 123
Hempel, C. 6, 8
hermeneutics 167–8, 169–71, 172–3; and positivism 170–1; and scientific empiricism 13
Himmler, Heinrich 80, 83
historical religion 71
history, Bacon on 69, 176; Kant on 42, 69–71; and mediation 112–13; poetry seen as imitation of 37, 38–9; and practical reason 48–50; as science 1; and scientific empiricism 9, 10, 13–15; seen as inferior to philosophy 38–9; seen as inferior to science 41
Hitler, Adolf 78; *Mein Kampf* 79
Hobbes, T. 35
Houston, J. 147–8
Hull, Clark 12–13, 23, 173
human activity, and society 172
human sciences, differentiated from natural sciences 5–6
human skills, and economic development 50–2
humanities, creative role 116; criticized by philosophers 127; dualism of with sciences 5–6; and scientific empiricism 16–23
Hume, David 4, 130, 131, 156, 174
Husserl, Edmund 172
Huxley, Aldous 105

ideas, of simple natures 29, 31; and veils of perception 31–2

ill effects of arts and sciences 98
illusion, and theoretical reason 68
imagination 59–61; and aesthetic creativity 58; Bacon on 37, 38, 39
immortality of the soul 46
impartiality and morality 165–6, 167
impersonality, in science 85–6
individual constants 5
individual variables 5
industrial revolution 99, 106
inequality 51–2, 54; of moral beings 93–4
initial conditions, of scientific theory 5
inner/outer distinction, in analysis of mind 26, 27, 34
insensitivity, and science 85–7
instinct, and reason 69; *see also* folk psychology
interpretation, canons of 144–7

James, William 123
Jaspersen, Dr H. 81
Jesuits 27
justice, development of system of 51

Kaiser-Wilhelm Institute of Anthropology, Human Heredity and Eugenics 79, 81
Kallman, F. 80
Kant, Immanuel 1, 19, 25, 26, 41–73, 74, 91–5, 98, 160, 176; contrasted with Descartes 43; definition of metaphysics 62; on differences between science and art 59; on knowledge 42, 43; and non-sciences 55–61; reaction of German philosophy against 42, chapter 4 *passim*; on rhetoric 59, 60, 61; and scientism 61–6; on tension between reason and feeling 55–6; theory of theoretical and practical reason 67–8; *Canon of Pure Reason* 46–7, 61–2; 'The Conjectural Beginning of Human History' 49–53, 54, 55, 66, 70, 73, 87;